DEMOCRACY IN DARK TIMES

DEMOCRACY IN DARK TIMES

Jeffrey C. Isaac

CORNELL UNIVERSITY PRESS / ITHACA AND LONDON

First published 1998 by Cornell University Press.
First printing, Cornell Paperbacks, 1998.

Printed in the United States of America.

Design and composition by
Wilsted & Taylor Publishing Services

LIBRARY OF CONGRESS CATALOGING-IN-PUBLICATION DATA
Isaac, Jeffrey C., 1957–
    Democracy in dark times / Jeffrey C. Isaac.
      p.   cm.
    Includes bibliographical references and index.
    ISBN 0-8014-3442-4 (cloth : alk. paper). —
  ISBN 0-8014-8454-5 (pbk. : alk. paper)
    1. Democracy.   2. Title.
  JC423.I77   1997
  321.8′09′04—dc21   97-25969

Cornell University Press strives to utilize
environmentally responsible suppliers and materials
to the fullest extent possible in the publishing of its
books. Such materials include vegetable-based,
low-VOC inks and acid-free papers that are also
either recycled, totally chlorine-free, or partly
composed of nonwood fibers.

Cloth printing   10 9 8 7 6 5 4 3 2 1
Paperback printing   10 9 8 7 6 5 4 3 2 1

For Adam, my Nikto pal

CONTENTS

This book is about democracy and about the need to rethink what democracy means in the conditions under which we live at the dawn of a new century. Developments in what many people have hailed as a "global resurgence of democracy" since the demise of Soviet-style communism are certainly of great import, but the celebratory manner in which many liberal political scientists and philosophers have viewed them hinders our efforts to appreciate their full significance. Both the promise and the fragility of democratic politics today are obscured by a perspective that seeks to fit the developments since 1989 neatly into a narrative about the ideological triumph of liberal democracy. This book is an effort to challenge that narrative, not in the name of antiliberalism but in the name of a robust and yet chastened conception of democratic praxis that may contribute to the reinvigoration of liberal democracy.

In developing this perspective I am building on ideas I worked out in *Arendt, Camus, and Modern Politics* (1992). My approach to democracy has been powerfully shaped by my reading of Albert Camus and Hannah Arendt, and their influence is quite evident in this book, some of whose chapters explicitly reinterpret Arendt's ideas. But whereas my last book was concerned principally with the exegesis of texts, this one is concerned more directly with the reading of contemporary political experience, with the application of a theoretical perspective to the practical difficulties in which we find ourselves.

While these essays pursue common themes and develop a common perspective, they are nevertheless diverse. Some were written for academic journals, others for more "public intellectual" ones. Some began as public talks, others as academic lectures. Some have previously been published, others were written expressly for this volume. With the help of my editors I have sought to weave them together into a book with a single, coherent theme. Yet I have deliberately avoided trying to make them fit together too neatly, for I wish to preserve some of their differences in genre and tone. Intellectual life today is dominated by two forms of writing, the academic journal article and the scholarly book, both of which typically seek, in their own ways, to present self-sufficient, fully worked-out theoretical arguments, and aspire to a kind of intellectual closure. Some of the essays here satisfy this aspiration, but others have a more open-ended and programmatic character. They are genuine *essays*, the venturing out into the world of ideas in pursuit of discussion, debate, and revision.

The essay is in many ways, I believe, the democratic form of writing par excellence. Unlike the scholarly article or book, it typically neither aspires to nor claims argumentative finality. Instead, the essay puts some ideas out into the public realm, with the full expectation that they will encounter readers and writers with other ideas, that they will provoke response and further discussion. Most of these essays were written in such a spirit, and two of them stimulated rich symposia as a result, exchanges from which I have learned much.

The life of the mind is in some respects deeply private, as anyone who has anxiously wrestled with ideas can attest, but in other respects intellectual inquiry is a public process, especially when one is writing political theory and seeking some kind of public voice. I have learned a great deal from the many friends and colleagues who have read parts of this book or have discussed with me the ideas contained in it, and it is my pleasure to acknowledge them: Charles Anderson, Ron Beiner, Casey Blake, Margaret Canovan, Dana Chabot, Aurelian Craintu, Mary Dietz, Jean Elshtain, Chuck Epp, Peter Euben, Judith Failer, David Glenn, Jack Gunnell, Russell Hanson, Ilya Harik, Jeff Hart, Bonnie Honig, Greg Kasza, George Kateb, Jim Miller, Mike Morgan, Derek Penslar, Sol Resnick, Jennifer Ring, Robert Rohrschneider, Mark Rosenbloom, Ian Shapiro, Carmen Sirianni, Marion Smiley, Rogers Smith, Dina Spechler, David Sprintzen, Gregory Sumner, Tracy Strong, Vladimir Tismaneanu, Michael Walzer, Michael Wrecszin, Bernie Yack, and Burt Zwiebach. I especially thank those who contributed to the symposia surrounding "The Strange Silence of Political Theory" and "The Poverty of Progressivism": Seyla Benhabib, William E. Connolly, E. J. Dionne Jr., Michael Gillespie, Elisabeth Kiss, Mark Levinson, Jane Mansbridge, Kirstie McClure, Joel Rogers, and Sean Wilentz. Lisa Disch deserves special thanks for her very helpful reading of the entire manuscript. Michael Walzer, Mitchell Cohen, and Brian Morton, my editors and colleagues at *Dissent*, deserve thanks both for their incisive criticisms and suggestions and for their hard work producing *Dissent*, a journal that has promoted a kind of political discussion we sorely need, and has afforded me a forum beyond the academy in which to develop my thinking. I also thank my editors at Cornell University Press—Roger Haydon, Barbara Salazar, and Lisa Turner—for their professionalism and generous assistance.

Many of the ideas contained in this book were first worked out in graduate seminars at Indiana University, and it is my pleasure to acknowledge the graduate students who, through their probing questioning and their own research, have enriched my thinking: Jacek Dalecki, Christiane Olivo, Matt Filner, Jason Bivins, David Korfhage, Maurice Meilleur, Nick Tampio, Charles Hoffman, and Chris Brooks. Special thanks go to Mike Baumgartner, who did indispensable research for an earlier incarnation of this book. Two undergraduates with whom I have worked closely also deserve mention: Noll Tufani, whose intellectual enthusiasm and relentless inquisitiveness are gifts that I have come to treasure even more since his departure for Paris; and Tun Myint, a Burmese refugee whose intelligence, integrity, and courage have been an inspiration to me.

As I have grown in experience as a teacher, my appreciation for my own teachers has deepened. It is my pleasure, as always, to thank Ray Franklin, Mike Krasner, Peter Manicas, and Lennie Markovitz for their kindness and inspiration when I was an undergraduate at Queens College, the most exceptional intellectual community I have ever known; and Dennis Young, Kurt Paul, Daniel Mahoney, and Barbara Brown, who introduced me to "humanities" in Jamaica High School. I am lucky to have studied democratic theory with Bob Dahl at Yale, an invaluable experience for which my appreciation increases with age. I was also blessed with the opportunity to learn from and know Michael Harrington, my teacher and later, briefly, my colleague at Queens College, one of the truly great public intellectuals and activists of our time.

I also thank my close friends Robert Orsi and John Efron. Our weekly breakfasts have been a source of insight and inspiration, and above all they have been fun. Steve Scott has been a good friend and an even better martial arts teacher, from whom I have learned much about what political theorists might call "agonism." Robin Murphy has offered me and my family invaluable support and counsel during the period when this book took shape. My *chavurah*—Rich Balaban and Julie Bloom, Jane and Andy Mallor, George Walker and Carolyn Lipson-Walker, and their children—has continued to enrich my life and that of my family. Judith Silverstein, my aunt, has inspired me with her poetry. My brother, Gary Isaac, and sister-in-law, Toni Gilpin, continue to engage me in stimulating political argument. And my parents, Hyman and Sylvia Isaac, continue to be sources of immeasurable support, emotional and material. I can only hope that one day my own children will be as grateful to me as I am to my parents.

Last, but surely not least, are my wife, Debbie, and my children, Adam and Annelise. Debbie continues to amaze me. She has managed to start a children's museum, host a weekly radio interview show, maintain an award-winning career as a freelance journalist, take care of the children, the dogs, the birds, and the gecko, and still be immeasurably supportive of my work. I thank her for her love, her support, and her inspiration. My children continue to enrich my life, Annelise with her graciousness and love of life, Adam with his relentless questioning and sharp wit. This book is dedicated to Adam, who through his iconoclasm and his courage has made me proud and has taught me more about the human condition than a million books of philosophy could ever teach.

Chapters 1, 3, and 8 are published here for the first time. The others, though they appear in revised form, have previously been published, and I thank the editors and publishers involved for permission to use the material here:

"The Strange Silence of Political Theory," *Political Theory* 23 (November 1995), 636–52.

"A New Guarantee on Earth: Hannah Arendt on Human Dignity and the Politics of Human Rights," *American Political Science Review* 90 (March 1996), 61–73.

"Oases in the Desert: Hannah Arendt on Democratic Politics," *American Political Science Review* 88 (March 1994), 156–68.

"The Poverty of Progressivism: Thoughts on American Democracy," *Dissent* 43 (Fall 1996), 40–50.

"The Meanings of 1989," *Social Research* 63 (Summer 1996), 291–344.

I also thank Ann Kjellberg and April Lamb, representatives of the estate of the late Joseph Brodsky, for permission to reprint "Bosnia Tune" in Chapter 8.

JEFFREY ISAAC

Bloomington, Indiana

DEMOCRACY IN DARK TIMES

INTRODUCTION

Democracy in Dark Times

We live at an interesting moment at which to write political theory. All moments are, of course, interesting in their own ways, and one of the greatest conceits of intellectuals is to imagine their own times to be somehow especially profound. It is a conceit to be avoided. And yet our times *are* profound, filled with meaning, and possibility, and also with danger.

The essays collected here were written in the wake of that complex and portentious ensemble of processes and events that has come to be called the Revolutions of 1989. In the blink of a historical eye the political authority of communist regimes in Russia and Eastern Europe precipitously and dramatically collapsed, tidal waves of popular discontent—most of it peacefully expressed—overwhelmed long-entrenched dictatorships, and the almost century-long saga of Soviet communism inaugurated by Lenin's fabled arrival at the Finland Station was brought to an end.

The consequences of these developments were profound. The Cold War, which had organized international relations for almost a half-century, concluded. With the collapse of the so-called Iron Curtain, which had long kept Eastern European citizens in and Western ideas and Western capitalism out, the way was open for the rapid incorporation of the former Communist lands into the "free world" of global media and global markets. And more or less liberal democratic regimes were established throughout the eastern half of Europe.

From the vantage point of most Western commentators and political scientists, these developments represented nothing less than a triumph of liberal values and democratic institutions. Indeed, these events in Eastern Europe were not isolated and, if the downfall of communism was the most important instance of democratization, it was by no means the only one. For during this period similar transitions took place throughout the world, in South Africa, the Philippines, and many parts of Latin America, constituting what has become known as a veritable "third wave" of democratic transformation.[1]

What can it mean, then, to speak of democracy in dark times? In what way are these times dark for democracy? And if they are dark, how dark are they? Is there no hope for democratic values?

To speak of democracy in dark times is to go against the grain of much current discussion about democracy; but only in a sense. For if the immediate response of many commentators was euphoria about "the end of history," it has become much more common for political scientists and policy analysts to express concern about the "third wave," to fret about whether it has crested, and to consider the possibility that it has produced an "undertow" that threatens to weaken or undermine the consolidation of democracy in those places where a transition to democracy appears to have been successful.[2] Furthermore, it is not just in those areas where democracy is new that its future is seen to be problematic. There is a widespread consensus among political analysts that liberal democracy in what used to be called "the West" is in decline, that liberal democratic regimes have proved themselves increasingly ineffective and decreasingly legitimate in the eyes of their citizens.[3]

Another way to put these observations would be to say that while the third wave of so-called democratic change resulted in the liberation of many societies from dictatorial regimes, it is less clear that it has resulted in the promotion of meaningful forms of political freedom for those so liberated. While something oppressive has indeed been left behind, it is less obvious that what lies ahead is any less disturbing. Indeed, that proposition is doubtful. Equally unclear is the issue of what institutions and practices democrats ought to aspire to achieve, for those institutions and practices long viewed as exemplary are now subject to widespread suspicion, and not just among critical intellectuals. Democracy, then, faces serious challenges and obstacles that it has not yet proved itself capable of overcoming, challenges that cast a dark shadow over the political horizon.

These challenges are numerous, but they can be boiled down to two basic issues. On the one hand, the socioeconomic processes increasingly prevalent in the world relentlessly jeopardize the security, livelihoods, and environments of ordinary people, displacing peoples and disrupting settled ways of life, putting the lie to the norms of legal and political equality so proudly proclaimed. On the other hand, the political institutions of even the most advanced liberal democratic societies seem incapable of regulating these processes or of promoting healthy and effective forms of political participation that might help to arrest them.

My prognosis for democracy is not heartening. I do not believe that we have entered a dawn of liberal democratic triumph or that antiliberal politics has been ideologically vanquished by liberalism, nor do I believe that there exist at present either the resources or the political will to strengthen or deepen liberal democratic forces or to master our difficulties in any more profound way. In my view, the best-case scenario for liberal democracy is a continuation of what the ancient Greeks called *stasis*, a persistent and noxious immobilism characterized by insecurity, meanness, and a deterioration of anything remotely resembling a genuinely democratic political culture or civic equality. The worst-case scenario is prefigured by the brutal "ethnic cleansing" carried out in Bosnia, a descent into increasingly fractious and violent forms of exclusion and conflict. In all likelihood, the future holds both possibilities simultaneously—hardly a catastrophe, but also hardly an edifying prospect for those who truly care about democratic values.

This prospect appears only bleaker in the context of another important result of the revolutions of 1989—the demise of what used to be called "the left." This is a complicated matter, and it is not the purpose of this book to explain it, except perhaps indirectly. But the demise of the left is a central horizon against which my thinking about democracy must be understood. Throughout much of the modern period liberalism has developed in a productive, even dialectical tension with the socialist left. Universal suffrage and the welfare state, to take two of the most important components of liberal democracy today, were the products of this fruitful tension, the results of powerful mobilization and agitation on the part of labor movements and socialist parties, and of the co-optation and incorporation of these efforts on the part of liberal political elites. The left has been perhaps the most crucial force behind the modern urge for social justice, and through its activities it has helped to extend and thereby to *democratize* liberalism. The narrative of social justice in the modern world is of course much more complicated than the above sentences indicate. It is important also to note that "the left" was never wholly unified; that it never spoke unproblematically for the working classes; that the very idea of "the working classes" or "working masses" in many ways obscures the heterogeneity and complexity both within and among producer groups; that other forces, such as abolitionism and the feminist, civil rights, environmentalist, and sexual liberation movements, also played crucial roles in the democratization of liberalism; that the idea of "the left," in other words, is part myth, and that this myth has had its own very powerful effects, many of them quite malign and some indeed barbarous. Yet it is also true that the myth of the left was grounded in a reality, the reality of a significant and in many ways "progressive" class politics that has contributed immeasurably to the freedoms now enjoyed, however imperfectly, by citizens of liberal democratic societies.[4] Indeed, the rise of Bolshevism and the onset of a global division between communism and social democracy in many ways reinforced at least the ideological vitality of the left in the West, providing it with a strong negative pole against which it could define itself, and offering grist for the mill of left-wing intellectual argumentation.

This socialist left is now terminally ill if not already lifeless, weakened in part by the ideological exhaustion engendered by the downfall of communism, in part by the global hegemony of capitalism that the demise of communism only hastened, and in part—this is important—by the rise of new political forces, "new social movements" that defied the conventions and "grand narratives" of socialism in any of its forms. These diverse new forces possess their own dynamism, and there is much about them that is heartening. In many ways they do represent new forms of genuinely democratic aspiration.[5] But they do not constitute anything like a unified left nor do they together make a force for change analogous to that once presented by the socialist left. I do not consider this lack a bad thing, and it is not my point to diminish or disparage these forces; their emergence and their surpassing of socialist class politics are part of what we might call the natural history of our time. My point is simply that these forces necessarily play what sociologists used to call a different historical role, and do not combine in such a way that they might exert significant pressure to resolve the serious and multiform problems confronting liberal democracy. This lack of convergence is not something to be bemoaned. But whether we like it or not, it is an accomplished fact. What some call "the left" today is at best a fractured collection of constituencies and organizations often at cross-purposes with each other, operating in a social setting that encourages fragmentation rather than coalition. At precisely the moment in which we confront serious political, economic, and environmental challenges on a truly grand scale, the prospects for an organized, collective will capable of addressing and seeking to resolve these problems are very dim.[6]

This is what I mean when I say that we live in dark times.

Most political analysts writing today have not taken the full measure of this darkness. One genre of political analysis that at least addresses contemporary

democracy as a problem is the outpouring of literature on consolidating and reforming democratic institutions. This genre takes its bearings from Joseph
Schumpeter's seminal work, *Capitalism, Socialism, and Democracy*, and it addresses itself to a set of important but limited questions: What are the most
mutually reinforcing institutional relationships between capitalism and democracy? What kinds of regime—presidential versus parliamentary, single-
member district versus proportional schemes—are most suited to consolidating transitional democratic regimes and to promoting effective governance
in more established democracies? What kinds of secondary associations, political parties, and party systems are necessary to ensure the stable functioning of a
liberal democratic regime?[7] These are significant questions, and it is necessary
to address them as part of the effort of public policy-makers and constitutional
engineers to help to promote liberal democratic governance. But they are also
limiting questions, for they assume that the establishment of stable "polyarchal" regimes is the principal task facing democrats today, and they construe
this task as a problem of institutional design. In its minimalism, this democratic
discourse too narrowly constricts the range of democratic possibility. It ignores
nonliberal traditions of thinking about democracy, and marginalizes the contemporary forms of democratic association and insurgency that stand outside
the normal working of liberal democratic politics and afford what are perhaps
more authentic forms of democratic participation. Its primary audience is public officials, lawyers, economists—political elites and those who advise them—
and its primary concern is the stabilization of liberal democratic institutions.
This is an important concern, but it does not have the ethical priority that its
proponents accord it. Much of the political science literature on democracy remains trapped in a discourse that is broadly positivistic and functionalist, even
when it addresses problems of legitimacy, a discourse that gives too little weight
to the utopian possibilities of democracy as an idea and as a kind of political
praxis. Ironically, however, in its instrumentalism and its faith in the possibility of deploying political science to stabilize the instability of our political world
by "engineering" official responses to it, this literature tends to be rather
overoptimistic, even naive, about the possibility of bringing things under control and of restoring or creating an orderly world of orderly liberal democratic
states.

    In Chapters 1 and 7 I criticize this genre, first by raising questions about the
genealogy of its silences, and second by challenging the ways in which it con-

stricts the range of historical possibilities. Ironically, a political science approach vaunted for its realism turns out to be based on unrealistic assumptions, and a discourse defined by its anti-utopianism discloses itself to be utopian in its belief that the future, in some fashion, belongs to liberalism.

Yet if one pole of political analysis today tends to be uncritically committed to a faith in liberal institutions, at least this mode of analysis has the virtue of being concerned with institutions in some fashion. The same cannot be said for much of what goes by the name of political theory today. American political theory has constituted itself as a discipline largely in opposition to positivistic and instrumentalist political science. In place of predictive science, political theorists have sought to analyze the deepest questions regarding human identity, conflict, and the possibility of justice; in place of institutional design, political theorists have sought to delineate and to advance transfigurative *visions* of political possibility. As a result, American political theory has managed to avoid the cynical liberalism characteristic of much political science writing on democracy, but at a price—a highly evolved cynicism of its own about the possibility of doing political theory in a way that clearly and meaningfully engages practical questions of political possibility.

A good deal of political theory today has thus retreated from the world of politics altogether, focused instead on those loftier—or sometimes subterranean— regions in which pure thought and textual exegesis can subsist virtually unaided. Chapter 2, "The Strange Silence of Political Theory," addresses itself to this failing of political theory as a field. In developing this line of criticism I do not mean to indict particular colleagues or approaches or to exempt myself from criticism; indeed, the silence of political theory has been promoted in many complex ways, and it exerts a powerful force over most theorists today. I believe it is a force that needs to be resisted, at least by those who take democratic values seriously, as I do. And this book can be read in part as an effort to practice this kind of intellectual resistance, to use historical texts and theoretically elaborated distinctions to help to make sense of current events and possibilities, and to identify meaningful forms of human agency that might perhaps arrest the forces of darkness that are upon us.

This is a kind of engaged political theory, but not in the sense in which leftist and existentialist writers of the 1930s and 1940s wrote about "engagement." For it does not assume that right and wrong, "progress" and "reaction," can be counterposed in any simple way, and it refuses to align itself with any side or movement that claims to speak unproblematically for "truth," "human emancipation," or "democracy." Such ethico-political concepts need continual interrogation. But they need to be interrogated in a pragmatic way that is alive to the practical difficulties of human living and to the range of possible approaches to these difficulties.

Yet if the chapters of this book represent exercises in a practically oriented political theory, it is also important to emphasize that I do not use the term "practical" in a narrow sense, to refer to forms of jurisprudential argument, public policy analysis, or schemes of institutional design. There is a kind of practicality that asks about these questions, that is concerned primarily with what public officials should do and with how the authority of the state should organize political affairs. These are important questions, and they have preoccupied certain kinds of policy analysts and legal scholars. But the practical questions that interest me are less juridical and less "authoritative," questions that have to do with the experiences and forms of political identity and civic initiative at cross-purposes with state authority and its exercise of juridical sovereignty. What concerns me are the forms of solidarity and power that are constituted by citizens themselves, and with effect, acting both in the civil societies of domestically bounded nation-states and in a global civil society that surpasses and problematizes the boundaries of the nation-state, and with the democratic potential of these forms of solidarity and power. These are not the only questions that might concern political theory, and there is no single way to address them. But they are vitally important questions that political theorists should, I believe, attend to if they aspire to speak meaningfully about politics.

In thinking about these themes I have turned to an unexpected source—the writings of Hannah Arendt. As I argue in Chapters 3, 4, and 5, Arendt is in many ways an unlikely source, for her work is not normally noted for its attentiveness to these questions. Indeed, her writing is famous for a series of distinctions that seem to call into question the very idea of democracy and of a democratically oriented political theory—such distinctions as the social versus the political, the private versus the public, truth versus opinion, and violence versus power. On an older, more dated but still prominent reading, these distinctions implicate an anachronistic, classical view of politics that is anathema not simply to democracy but to modernity itself. This reading of Arendt has been challenged. Indeed, in many ways it is no longer the received view among political theorists, who have developed a veritable cottage industry of Arendt commentary devoted to demonstrating Arendt's relevance to the most contemporary and sometimes avant-garde concerns in philosophy and social theory, such matters as the importance of language, the character of intersubjectivity, and the very nature of human identity.[8] But here too it is often difficult to discern any practical concern in Arendt's writings, any sense that Arendt allows us to understand the forms of association, power, and contestation that have assumed such prominence in our world.

As I read Arendt, the specific forms of powerlessness and power characteristic of the present are at the center of her thinking. Of course her present is not our present; indeed, it would be absurd for an argument premised on the importance of historically grounded political analysis to ignore this fact. But it is also true that our present is not so different from Arendt's present. There are important elective affinities between the postwar setting of her writing and our own postcolonial and post–Cold War setting, both in the characteristic forms of injustice and danger that we confront and in the sense of uncertainty that engulfs us. The title of this book is an allusion to Arendt's own collection, *Men in Dark Times*. In the preface to that book she tells her readers that she borrows the specific metaphor of "dark times" from Bertolt Brecht's famous poem "To Those Born Later," a poem which, in her words, describes "the disorder and the hunger, the massacres and the slaughterers, the outrage over injustice and the despair 'when there was only wrong and no outrage.'" What disturbs Brecht and Arendt is that such violence and injustice could take place in public, in plain view, yet it could not be seen and could not engender sufficient outrage or appropriate legal and political responses, for "it was covered up not by realities but by the highly efficient double-talk of nearly all official representatives who, without interruption and in many ingenious variations, explained away unpleasant facts and justified concerns." If an authentic public realm throws "light on the affairs of men by providing a space of appearances in which they can show in deed and word, for better and worse, who they are and what they can do," she continues, "then darkness has come when this light is extinguished by 'credibility gaps' and 'invisible governments,' by speech that does not disclose what is but sweeps it under the carpet, by exhortations, moral and otherwise, that . . . degrade all truth to meaningless triviality."[9] It would be foolish to propose that our own forms of darkness are exactly the same as the ones that troubled Arendt. The end of the Cold War has brought an end to the nuclear balance of terror that loomed so large in her own pessimism; and our age is, after all, an age of so-called demo-

cratic transformation, in which genuine and somewhat heartening changes
have been effected. And yet the injustice and corruption persist, in liberal democratic societies and in those societies less fortunate, as does the obscurantism
and trivialization that define our political discourse. Indeed, the level of dis-
simulation, deceitfulness, and outright cynicism about the very idea of real
suffering and real solidarity has only increased in our time.[10] Arendt's work
speaks to these phenomena in powerful ways.

Yet the relevance of Arendt extends beyond the affinities between her time and
our own. There are also important linkages between the kind of rebellious politics that she prized, a politics modeled on the experience of "resistance" to totalitarianism, and many kinds of association that have arisen as a crucial part of the
very process of democratization. It is not just that Arendt's ideas and interpretations of rebellious politics have influenced democratic activists, from Martin Pa-
lous and Adam Michnik in Eastern Europe to Ernie Cortes, Leo Penta, and Bob
Moses in the United States. It is that, as I argue in Chapters 4 and 5, her conception of democratic politics as the development of "oases" in a political "desert"
resonates with so much contemporary democratic civic activity that it helps us
to make sense of such activity, and to appreciate its value and its possibility.

To say that Arendt offers us a vital conception of democratic politics is not to
say that she offers a systematic theory of democracy or a normative account of the
range of concerns relevant to democracy. Her theory is not juridical. Its principal
concern is not with the legal organization of the public authority of states but
with the possibilities for embodying and sustaining a spirit of independent association and initiative outside of the state, with generating nonjuridical forms of
power and resistance to authority. Thus she is not a theorist of constitutionalism
narrowly understood, nor is she a theorist of rights, not because she dismisses
the importance of these concerns but because she wishes to push a different set
of concerns, concerns that sometimes counter but also often enrich the workings of legally constituted authority and the politics of rights that such authority
encodes. She is a theorist of "extraordinary" rather than "normal" politics, but
not in the sense that she prizes episodes of profound political uncertainty or extraordinary disruption—the kinds of episodes usually associated with large-
scale upheaval, rioting, or revolution—but in the sense that she prizes those initiatives, typically modest ones, that are literally extraordinary, beyond the
bounds of the anticipated and the routine, that are innovative, different, and
challenging. Those commentators who see Arendt as a partisan of a vitalist "po-

litical existentialism" that prizes chaos and danger egregiously misread her.[11] The fact that they misread Arendt is of incidental significance; but in doing so, they theoretically foreclose the possibility of an important and valuable kind of contemporary politics.

This is a kind of *democratic* politics, a kind of politics concerned, in her words, with "the average citizen's capacity to act and form his own opinion," with the political spaces and forms of association, outside of the corrupt forms of mass politics, that might foster such capacities and their exercise. But to say that it is a kind of democratic politics is not to say that it exhausts the kinds of democratic politics that might concern us as theorists or as citizens. Here it is necessary to be as clear as possible.

For a long time it has been customary for political theorists of many persuasions to write about "democratic theory" and to specify, usually by simple assertion, that "democracy means x" or "democracy is y." There is a tendency to imagine that "democratic theory" concerns itself with a single problem or set of problems, and that it is the task of the "democratic theorist" to address these problems exhaustively, or at least to order them in some hierarchy, so that it is possible to say how the political authority of the state and those institutions beneath it should be organized. But the fact is that, to paraphrase Robert Dahl's classic *Preface to Democratic Theory*, there has never been a single enterprise called democratic theory but only a plurality of theories of different aspects of democratic politics, just as there has never been a single project of democratic politics, but rather a complex plurality of democratic projects. The idea of democracy has never been unproblematically associated with any clearly defined set of institutions or even problems. The history of the idea of democracy, since its inception in the ancient Greek world, has been a history of its association with a range of projects, from city-state institutions to liberal representative institutions to socialist, social democratic, Communist, anarchist, and perhaps even neo-fascist visions and schemes.[12]

Since the end of the nineteenth century the principal vehicle of democratic aspirations in the modern world has been the liberal democratic system of representative government, with its electoral institutions, its mass party organizations, and its parliamentary conventions. The forms of "totalitarian" or "populistic democracy" that sought to defeat it in the twentieth century, whether Communist or fascist, have now been thoroughly vanquished. And social democratic aspirations have been just as thoroughly incorporated, however imperfectly, within liberal democracy, encoded in the rights of trade unions, the forms of corporatist intermediation, and the systems of public provision and economic regulation characteristic of the advanced liberal democracies. In this sense it is fair to say that we are witnessing an "end to ideology" in the normative sense. Marxist socialism, liberalism's most prominent ideological antagonist, has largely passed from the historical scene. And liberal democracy has proven itself, as a matter of historical durability but also as a matter of any reasonable conception of justice, to be the most compelling and thus "valid" way of organizing public offices and distributing civil and political liberties at the level of the nation-state.

But liberal democracy has also proven itself to be a deeply flawed and increasingly illegitimate form of public authority. Its illegitimacy has not resulted in a generalized political crisis of legitimacy. In the places where it exists it is likely to continue to exist, in however debilitated and traduced a fashion, and this is a good thing. But we should recognize that liberal democracy has lost its utopian charm, and ceased to have "a transforming effect upon the existing historical social-order," that it has become in many ways a conservative ideal, perhaps even a simulacrum of political freedom rather than the real thing.[13] However much it remains an aspiration not yet achieved in many parts of the world, it also increasingly rings hollow as a repository of utopian impulses or as a meaningful vehicle of self-government. This is not to dismiss its importance; in a world of "ethnic passions and decaying states" liberal democracy is itself an important achievement.[14] But it is also a limited one, both in the sense that it does not inspire confidence and in the sense that does not seem able to master the difficulties that it confronts. Indeed, the extent to which it recommends itself precisely by virtue of its antithesis to outright barbarity betrays its very minimal, and hardly inspiring, ideological foundations. Again, it is worth emphasizing that edification is not the principal political good, and it hardly counts against liberal democracy that it *does* provide for a minimum of personal security and material well-being. But recent events surely pose questions about the "health" and effectiveness of a regime that rests on such slim foundations and inspires such minimal civic confidence.

It is in this light that we need to consider and to theorize other forms of democratic politics, other vehicles of democratic aspiration, not as replacements for the liberal democratic state but as adjuncts to it, ways of challenging the injustices to which it is insufficiently attentive and ways of promoting forms of exit, loyalty, and especially *voice* in a system increasingly beset by immobilism and sclerosis.

The kind of democratic politics that I explore in this book is exemplified by several contemporary forms of association and initiatives, groups such as Charter 77, Solidarity, and Charter '91, Amnesty International, the Helsinki Citizens' Assembly, and Médecins sans Frontières, the Industrial Areas Foundation, the Citizens' Clearinghouse on Hazardous Waste, and the Algebra Project. These groups and others like them do not share a common project beyond the general aspiration to empower individuals, through their own concerted action, to resist the injustices and insecurities that confront them. What they share are certain self-understandings and commitments to civic responsibility, on the one hand, and a certain improvisional and grass-roots form of activity on the other. Whether they work at the level of a geographic region or locality or the world as a whole, they represent informal means of influencing public opinion and effecting governmental change but, most important, of giving life to the spirit of direct, practical, palpable democratic participation itself, of making real the sense that individuals can make a difference in their own social lives.

These are not the only kinds of groups that one might analyze from the standpoint of democratic aspirations, though in their courageousness and also in their modesty and partiality they represent particularly apposite forms of association in the face of the desert that is our political landscape. Yet if they do not exhaust the range of democratic possibility, they do represent, I believe, a crucially important form of democratic politics at a time when the more normal and authoritative forms are in disrepute.

My argument here has close affinities to the approach developed by Jürgen Habermas and extended by Seyla Benhabib, Jean Cohen, and Andrew Arato.[15] Like these writers, I proceed from an awareness of the "exhaustion of utopian possibilities" associated with liberal democracy and with the welfare state that represents the most advanced form of liberal democracy. Like them, I believe that the currently dominant political and economic forces—what Habermas calls the "systems" mechanisms governed by the media of "bureaucratic power" and "money"—produce at once social insecurity and political alienation. Yet like them I also believe that there exist resources for resisting these mechanisms and for constituting more meaningful and effective forms of democratic self-organization, resources associated both with the legal forms of the constitutional state itself and with the forms of intersubjectivity and solidarity that still exist in what Habermas calls "the lifeworld" of society. In civil society, then, it is possible to locate what Habermas calls "autonomous public spheres," that sometimes achieve "a combination of power and intelligent self-restraint" that renders them capable of making political and economic institutions "sensitive to the goal-oriented results of radical democratic will-formation."[16] Jean Cohen and Andrew Arato offer an encyclopedic treatment of how such "public spheres" do and might emerge, and they argue, in my view correctly, that it is through initiatives like the ones I cited above, along with social movements such as feminism and environmentalism, that meaningful forms of "democratic will formation" can be mobilized. Cohen and Arato also offer a sophisticated account of the different ways in which such "public spheres" and civil society associations can influence public opinion and indeed achieve forms of political power itself. On their view it would be wrong to counterpose a politics of democratic associations in civil society to more normal forms of liberal democratic politics, and they thus endorse a "dualistic" conception of the way that such associations operate.

The general account that they provide is one that I find quite congenial to my own view, and yet there are significant differences between their argument and my own. While, following Habermas, they identify civil society with the resources of an egalitarian intersubjectivity, they fail to pay sufficient attention to the forces of resentment, acrimony, and authoritarianism equally latent within modern civil society. As a result they overemphasize the democratic potential of a politics rooted in civil society, and underemphasize the challenges posed to democracy by the cross-purposes and antagonisms that are endemic to social life. This tendency to present an overly optimistic narrative of civil society is reinforced by a second feature of their analysis, their reliance on an elaborated social theory of the contradictions and legitimation problems of postindustrial capitalism, which leads them to view modern industrial society as containing not simply untapped "communicative reason" but the latent structural foundations for the flourishing of vital social movements themselves. While it goes well beyond the scope of this book to demonstrate this point, I should say that their reliance upon such an elaborated theory is one of the great strengths of their book.[17] But it is also a great weakness, for it does not sufficiently take account of the dehydrating effects of modern consumer society, particularly the ill effects of the mass media and the forms of cynicism that these media promote. Arato and Cohen's view is thus much less dark than my own, and where they discern new prefigurative possibilities, I see more fragile and improvisational forms of resistance, confronting both the power of entrenched political elites and institutions and the growing meanness and divisiveness of public life.

In my appreciation of these forms of power and resentment, and of the difficulties they create for democratic politics, my view overlaps with the conception of "agonistic" democracy developed by William Connolly, Bonnie Honig, and others.[18] On this view, the forms of identity, responsibility, and organization that are engendered by democratic civic initiatives and social movements are inherently partial and agonistic, both in the sense that they inevitably come into conflict with equally powerful forms of identity and association that oppose them or cross-cut them and in the sense that they come into conflict with parts of the very selves who promote them. Such political practices thus occupy an inherently antagonistic terrain. And those who practice them are inherently susceptible to two forms of overreaching—the tendency to villify and marginalize those other political identities against which one competes, and the tendency to resent and marginalize those aspects of oneself that are not wholly expressed by one's politics, further repressing hesitation or doubt and projecting one's anxiety all the more rancorously onto one's political opponents. Like Cohen and Arato, such agonistic democrats thus emphasize the importance of an attunement to difference and an ethic of self-restraint.[19] But on their view such a sensibility becomes all the more difficult to achieve, and it becomes as much a psychic as it is a strategic problem, one that is endemic to the inevitably complex interplay between identity and difference that constitutes political life.

It is thus the "closures" of politics that most concern these writers, and their conception of agonistic democracy is a way of conceiving politics as "simultaneously a medium through which common purposes are crystallized and the consummate means by which their transcription into musical harmonies is exposed, contested, and unsettled [and] unequivocal practices of responsibility are compromised and confounded."[20] Resistance, both its possibility and its practice, is thus central to this agonistic approach, much as it is to the approach that I develop in the essays below. As Connolly writes, such efforts as the movements on behalf of gay rights, femimism, homeless people, and prisoners' rights symbolize the importance of new forms of contestation that go beyond the bounds of normal liberal politics; "these protests and movements, however ineffective they may be on occasion, simultaneously signify a broadening and deepening of institutional investments in the life of the self and a corollary politics of resistances, disinvestments, and subversion on behalf of individuality."[21] In challenging important and taken-for-granted forms of power, such efforts represent "political practices of amendment and resistance" that interrelate in complex and unpredictible ways, involving individuals in a "continual renegotiation of [their] boundaries and affiliations in relation to a variety of (often incommensurable) groups, networks, discourses and ideologies."[22]

In the chapters that follow I develop a conception of democratic politics that shares the agonistic sense of the ineliminability of contentious and fractious conflict and of the difficulties confronting any kind of associational politics in civil society. Yet my own view differs from this approach in some important ways that are worth noting, though it goes beyond the scope of this introduction to explore them fully. In part the difference is merely one of style and inspiration. Many agonistic theorists situate themselves in a loose tradition of Nietzschean inspiration whose principal expositors are Michel Foucault, Jacques Derrida, and Jean-François Lyotard; my own view takes its bearings from a more avowedly humanistic tradition that includes such writers as Albert Camus, C. Wright Mills, and Arendt.[23] But there are more substantive differences as well. In part this is a question of a different political orientation. Whereas agonistic writers, following Foucault, are most often concerned with the kinds of politics that counter culturally sustained forms of normality—the politics of sexual identity, or prisoners' rights, or drug enforcement—my own writings take their bearings from less culturally radical forms of political association, whether they be human rights campaigns on behalf of persecuted dissidents or forms of community-based economic organization.

Again, this difference is partly a matter of style rather than substance, for there is nothing that in principle prevents more "postmodern" writers from addressing these phenomena, just as there is nothing that prevents me from addressing the politics of cultural identity. But it is more than a matter of style. For the way most agonistic writers usually define their problem differs from my own. For them, again following Foucault, and perhaps Weber and Adorno as well, the central problem facing us in the late modern world is the problem of closure, the problem of too much organization and too much coherence, too much virtue, too much "responsibility." As Connolly puts it, a whole range of contemporary phenomena, from corporate drug-testing to new forms of computerization, "signify a regularized politics of normalization through observational judgment and anticipatory self-policing," and present "threats to individuality ... [residing] in the normal operation of a political economy of productivity within a society of increasing surveillance and normalization."[24] Now, these are real issues, and the forms of contestation that have emerged to address them are real too, and often valuable. But my own conception of the central problems confronting us today is rather different. We do inhabit a world of extraordinary regulation and constraint, but the forms of regulation and constraint that are operative in the world today are distinguished less by the "normalization" than by chaos, barbarity, and pervasive insecurity, and the pervasive indifference to these phenomena, that they engender. "Responsibility" is, to be sure, a kind of virtue, a form of self-restraint that might always turn into its opposite, and ought to be treated with care. But in my view the problem today is not too much responsibility but too little, not too much normality but too little. But in working from this perspective it is important to keep in mind the point on which agonistic theory and my own Arendtian approach converge—that the kinds of responsibility that might be constructed are complex and plural, and are subject to continual renegotiation. None of them has the sanction of Nature, or Reason, or History.

So, while I do not disparage the agonistic concern with cultural normality or dismiss the political phenomena that have emerged to contest such normality, the approach I develop here is rather more humanistic, for good or ill. And the kinds of democratic initiatives that most concern me are those that represent modestly constructive efforts to develops forms of civic identity, responsibility and agency that might resist not so much the normalization but the profoundly deracinating disorderliness and irresponsibility of our world, a disorderliness that has a certain logic, to be sure, but whose logic demands new forms of solidarity and control.[25]

This, at any rate, is the guiding thread that runs through this book.

The chapters fall roughly into three categories. Chapters 1 and 2 concern themselves with different forms of intellectual practice, with ways of thinking about doing political theory, and with ways in which political theory might help us to address the problems confronting us today. In Chapter 1 I address myself to the kind of "democratic theory" developed by empirical political scientists in the United States after World War II, an approach that is currently being deployed to help explain the "third wave" of democratization and the problems associated with transitions to democracy. I argue that this democratic theory is not without merit, and it is easy to understand why it assumed prominence in the postwar period, but that it is a limiting approach that narrows the range of democratic possibility and inhibits us from understanding either the current upsurge of democratic impulses or the resurgence of new forms of authoritarianism that recently have reared their ugly heads.

In Chapter 2 I address the parallel failings of American academic political theory, which has proved itself equally unable to address contemporary democratic developments in a meaningful way. If empirical political science evacuates any utopian aspiration from its understanding of democracy, political theory suffers from its relentless anti-empiricism, its refusal to engage problems of political life in their mundane and messy materiality. In both cases characteristic methodological commitments have rendered it difficult to appreciate the significance of one of the most important developments of our time, the revolutions of 1989.

The next three chapters together compose a kind of argument, understood loosely, on behalf of a different way of doing political theory. The way in question is associated with the writings of Hannah Arendt, and it might be called an Arendtian political theory. In all honesty, however, what these chapters present is not unadulterated Arendt but a reconstructed or interpreted version, my version, and they are as much an exemplification, for good or ill, of my own view of how to do political theory as they are an exegesis of Arendt herself.

The Arendt that is presented here is someone who is exemplary in her engagement with the most important events and processes of her day, a writer alive to some of the most pressing problems of twentieth-century political life. Chapter 3 treats her as what Michael Walzer has called a "connected critic," though one distinguished by her adamant refusal of ideological labels and by a genuinely iconoclastic independence of mind. In her own defiance of the dominant frames of reference presented by the Cold War, her way of thinking about politics is perhaps uniquely relevant to our own post–Cold War moment. Chapter 4 treats Arendt as a theorist of the distinctively contemporary problem of rightlessness, and argues that this pressing ethical problem of human dignity framed her conception of politics. And Chapter 5 follows this line of thought by arguing that in Arendt one finds a powerful and distinctive conception of democracy, an emphatically anti-majoritarian conception, in which democratic agency is associated with a plurality of associations existing beneath and beyond the boundaries of the nation-state.

The next three chapters offer what might be called applications of these ideas to some of the important issues concerning us today. Chapter 6 addresses the decline of liberalism and the left more generally in American politics, and what in my view are the exceedingly dim prospects for their renaissance. Here I gesture at what a scaled-back democratic politics of "oases in the desert" might mean for American democracy at the turn of the next century. Chapter 7 is concerned with an analogous problem, one that is in fact the single overriding concern of the book as a whole—the meanings of the revolutions of 1989 in Central Europe. Here I argue that the initiatives pioneered by Charter 77 in Czechoslovakia are of continuing relevance not only in Central Europe but also in the more established liberal democratic world, and that they represent a kind of associational politics that is supremely relevant to the legitimacy crises confronting liberal democracy today.

Chapter 8 addresses itself to another aspect of the same phenomena, to the emergence of disturbingly antidemocratic movements and possibilities, and to the depressing and literally pathetic measures that liberal democracy has been able to muster in response to them. My problem here is what I call the meanings of Bosnia, but I am concerned with Bosnia less as a place than as a symbol. In this sense Bosnia stands for the darkness that this book's title evokes, for the profound challenges facing democrats at the dawn of a new century, challenges posed by violence and exclusionism and cynical indifference to the plight of others.

The book thus ends on a chastened, indeed a pessimistic note, but not a despairing or a hopeless one. For I do believe in what Camus called "the modest thoughtfulness which, without pretending to solve everything, will always be ready to give human meaning to everyday life."[26] Such a thoughtfulness, in its modesty and in its courage, in its disappointments and in its tenacity, has proved itself a vital if limited force in our time. And as long as it remains with us, as it does, there is yet cause for hope.

1

> We have acquired powerful skills, proliferated subdisciplines,
> and have extended our influence all over the world . . . [people are]
> turning to Western-style political science . . . It is at this moment
> of the vindication of the Western political science tradition that I
> want to remind my colleagues of the state of the discipline . . .
>
> GABRIEL ALMOND,
> "The Nature of Contemporary Political Science"

> And indeed, as he listened to the cries of joy rising from the town,
> Rieux remembered that such joy is always imperiled. He knew
> what those jubilant crowds did not know but could have learned
> from books: that the plague bacillus never dies or disappears for
> good; that it can lie dormant for years and years in furniture and
> linen-chests; that it bides its time in bedrooms, cellars, trunks,
> and bookshelves; and that perhaps the day would come when,
> for the bane and the enlightening of men, it would rouse up
> its rats again and send them forth to die in a happy city.
>
> ALBERT CAMUS, *The Plague*

On March 29, 1994, the citizens of Italy voted into office a right-wing Popular Front led by Silvio Berlusconi, who declared in his victory speech that "we have consigned our country to a future of democracy and freedom." Two days later Gianfranco Fini, the leader of the neo-fascist National Alliance—Berlusconi's coalition partner—declared that Benito Mussolini was "the greatest statesman of the century." Italians would be waiting, said Fini, to see whether Berlusconi stacks up to Mussolini's mettle. Berlusconi, it turns out, did not stack up well; in virtually no time he was unseated, a casualty of a notorious financial scandal in which his business empire was implicated; and the coalition of which he was a part quickly unraveled.

Nonetheless, the resurgence of Italian neo-fascism was profoundly disturbing to democrats of all stripes, particularly in light of the ascendancy of similarly neo-fascist and xenophobic movements in France, Germany, Austria, and elsewhere throughout Western Europe, the heartland of the formerly so-called West. "We have said time and again that Fascism was a part of history that finished 50 years ago. This is not the moment to talk about history, but to look to the future," insisted one Italian neo-fascist leader. Yet the legacies of the past obviously persist. The rhetoric of right-wing authoritarianism still resonates in many parts of the "free world," condemning visible forms of corruption, offering a vicarious sense of empowerment to those without power, and a secure sense of identity to those beset by insecurity. Purporting to speak for "the people," right-wing populism presents a serious challenge to civil liberty, to political pluralism, and to democratic politics itself.

It is time to look to the future. In 1989 Francis Fukuyama, writing in *The National Interest*, declared that mankind had come upon the "end of history." Echoing Daniel Bell's "end of ideology" thesis of the 1950s, Fukuyama claimed that Western liberal democracy had triumphed over its ideological competitors—principally communism—and had proved itself the only viable form of politics consistent with human freedom. We had reached, he insisted, "the end point of mankind's ideological evolution and the universalization of Western liberal democracy as the final form of human government."[1] Fukuyama's thesis was widely echoed. Marc Plattner, coeditor of the newly founded *Journal of Democracy*, declared that we were living through a watershed in world history, "the democratic moment." In the wake of the revolutions of 1989 we find ourselves in "a world with one dominant principle of political legitimacy, democracy."[2] The National Endowment for Democracy, a U.S.-government-supported agency set up to "promote democracy" worldwide and the sponsor of the *Journal*, declared that a "democratic tide" is sweeping the world.[3] *Time* magazine called this "an irresistible tide"; *Newsweek* named the 1980s the "Decade of Democracy," and *U.S. News & World Report* proclaimed that "the battle for democracy" is successfully being waged across the globe.

Public officials and politicians sounded similar themes. "A new breeze is blowing and a world refreshed by freedom seems reborn; for in man's heart, if not in fact, the day of the dictator is over," declared George Bush in his 1989 presidential inaugural address.[4] "Democracy is on the move everywhere," announced Colin Powell.[5] Democracy "is taking off like prairie fire," exclaimed Representative Henry Hyde.[6] James Baker, then U.S. secretary of state, spoke the conventional wisdom when he noted that "the quest for democracy is the most vibrant fact of these times."[7]

This euphoria about an irresistible and irreversible democratic tide sweeping us along in a triumphal quest for freedom was not wholeheartedly embraced. Many commentators expressed skepticism toward the Hegelian optimism underlying this view. Questions were raised about the timing of the triumph of liberal democracy, the remaining obstacles here and there, the policies whose implementation would be necessary to insure the institution of liberal democratic regimes over time. "It would be a profound mistake," maintained Representative Stephen Solarz of New York, "to take the survival and success of democracy for granted."[8] "The road will not be smooth," and some backsliding is likely, insisted Joshua Muravchik of the American Enterprise Institute.[9] "There was cause to rejoice at the end of the eighties," maintained Jean-François Revel, "but there was also cause to worry about an overhasty assumption that the movement toward democracy represented a sort of reverse millennium, the arrival of the eternal kingdom of liberty."[10]

Perhaps the most serious and systematic statement of this skepticism was Samuel P. Huntington's critique of Fukuyama, titled "No Exit: The Errors of Endism." "To hope for a benign end of history," he writes, "is human. To expect it to happen is unrealistic. To plan on it happening is disastrous."[11] While we are indeed riding a "third wave" of democratic transformation, Huntington argues, there are many obstacles in the way of its full success, and many possibilities for stasis or reversal. For this reason we must pay much more careful attention to the problematics of democratic transformation, in the name of accurate political science but also in the name of realistic, strategic thinking about the best ways to assure the triumph of democracy that Fukuyama prematurely heralds.

Yet beneath the surface of these disagreements about the end of history rested a larger agreement about liberal democracy—that it represents the most "progressive" or advanced form of politics, that it is the wave of the future to the extent that there will be a future worth having. Even among those who took issue with this or that aspect of Fukuyama's thesis, congratulatory sentiments like those expressed by Gabriel Almond were fairly widespread among liberals, and certainly among liberal political scientists. Western empirical political science, it was widely believed, had proved itself the necessary and sufficient condition of understanding liberal democracy, the conditions for its emergence and flourishing, and the kinds of political engineering required to create these conditions—a veritable riddle of history solved.[12] While political scientists and constitutional engineers may have disagreed about whether or not the advent of democracy had fully and finally been assured, there was little disagreement about the fact that liberal democracy "is now a universal reference and goal," and that "the whole world is aware by now of the superiority of liberal democracy as a political and social system."[13] Whether as Hegelians, Kantians, or Weberians, liberal writers across the political spectrum agreed that liberal democracy is the moral apotheosis of world history, and that the experience of successful democratization in the West, and the wisdom that has been gained through analyzing this experience, furnish the key to effecting a global democratic transformation.

Yet today, but a few years later, such optimism about liberal democracy, and about "Western"—principally American—political science as the truth of political freedom apprehended in time, rings hollow.

It's not just what's happening in Bosnia or Burundi or the countless other violent and depressing conflicts around the world; nor is it the fitful, problematic advance—one step forward, two steps back?— of liberal democracy in Russia, a process symbolized by the rise to prominence of Vladimir Zhirinovsky and others like him.[14] Nor is it the return of fascists to respectability a half-century after the defeat of the Axis. As significant as these phenomena are, the problem cuts much deeper. As the *New York Times* reported a few years back: "in practically every democracy you can think of, established political parties are in deep trouble, their legitimacy suspect, and their leaders susceptible to attack by populists who preach simple, emotional answers to the complicated questions of the post-cold war age."[15] Recent events have exposed fissures and faults in the seemingly secure foundations of liberal democratic politics in the places where it lives, in Italy, Germany, and Japan, but also in France, Great Britain, and the United States, long considered the avatars of liberal democratic triumph. They indicate, as Philippe Schmitter has observed, that "far from being secure in its foundations and practices, democracy will have to face unprecedented challenges. Its future . . . will be increasingly tumultuous, uncertain, and very eventful."[16]

That liberal democracy confronts significant challenges is hardly something new. The future may belong to democracy and freedom, Keynes's famous dictum about the long run notwithstanding. But it is a sobering thought that mature, functioning Western liberal democracy is of fairly recent vintage. The United States and Western Europe have enjoyed fifty years of stable democratic government and economic prosperity. But it was not so long ago that Europe lay

in shambles, and the world was reeling from the experience of world war, Holocaust, and totalitarian ascendancy.

Intellectuals responded to this experience in many ways. Some articulated a
powerful sense of pessimism and sometimes even despair about the future,
viewing the war as the apotheosis of the destructive impulses—now hidden,
now open—at the heart of modern civilization. Hannah Arendt, Leo Strauss,
George Orwell, Theodor Adorno, Arthur Koestler, Albert Camus—in spite of
the significant differences between these writers, they shared in common, along
with many contemporaries, a sense of foreboding about the future of a civilization in crisis.[17] Skeptical of the Enlightenment, and of the Baconian project of
using scientific knowledge to enhance human power, these writers urged a profound reorientation of modern political theory. As Arendt wrote: "On the level
of historical insight and political thought there prevails an ill-defined, general
agreement that the essential structure of all civilization is at the breaking point.
Although it may seem better preserved in some parts of the world than in others,
it can nowhere provide the guidance to the possibilities of this century, or an adequate response to its horrors."[18]

Such skepticism about the possibilities of modern politics was powerful
among intellectuals such as Arendt, who had experienced persecution, displacement, and forced exile from a Europe once considered the heart of "civilization."
But for the same reasons it was a marginal sensibility for those political scientists, mostly American, who had been spared that experience, and who were concerned with developing a "democratic theory" appropriate to the task of postwar
reconstruction. If for such thinkers as Arendt, Strauss, and Adorno the war sig-
nified a profound crisis of modern politics and made necessary new and more
chastened ways of thinking about politics, for these democratic theorists it indicated the need for a redoubled effort to defend the tried and true ideals of liberalism and the institutions of representative government that had survived the war.

Writers in this idiom were also traumatized by the experience of the war. They
were revolted by the mass mobilization, ideological absolutism, and populistic
antiliberal rhetoric that characterized Bolshevism and Nazism. The horrifying
convergence of these two antagonistic regimes, marked by the theory of "totalitarianism," was a central preoccupation of postwar political science.[19] Democratic theorists sought to deploy scientific reasoning against fanaticism, and to
arrange the institutions of representative government to limit the appeal of
antiliberal "ideologies" and to sustain an "open society."[20] On this view totalitar-

ianism constituted the danger, the enemy to be combatted, and democracy was
its antithesis. If totalitarianism was extreme, democracy was moderate; if totalitarianism was ideological, democracy was pragmatic; if totalitarianism prom-
ised authenticity, democracy represented sobriety and realism.

In what follows I am interested not in criticizing any particular theorist but in
delineating a *mentalité* widespread among right-thinking, scientific, empirical
researchers of politics. It is this mentalité that Almond celebrated in his 1990 remarks, a world view distinguished both by its methodological sophistication
and by the powerful institutions it has spawned. Yet while it seemed in the aftermath of the Eastern European revolutions of 1989 that this political science
tradition had been vindicated, today such optimism can, I think, no longer be
sustained.

The mood of postwar democratic theory mirrored the prevalent mood of postwar reconstruction in Europe. Battered by the experience of the war, liberal democrats looked forward with anxious anticipation to a future of political normality
and economic prosperity under the leadership of the United States and the Atlantic Alliance. This was not a mood of unadulterated optimism, but it was a
spirit of hopefulness about a "postideological" age in which the traumas of the
past could be left to lie safely in the past. Camus wrote against the grain of this
hopefulness when he noted with foreboding that "the jubilant crowds" overcome with the joy of liberation were forgetting that the plague "never dies," that
it can "lie dormant for years and years," and that, "for the bane and the enlight-
ening of men," it can recur.

My thesis is a simple one. The experience of Weimar, the ascendancy of totalitarianism, and World War II represented a crisis of the form of government—liberal representative democracy—that is also the modern world's greatest political achievement. This form of government promises civil liberty,
political stability, and accountable government. It is also endemically prone to
bureaucratization, corruption, and sclerosis. While it claims to stand for equality before the law, it permits and indeed promotes extensive and dramatic social
and economic inequalities. While it claims to embody the will of the people, it
lacks channels of healthy civic participation, and thus tends to promote—or at
least is perpetually vulnerable to the emergence of—political alienation and resentment. Such alienation and discontent do not necessarily eventuate in fascism and totalitarianism. These phenomena, the products of many complex
causes, were unique to the interwar period; it is doubtful that they can recur in

the same form. To this extent liberal democracy *has* put them behind us. But the alienation and resentment that helped to pave their way are endemic to liberal democracy. Because postwar democratic theory did not incorporate these factors into its understanding of democratic politics, in important ways it has failed. The return of the repressed makes evident these failures, and also makes pressing the development of richer conceptions of democratic citizenship.

The Discourse of Democratic Theory

What, indeed, *is* democratic theory? Writers of course have long debated the virtues—and vices—of democracy.[21] Very few of these writers have considered themselves democrats, and even fewer have thought of themselves as participants in a discourse called democratic theory. And yet after World War II, in the wake of totalitarianism, collaborationism, the Holocaust, and the atomic bombings of Hiroshima and Nagasaki, *and* in the wake of the Allied victory over the forces of darkness in the heart of Europe, a new discourse emerged, calling itself democratic theory. Robert Dahl's *Preface to Democratic Theory* (1956), Giovanni Sartori's *Democratic Theory* (1958), and Henry Mayo's *Introduction to Democratic Theory* (1960) were but three of the classic statements of this new paradigm.[22]

This paradigm had two principal concerns. One was the way liberal democratic regimes actually function. What is the typical role of political parties, interest groups, social "cleavages" (a term used sometimes as a benign synonym for class conflicts, sometimes as a marker for antagonisms that cross-cut class), of legislatures and executives? What are the variations in the civic cultures of liberal democracies? How is public opinion safely channeled into party platforms and public policy (a process called "interest aggregation" in the parlance of political science)? The second concern was the development of a persuasive, and at the same time "realistic," normative justification for liberal democracy, one that would make sense of, and provide a rationale for, the practices taking shape in the postwar West.

It is important to see how compelling these problems were to political scientists concerned with being relevant. Fascism had only recently been defeated. The Cold War was at its height. The task of providing a penetrating—and convincing—account of liberal democracy seemed pressing indeed. And yet from the outset this democratic theory rested upon a deliberate narrowing of vision that would, in time, come back to haunt it. Such a narrowing took a number of forms.

/ / / HISTORY. First, the theory willfully—and anachronistically—constituted itself as a continuous historical tradition of argumentation, beginning with Pericles, Plato, and Aristotle and continuing into the present day, a tradition whose central figures were John Locke, John Stuart Mill, and Alexis de Tocqueville. Now the most astonishing thing about this group is that, with the possible exception of Pericles, *not a single one of them* considered himself a democrat or plausibly can be construed as an unequivocal advocate of democratic politics. It is true that these men participated in a discourse about democracy, a discourse largely about the *dangers* of democracy and the need to mitigate those dangers through the preservation of institutions that insulated political authority, keeping it at a healthy distance from ordinary citizens and thus limiting the exercise of political power.[23] I don't mean to dismiss these concerns, or to question the project of incorporating the insights of such writers into relevant theorizations of democracy. But I do mean to question the historically misleading linking of these thinkers together as democratic theorists. For such a linkage implies a much greater degree of common concern and shared theoretical focus than was in fact the case for this heterogeneous set of thinkers.

If the reappropriation of "democratic theory" involved the misleading construction of a tradition through a process of inclusion, it also relied upon a symmetrical process of *exclusion* that marginalized or co-opted antiliberal approaches to the subject of democracy. Thus left-wing political thought—Marxist, socialist, anarchist—was virtually banished from the purview of democratic theory.[24] And fascist political thought was either domesticated or ignored. The idea of political elites, for example, was taken up by democratic theorists in their efforts to identify the major characteristics of liberal democratic political leaders. But the critique of parliamentary institutions, and of liberalism more generally, to be found in the writings of Vilfredo Pareto, Gaetano Mosca, and Robert Michels, who had originated the idea of political elites, was virtually ignored or else peremptorily dismissed.[25]

It is easy for us to imagine that liberal democracy rests on deep and secure intellectual and historical foundations, but before 1945 the very idea of liberal democracy was anathema. Critics on the left and the right assailed liberal democracy for its ineffectiveness at solving social problems, its corruption, and its distance from the masses. Many of these critics, Communists like V. I. Lenin but also fascist sympathizers such as Carl Schmitt, George Sorel, and Robert Michels, drew inspiration from Rousseau, and many considered themselves democrats, *authentic democrats*, democrats untainted by liberal reservations about popular mobilization and participation and unqualified by liberal commitments to civil liberty and parliamentary deliberation.[26]

Schmitt's *Crisis of Parliamentary Democracy*, originally published in Germany in 1923, is emblematic, both because of the power of his critique of liberal democracy and because of the recent revival of its arguments, which have found adherents both among certain avant-garde intellectuals and among the most chauvinistic political movements in European politics.[27] Representative government, Schmitt writes, has "already produced a situation in which all public business has become an object of spoils and compromise for the parties and their followers." Modern mass democracy has rendered public debate "an empty formality," for politics has come to be dominated by "social or economic power-groups calculating their mutual interests and opportunities for power," and political parties seek the support of the masses "through a propaganda apparatus whose maximum effect relies on an appeal to immediate interests and passions."[28]

Drawing on Rousseau, Schmitt argues that democracy "is correctly defined as the identity of governed and governing," and that liberal democracy, with its mediating institutions, its partisan antagonisms, and its parliamentary maneuverings, impairs such an identity. Schmitt thus condemns liberal democracy in the name of the unmediated and unconstrained rule of the people. Such rule may be "dictatorial and Caesaristic," and it surely will be antiliberal, but precisely by virtue of this antiliberalism it will be authentically democratic. Schmitt acknowledges that such a "general will" requires an extraordinarily high degree of "homogeneity," and that the people can exist only in opposition to its others; true democracy, he chillingly allows, requires the "elimination or eradication of heterogeneity." The "enemies of the people" are an important foil to "the people," and must be combated in the name of popular sovereignty.

Schmitt maintains that there are two versions of authentic democracy, Bolshevism and Fascism, one relying on a myth of class unity, the other on a myth of ethnic or racial unity. The reasons for Schmitt's preference for the fascist version—its cult of violence, its "superior energy," its irrationalism—are less important than the fact that Schmitt presents a powerful, coherent justification for what Jacob Talmon later called "totalitarian democracy," a regime that Schmitt justifies on the grounds that liberal democracy is an inherently banal, inefficient, and corrupt form of rule.[29] The masses, Schmitt holds, seek identification. They want their sense of themselves and their values to be confirmed by the law and by their political leaders. Liberal democracy obstructs this process. Totalitarian democracy promotes it. The rule of the people under such a regime is vicarious, to be sure, based on plebiscite rather than the banal "statistical apparatus" of representative government or the more palpable forms of participation originally envisioned by Rousseau. But, he maintains, "the will of the people can be expressed just as well, and perhaps better, through acclamation, through something taken for granted, an obvious and unchallenged presence . . . The stronger the power of democratic feeling, the more certain is the awareness that democracy is something other than a registration system for secret ballots."[30]

The connection between this mode of reasoning and the totalitarian terror practiced by the Hitler and Stalin regimes is obvious, and it is both commendable and unsurprising that postwar liberal democrats would seek to formulate a convincing alternative. But the historical framework through which it approached this task was severely constricted. Many of the arguments advanced by the critics of liberal democracy were not taken seriously, and as a result, the defects of liberal democracy to which they pointed received too little attention. The legitimation problems that brought down the Weimar Republic, and that in a more restrained way plague liberal democracies today, were brushed to the side. Powerful arguments about the limitations of representative democracy and the need for more compelling forms of civic identification and engagement were reinterpreted as "irrationalist" and anti-democratic, beyond the pale of serious theoretical inquiry. Indeed these defects of liberal democracy—alienation, strategic maneuvering, corruption—were reinterpreted, by sleight of hand, as *virtues* of liberal democracy. In almost Orwellian fashion, weaknesses thus became transformed into strengths.

/ / / VISION. What is democracy? What ideals does it embody? How might democratic self-government afford opportunities for the participation and empowerment of ordinary people in the direction of their own affairs? Postwar democratic theorists understood that the history of the democratic idea in the modern era is a history of contestation. And yet as they reconstructed a historical tradition of inquiry, they sought to narrow the range of vision considered appropriate in the names of realism and pragmatism.

Democracy was thus defined exclusively as *liberal*, representative democracy. While other conceptions of democracy were acknowledged, they were considered unrealistic when not proto-totalitarian. The "populistic" model of democracy, which imagined that democracy should involve the realization of the "will of the people" rather than the will of some particular group, introduced, it was argued, unrealistic assumptions about the homogeneity of "the people." Thus, the argument that a society in which particular groups hold sway is undemocratic was undermined, for the vision of democracy on which such a criticism rests had—purportedly—been shown to be impossible.[31] Similarly, participatory conceptions of democracy as involving high degrees of civic participation were rejected on the grounds that such participation is simply inconceivable given the size, scale, and complexity of modern society, and modern man's typical preoccupation with private life.[32] Associating populistic appeals to the common good and intense popular mobilization with totalitarianism, postwar democratic theorists produced a conception of democracy in which these features played little or no role, a conception indeed in which these were viewed as dangers to be avoided. The main features of this conception are well known, but they are worth summarizing.[33]

First, it is an exclusively *political* model. In other words, the principle of democracy is held to apply only in the autonomous realm of politics, the sphere of governmental affairs. What makes a society democratic, on this view, has to do with the operations of its state or government, not with the institutions of civil society and the sense of responsibility or irresponsibility, power or powerlessness, equality or inequality, that these institutions foster.

Second, it is a *representative* democracy, in which the political power to make and enforce governmental decisions rests in the hands of a set of public officials who alone are authorized to legislate and execute such decisions. The system is considered democratic not because the people rule in any literal sense, but because it can be said that they rule figuratively or metaphorically through the public officials whom they select through a fair and undisturbed electoral process.

In what sense can it be said that they rule figuratively? What grounds the claim that it is the people in some sense who rule rather than the elites who hold office and exercise official power through the state? Here we come to the third and fourth features of the liberal democratic vision.

The third is that public officials are selected through an electoral process in which public office is open to a broad pool of potential candidates and in which virtually all resident adults are given the right to vote through the institution of *universal suffrage*. Because, presumably, class, race, gender, and other sources of difference of wealth, status, and power in society are not considered criteria for exclusion—in other words, because the electorate is inclusive—it is assumed that no particular social or economic group is afforded any political privilege. All adults are able to vote, all votes are accorded the same weight, and candidates for office are thus compelled to appeal to a broad base of the electorate. Because there exist no legal exclusions on political participation it is possible to describe the liberate democratic state as a neutral apparatus that remains responsive to the felt concerns of a citizenry free to associate and mobilize as it chooses.[34]

Fourth, what compels candidates to appeal to such a citizenry is the system of political competition that is ensured by a *liberal system of rights*. As democratic theorists have often noted, there are many examples of political systems in which universal suffrage plays the role of ratifying the continued rule of a single party or elite. What distinguishes a liberal democracy is that the institution of universal suffrage is combined with a genuinely competitive system of elections. Because individuals enjoy basic freedoms of expression and association, they are able to organize a multitude of political organizations and parties that reflect the diversity of a modern society. The system thus allows, and indeed fosters, political competition. Candidates need to appeal to public desires, and public officials need to remain continually sensitive to such desires, because if they offend the electorate they will not be returned to office. The desire to secure public office and the ever-present possibility of alternations of office thus force a certain level of accountability upon public officials.

This does not mean that "the people rule" in any meaningful sense, or that "the will of the people" is realized, for a variety of reasons frankly acknowledged by "democratic theorists": (1) popular rulership is mediated by public officials; (2) the citizenry is typically divided along multiple lines; (3) the voting public is likely to be only a proportion, sometimes a small proportion, of the electorate; and (4) the electoral process translates popular preferences and demands in only a gross fashion, narrowing a wide range of choices into the choice between a small group of parties or candidates.

As theorists such as Joseph Schumpeter, Robert Dahl, and Anthony Downs argued, the public sphere of liberal democracy is like a marketplace.[35] Politicians are entrepreneurs who present themselves as candidates for office. Seeking public support, they offer sets of proposals and promises to the electorate. Citizens are consumers of these platforms. Seeking to satisfy their wants, they register their preferences through the act of voting, hoping that the electoral outcome will minimize dissatisfaction and maximize satisfaction. To the extent that this is the result, majorities, or at least pluralities, will return public officials to office at the next election. To the extent that it is not, incumbent officials will be rejected in place of candidates deemed more likely to do a "better" job, candidates themselves perpetually subject to the competetive electoral process.

Such a democracy is distinguished less by the empowerment of ordinary citizens than by a certain accountability of public officials. The possibility of gaining office and the threat of losing it serve to constrain public officials, inclining them to act according to the "popular will" as expressed through elections and by interest groups in between elections, or at least to *seem* to do so. As Dahl put it, the procedures of liberal democracy "are crucial processes for insuring that political leaders will be somewhat responsive to the preferences of some ordinary citizens."[36] *Somewhat* responsive to the preferences of *some* ordinary citizens. These qualifications mark the severe narrowing of vision that characterizes this model of democracy.

/ / / EMPIRICISM. Part of the justification for this narrowing of vision was methodological. As a mature science, political science was said to be beyond idle speculation about utopian schemes of popular sovereignty, democratic participation or the end of alienation. In the name of empirical research, democratic theorists were enjoined to focus their attention on the actual. Approaches that, in the words of Henry Mayo, were "neither descriptive of nor feasible in any modern state" were thus to be rejected. While edifying perhaps for dreamers, they were unproductive for scientists of politics. Democratic theory in the postwar world was above all "realistic," which is to say that it was wedded to the status quo. Liberal democracy might have its problems. It might be banal, remote, unedifying. But it was practical, it was stable, it was real. In a world still recovering from fascist and communist mass mobilizations, this genuinely seemed sufficient.

But how real *was* liberal democracy, and how empirical *was* the postwar theoretical justification of it? When revisiting postwar democratic theory it is impossible not to be struck by its anxiously *prescriptive* character. In the guise of a realistic, empirical theory, political science was promoting a vision of democracy that was relatively new and not yet popular. Consider the following:

[1] The proof text for this empirical theory was Joseph Schumpeter's classic *Capitalism, Socialism, and Democracy.* Schumpeter argued against the so-called classical view, derived from Rousseau, which linked democracy with widespread and intense civic participation. He put forth a more empirical theory, suppos-

edly "much truer to life," according to which democracy is simply the right to vote for the candidate of your choice.[37] This theory represented a severe reduction of the idea of democracy. Indeed, it is clear that Schumpeter's belief that his revision "salvages much of what sponsors of the democratic method really mean" can be considered true only on the basis of an incredibly permissive definition of the word "much." All of these limitations have been widely remarked upon.[38] What I wish to note here is something that is less widely noted by so-called democratic theorists and their critics—that this book was published in 1942. In 1942 a war was raging across the globe. Italy, Germany, Japan—later bulwarks of "the free world"—were all governed by fascist autocrats. France was occupied by the Nazis and governed by a military dictator. England was under siege, the United States governed by a corporatist regime engaged in a massive military mobilization. In what sense can Schumpeter's model of competitive elites be considered "truer to life," a more empirically accurate conception of a democratic politics? In 1942 a political theory concerned with being "truer to life" would surely have endorsed some variant of totalitarian dictatorship.

Schumpeter's model, in short, was, appearances to the contrary, not empirical at all. It was less a description of actually existing democracy than a *prescription* about the only kind of halfway decent politics that might, it was believed, avoid the evils of totalitarianism. Far from bringing theory into accord with reality, Schumpeter's revision was intended to help bring reality into accord with a theoretical vision. Again, he may have had good reasons to wish to do this. But the way he did it involved a kind of subterfuge. In the name of realism he put forth a particular normative vision as an empirical description, and disparaged alternative visions and excised them from serious inquiry. And what inspired and gave credence to this "realism" was the prospect of an especially grim alternative that was believed to be the only other way that democratic politics might be reconfigured.

[2] After the war writers such as Almond, Sartori, Dahl, and Seymour Martin Lipset sought with barely constrained anxiety to promote a liberal model of democracy in the face of the appeal of more populist models, especially in countries such as Italy and France, that had a legacy of fascism or right-wing authoritarianism and had strong Communist parties. This is clear in Sartori's *Democratic Theory*, which contrasts "rational democracies" such as Italy and France—countries whose ideologies strongly associate democracy with unmediated popular sovereignty and the good of the people—and "empirical democracies" such

as England and the United States. The former are illiberal and impractical, for "the empirical mind is best suited for the requirements of a democratic modus vivendi." Whereas "rationalists" expect too much from democratic politics, "empiricists" see that politics is a mundane and thoroughly practical way of solving specific problems through negotiation, calm, levelheaded bargaining, and compromise.[39] But of course here "empiricism" is being used as a prescriptive term, to recommend an attitude of mind that is not as widespread as it purportedly should be, an ethos supposedly necessary if democracies are to approximate the liberal model exemplified by England and the United States, the model considered most "workable."

One finds a similar point made by Almond and Sidney Verba in *The Civic Culture*, which presents the civic attitudes found in the Anglo-American liberal democracies—instrumentalism, a low level of ideological intensity, a "realistic" sense of what reasonably can be expected from government—as the most fully developed, "mature" form of democratic political culture, the form of culture to which others should aspire.[40] These arguments merge with Dahl's critique of "populistic democracy" in *A Preface to Democratic Theory*. The point is that only liberal democracy is realistic democracy. But the point is emphatically normative, and it is made in the face of an enormous obstacle—that, in Sartori's words, the appeal of the liberal conception of democracy "is not very strong."[41] So-called empirical democracy was not, circa 1960, hegemonic at all, and one reason why it was not is that many people and political organizations throughout Europe had come to expect more from politics than the right to vote for the candidate of their choice. Empirical democracy was above all dedicated to repudiating any such expectations. In combating the "rationalism" of Continental democracy, democratic theorists sought to purge democracy of the legacy of antiliberal sentiments associated with the defeated fascists and with those Communist parties that were still powerful political competitors in the postwar years. What they sought above all was a "post-ideological" politics, in which serious normative challenges to liberalism would be marginalized, and in which a more instrumentalist politics based on distributing the fruits of postwar prosperity was hegemonic.

The Limits of Democratic Theory

It would be both misleading and unjust to present this narrowing of the field of vision as a self-conscious scheme to promote Western liberalism or capitalism. There were good historical reasons why this version of democratic theory acquired such prominence and plausibility, and became the common wisdom of political science. From the perspective of the postwar world, the most vivid and powerful conception of populistic democracy or unmediated popular rule was fascism. In the name of the *Volk* liberal freedoms had been abolished, parliamentary institutions traduced, and savage repression and mass murder undertaken. It was not the ideas of Rousseau or of the anti-Federalists but those of Carl Schmitt and many others like him that postwar democratic theorists sought to delegitimize.[42] After the defeat of fascism the only other powerful competitor of liberal democracy was communism. Like fascism, in theory communism was inspired by a revolutionary vision, a democratic vision—"proletarian democracy"—of mass mobilization and popular empowerment. And like fascism, in practice communism had disparaged liberal proceduralism and destroyed civil liberties, instituting new forms of coercion and terror in the name of "the people."[43]

In the light of these experiences liberal democracy clearly had much to recommend it. The popular enthusiasms on which totalitarian regimes had been carried into power certainly suggested that a lower level of mass participation might be beneficial. The grandiose ideological objectives sought by totalitarian power seemed to recommend a more pragmatic, indeed instrumental, political culture, in which citizens acted like calculating political consumers and political elites like savvy entrepreneurs. A liberal, representative democracy seemed most consistent with civility and political stability. It did not offer grand schemes of existential fulfillment, but it offered a modicum of comfort and security. It was not immune to problems, but it surely seemed advisable to view these problems "realistically," with a clear sense of what was possible and what impossible. As Churchill once quipped, liberal democracy is the worst form of government, with the exception of all other forms. If we see things in this way, we will not abandon our efforts to fine-tune this political machinery, but we will cease to judge this machinery in terms of impractical or unrealistic ideals of democratic participation.

The proof of the pudding was in the eating. Western liberal democracy, and the democratic theory that supported it, enjoyed a quarter-century of unparalleled success. In comparison with revolutionary turmoil in the Third World, liberal regimes experienced stability, even in Italy, which saw the incessant rise and fall of governments. While the subjects of communism in Russia, China, and Central Europe experienced stultifying repression, the citizens of liberal re-

gimes enjoyed a measure of political freedom. Radical political parties, even
Communist ones, had been incorporated into the system of political competition and elite bargaining. Adjusting to the imperatives of the political marketplace, they increasingly sacrificed their ideological commitments to the requirements of the electoral process.[44] And liberal democracy was not simply a political
success; it was also an extraordinary *economic* success. The conditions of postwar
growth certainly contributed to the sense that liberal democracy had been vindicated and the end of ideology had arrived.[45]

The glorious Central European uprisings against communism in 1989
seemed like icing on the cake. It had long seemed clear that liberal democracy
had triumphed normatively. Its only twentieth-century ideological competitors,
fascism and communism, were thoroughly discredited. Throughout the Cold
War the Soviet Union stood poised menacingly westward, as the symbolic incarnation of totalitarianism, and the United States, its global opposite, seemed by
virtue of this opposition to represent the very essence of democracy and freedom. And with the downfall of communism in Europe this normative victory
became, it seemed, a practical political victory. It made good sense to proclaim
the end of history, even if Francis Fukuyama's proclamation was a bit prema-
ture. For liberal democracy did seem to be the only live, the only compelling version of democracy, and its triumph in Europe seemed to inaugurate a new wave
of democratic transformation.[46]

Yet the victory of liberal democracy seems to have been Pyrrhic, for at the very
moment of its triumph, at the point at which its legitimacy should have been ensured, liberal democracy seemed beset by difficulty. The holy trinity of pragmatism, permanence, and prosperity upon which postwar liberal democracy rested
was now in doubt. This is not, to be sure, a crisis like that of the 1930s, but it is
serious nonetheless. Established parties and established political processes are
in deep disrepute. Writing in *Foreign Affairs*—a publication of the Council on
Foreign Relations and a bellwether of elite opinion if ever there was one—
Charles Maier has argued that Western democracy is plagued by a wave of civic
discontent that constitutes nothing less than a "moral crisis."[47]

While this "crisis of confidence" is unlikely to threaten the foundations of liberal democratic regimes, it presents some serious and perhaps intractible problems that such regimes will be forced to confront. And the fact that these problems are not cataclysmic in no way reduces their significance.[48]

Perhaps the most serious such problem is what might be called a crisis of national identity. Economic transformations, new forms of global mass media, and dramatic demographic shifts have all conspired to call into question the meaning of membership in a national community and of democratic citizenship in a nation-state.[49] How is political community defined in a multicultural age? Who is fully a member of the community? To what rights are they entitled? Are these rights without cost, and if not, who is to bear the economic burden of supporting them? These questions, seemingly unanswerable, plague liberal democracies today. The most malignant form this identity crisis has taken is the rise of ethnic chauvinism and calls for ethnic and cultural homogeneity, exclusion, or "cleansing." A closely related phenomenon is the rise of right-wing populist movements and parties that claim, in the name of the true or authentic people—the true Italians or French, the real Americans—to terminate undue "foreign influences," put an end to waste and corruption, end governmental gridlock and *make things work*. On this view constitutional formalities and the imperatives of parliamentary deliberation and negotiation need to give way to effective and above all decisive governmental action. This is the discourse of Berlusconi and his neo-fascist allies, but also of Jean Le Pen, Ross Perot, and countless others.[50]

This right-wing populist discourse articulates a profound disenchantment with the established procedures of liberal democracy. Above all it expresses a sense of disconnection from political power, which is considered remote, unaccountable, corrupt. Conservative populist rhetoric taps into this sense of alienation and disempowerment. It articulates a romantic conception of communal membership and a vicarious sense of participation and empowerment through identification with *this* community and its leader and against aliens of various kinds.[51] This is the most malignant form that the current crisis of national identity has taken, but it is by no means the only one. For the anxieties about "foreigners" and "foreignness" given such mean-spirited and dangerous voice by right-wing populist rhetoric are pervasive across the political spectrum, and they are engendered by global changes and challenges to which liberal democracies will have to muster a response.[52]

This crisis of national identity is related to an equally serious "crisis" of political and economic adjustment. As has been widely commented upon, we are currently living amidst a dramatic transformation of economic life. The social contract that legitimated postwar liberal democracy and the conditions of economic growth and middle-class prosperity that supported it have been destroyed by new forms of "postindustrial," "third wave" technologies and new forms of "lean and mean" global production and marketing.[53] Economic globalization has produced serious unemployment and promoted equally serious economic inequality and worsening economic insecurity. Coincident with these developments, and related to them in complex ways, is the proliferation of pressing and severe ecological challenges associated with the nuclear, chemical, petrochemical, and biological technologies that have assumed such prominence in economic life. The need to address these problems and to distribute the costs associated with their risks constitutes what Ulrich Beck has called "a profound institutional crisis of industrial society itself."[54] Such problems as hazardous waste and nuclear waste disposal, the control of acid rain and the cross-national distribution of its costs, and the licensing and regulation of the new genetic engineering technologies demand solutions. The demand is politically mediated, to be sure, but it is also imposed by the imperatives of a natural environment that imposes its own constraints, associated with such taken-for-granted, supposedly "free goods" as the air we breathe, the water we drink, the foods we eat, and the parts of the earth we inhabit.

These social, economic, and ecological problems, in short, present a profound test of commitment for the politics of liberal democracy. They require, it would seem, a significant exertion of collective will and public provision. And yet liberal democratic states seem less capable than ever of generating such collective resources or of addressing such problems. For the welfare state project of generating democratic legitimation and deploying public power to address pressing social problems is in disrepute, the casualty of its own inadequacies and of almost two decades of neoconservative government committed to its dismantlement.[55] As Jürgen Habermas has put it: "Today it seems as though utopian energies have been used up, as if they have retreated from historical thought. The horizon of the future has contracted and has changed both the Zeitgeist and politics in fundamental ways. The future is negatively cathected . . . the responses of the intellectuals reflect as much bewilderment as those of the politicians . . . What is at stake is Western culture's confidence in itself."[56]

As a result, liberal democracy today is plagued by immobilism and ungovernability, problems long noted since the fiscal crises of the 1970s.[57] On the one hand, the agencies of the democratic state are "colonized" by interest groups who engage in what economists call "rent seeking," striving to derive special private advantages from the exercise of public power. On the other hand, the traditional means of organizing broader public agendas—labor movements and political parties—seem to be in serious decline as sources of political identification and what political scientists call "interest aggregation." In short, elected governments lack both the coherent base of political support and the fiscal resources to address pressing social, economic, and environmental problems. As a result, liberal democratic citizens are restive. They have little faith that the political system can "process" their inputs into effective and satisfying outputs, and they have even less faith in the political class whose entrepreneurial spirit has long been put forth by democratic theorists as the heart of democratic politics. Such citizens do not like paying taxes, they are quickly disenchanted with incumbents, and they are deeply cynical about political representation.

This is the reality of liberal democracy at the dawn of the twenty-first century. Governmental gridlock. Ineffective public policy. Declining faith in political institutions. A growing appeal of right-wing populism and antiliberal sentiments. These are the results of a political system that rests on a lack of direct participation and civic initiative, supports manifold forms of social inequality and corporate economic privilege, and thrives on the energies of a class of political entrepreneurs who mobilize extraordinary financial resources and propaganda machines to manipulate a largely passive and disempowered electorate.

Liberal democracy is an important historical achievement, and clearly its constitutional liberties and system of political competition are necessary conditions of any democracy worth having. It is to the credit of Western political science that it has advanced our knowledge of such a regime and how to organize it. But the approach to democracy that emerged in Western political science after the war affords us the means of neither understanding nor remedying the serious difficulties that currently beset liberal democracy. For while it offers great insight into the dynamics of political competition, representation, and public opinion, it pays insufficient attention to problems of democratic legitimacy and political identity that have moved to the forefront of political life today.

The empirical theorization of democracy promoted by writers such as Dahl, Lipset, and Sartori was exemplary in its effort to address the problems of its time as its chief proponents defined these problems. In retrospect it is possible to appreciate this way of defining an intellectual problem field. But in retrospect it is also possible to see just how limiting this definition was. In the name of an interest in the empirical, a narrow canon of empiricist methods was instituted, purging political inquiry, and indirectly purging the idea of democracy itself, of its speculative and visionary impulses. In the name of realism the range of histori-

·cal experience and historical possibilities associated with democracy was severely and unjustifiably narrowed. In an effort to distance liberal democracy
from the populist fanaticism associated with Hitlerism and Stalinism, this
"democratic theory" described—and prescribed—a thoroughly domesticated,
normalized kind of democracy, a democracy in which a clear division of labor existed between politicians and citizens, in which significant ideological conflicts
were abated, and in which government could distribute its benefits to an eagerly
consuming public.[58]

Such an understanding of democracy left little room for the popular mobilizations and collective insurgencies—abolitionist movements, labor movements,
feminist movements—that played such an important role in achieving democracy in the first place. It had little to say about exemplary forms of democratic activism practiced in its own time, such as the resistance to totalitarianism during
World War II, or the Hungarian uprising against communism, or the American
civil rights movement. The theoretical counterposition of totalitarianism and
democracy admitted no such complexities. And so this approach to democracy
was ill prepared for the upsurges of the 1960s, and for the rise of the new social
movements, on the left and the right, that have so disturbed liberal democratic
normality in the aftermath of that decade.[59] From the perspective of democratic
theory, such phenomena were anomalous forms of participation and contestation that went beyond the bounds of the conventional politics of interest-group
bargaining and elite representation, forms of political praxis that sought more
palpable forms of democratic empowerment, and yet forms of politics that were
in no way totalitarian. They were *democratic* forms of politics, not directed toward the overthrow of liberal constitutional regimes, but seeking to effect sub-
stantial ethical and political changes nonetheless.

Recent developments in political science attest to the obsolescence of the
model of normal politics promoted by democratic theory, and to the need for a
greater sensitivity to phenomena such as those mentioned above. As the opening pages of this chapter indicate, and as subsequent chapters will demonstrate,
such developments have by no means displaced the more conventional view of
democracy. But they are signs of a genuine theoretical *apertura*, or opening, of a
serious scholarly reconsideration of the nature of democratic politics.

One example is the movement of many prominent empirical theorists toward
a more critical view of liberal democracy and the ways in which its own functioning frustrates political equality and meaningful public participation, a develop-

ment marked by the 1991 publication of Robert Dahl's *Democracy and Its Crit-ics*.[60] Another example is the growing interest in "deliberative democracy" on the part of normative political theorists but also more empirically inclined re-searchers attuned to the legitimation deficit of liberal democracies today.[61] A third is the research on "social capital" and its decline that has been sparked by Robert Putnam's work, and the extraordinary attention this work has received from scholars thirsty for insight into the problems plaguing liberal democracy today.[62] Indeed, a heightened interest in civil society is one of the most impor-tant features of contemporary political theory. If postwar democratic theory emerged in reaction to the experience of totalitarianism and was animated by a fear of political power, contemporary democratic theory is concerned above all with the generation of new spaces of civic responsibility and new forms of civic empowerment that might provide ordinary citizens a sense of efficacy and in so doing enhance the workings of liberal democracy.[63]

As we reflect on the development of political theory in the years since the end of World War II, it is not hard to appreciate the truth in Almond's observation about the vindication of political science. Liberal democracy has surely achieved a prominence that could only be hoped for fifty years ago; and the totalitarian re-gimes that so darkened the horizon of world politics seem to have been thor-oughly vanquished. And yet democracy today faces new challenges, challenges due to problems of legitimacy that the postwar period only *seemed* to have tran-scended. Now that these problems have surfaced, it is possible, from the vantage point of the present, to appreciate the power of postwar democratic theory and its limitations. To ignore the former is to ignore an important moment of recent intellectual history; to ignore the latter is to substitute self-congratulation for the serious inquiry that our current challenges demand.

2

> Main deficiency of active people. Active men are usually lacking
> in higher activity—I mean, individual activity. They are active as
> officials, businessmen, scholars, that is, as generic beings . . . Active
> people roll like a stone, conforming to the stupidity of mechanics.
>
> FRIEDRICH NIETZSCHE, *Human, All Too Human*

Just a few short years ago, exactly two hundred years after the start of the French Revolution, "when modern times began to the accompaniment of the crash of falling ramparts" (Camus), the walls of communism came tumbling down in Central Europe and the former Soviet Union. The "Revolutions of 1989" took the world by storm. Even their participants failed to anticipate how quickly the power of Communist regimes would dissolve in the face of mounting crisis and determined opposition.[1] In a few months the face worn by world politics for five decades was transformed. The Cold War was over, and the dramatic ideological antagonism between communism and liberalism, which had defined the politics of the twentieth century, was concluded with a Communist plea of "no contest" and the exultant triumph of Western liberalism.[2]

One would have expected that such dramatic and consequential events would have been grist for the mill of American political theorists. The power of ideas in a world of cynicism and manipulation. The relevance of an avowedly humanistic vocabulary in a postmodern age. The nature of democratic movements, the strategies they employ, the choices they face, the kinds of politics they aspire to construct. The emphatic political revival of liberalism at a time of deep philosophical skepticism, a renewed preoccupation with political foundations at a time of anti-foundationalism. The "meanings" of the revolutions of 1989. The possibilities are virtually endless. And yet, surprisingly, American political theory responded to these events with a deafening silence.

Some simple statistics: In the years between 1989 and 1993 *Political Theory*, "an international journal of political philosophy" that is certainly the premier journal of American political theory, published 108 full-length articles. Of these only one had anything to do with 1989.[3] During the same period *Polity*, the most important American political science journal regularly publishing political theory, published 61 articles in the area, with but a single review essay on 1989.[4] The *American Political Science Review* published 30 articles of political theory, with nothing on the subject. *Philosophy and Public Affairs* ran 76 articles and *Ethics* 109, including symposia on objectivity in ethics and the nature of personal responsibility; but neither journal of contemporary moral philosophy published a single piece on anything connected to the dramatic breakthroughs of 1989.

If we consider these the major American outlets of academic political theory broadly construed, then in the four years following the revolutions of 1989 political theorists published a total of 384 articles, of which a mere two—roughly one half of 1 percent—dealt with dramatic current events of earth-shattering importance.

That is not to deny that attention has been paid to these events. Political scientists, especially comparativists, have written scores of articles on the subject, and indeed a prominent journal, the *Journal of Democracy*, was established in part to deal with it.[5] Public intellectual journals including *Dissent*, *The Nation*, *Praxis International*, and *Social Research* have published numerous essays, some written by political theorists. Yet the principal academic journals of the field, the main organs of scholarship and intellectual exchange, have been silent. When academic political theorists have written scholarly papers or made presentations at scholarly conferences, they have consistently avoided dealing with the revolutions of 1989 and their implications.

This avoidance strikes me as a shocking indictment of academic political theory. How can it be? How can a form of inquiry that claims to be the heir of Plato, Machiavelli, Tocqueville, and Marx, thinkers profoundly caught up in the events of their day, be so oblivious of what is going on around it? A variety of possible justifications present themselves. While each has a certain plausibility, in the end none is convincing.

[1] Perhaps the events of 1989 are so contemporary, so recent, that it is too early to expect them to be incorporated into scholarship. Perhaps more time needs to pass before theorists truly can assess the significance of these events. It seems reasonable to imagine that theorists will assume a more detached, a more profound view of current events than that proffered by pundits, that they will not rush into print on passing fancies and rapidly unfolding events. And yet this ex-

planation will not do. For surely one of the most distinctive characteristics of American political theory as a field is the proliferation of critical commentary on the most recent, celebrated books and articles. The most current publications of Jürgen Habermas and Jacques Derrida, Charles Taylor and William Connolly are quickly consumed, digested, and regurgitated by political theorists eager to make their mark by contributing to the growth of theoretical knowledge. A discipline that is itself so intellectually faddish can hardly plead patience and caution when it comes to interpreting current events.

And how ironic is this reluctance to interpret current events! Is it even possible to imagine such a posture being assumed by Locke or Paine, Kant or Hegel? Historical caution, a determination to let time pass and truly, "deeply" process events, never deterred the "great" theorists of the past upon whom we worshipfully comment again and again. Recall Kant's observation on the French Revolution: "even if the end viewed in connection with this event should not now be attained, even if the revolution or reform of a national constitution should finally miscarry, or, after some time had elapsed, everything should relapse into its former rut . . . that event is too important, too much interwoven with the interest of humanity, and its influence too widely propagated in all areas of the world to not be recalled on any favorable occasion by the peoples which would then be roused to a repetition of new efforts of this kind."[6] What R. R. Palmer has called the age of democratic revolutions—1776–89—was one of the founding moments of modern political thought.[7] Current events, unprecedented revolutions, provided the raw material, the inspiration behind some of the most seminal theorists of the period—Jefferson and Madison, Paine and Wollstonecraft, de Maistre and Burke, Kant and later Hegel. How to classify such writers? Are they philosophers, politicians, essayists, journalists? Does the classification "political theorist," with its heavily academic connotations, really suffice? There is a striking discrepancy between the passionate engagement in current events that characterized most of the foundational writers of contemporary political theory and the disconnection of contemporary political theorists themselves.

[2] Perhaps the inattention to the revolutions in Central Europe and Russia has another source, linguistic and more broadly cultural. Political theory today is, after all, principally a Western European idiom. Many American theorists have been trained to move comfortably in French, German, Italian; how many are familiar with Czech, Hungarian, Polish, or Russian? Perhaps Central Euro-

pean culture and historical experience is sui generis, as Milan Kundera has suggested, or at least constitutes a sufficiently distinctive reality to be terra incognita to theorists grounded in Western European culture.[8]

Linguistic and cultural unfamiliarity seems to offer a plausible explanation for the silence of political theory about Central Europe. But on deeper consideration this explanation falls apart. For language barriers have never really constrained political theorists from offering interpretations of texts or the events to which they are related. While for highly esoteric kinds of historical scholarship reading in the original is important, the most important textual commentary in American political theory is done on the basis of translations. How many of the numerous recent accounts of the writings of Habermas or Foucault, Augustine or Hegel, do you suppose, are based on a reading of the author in the original? A cursory glance at footnotes reveals that the answer is few indeed. Question most self-respecting political theorists about Machiavelli, for example, and they will offer you some interpretation. Can you imagine many political theorists saying that they could not comment on or write about Machiavelli because they could not read Italian or grasp sixteenth-century Florentine idioms in the original? The writings of the principal Soviet-bloc democratic oppositionists—Vaclav Havel, Adam Michnik, Jan Josef Lipski, George Konrad, Ivan Szelenyi, Andrei Sakharov, et al.—have amply been translated into English. They have long been available to the English-speaking world, and there is no linguistic excuse for having avoided them.

The cultural distinctiveness argument is no stronger. It may well be that there is a Central European culture. It is certainly the case that, with the partial exception of certain Marxists such as George Lukacs and Rosa Luxemburg, no Central European writers have been admitted into the hallowed canon of modern—Western—political thought as it has been constructed by American political theorists. But even a surface familiarity with the democratic oppositionists in Central Europe makes clear that, in spite of cultural particularities, the most striking feature of their writings was their profound affinity toward and avowed connection with familiar idioms of Western political theory, whether Jeffersonian, Kantian, Tocquevillean, Heideggerian, or Arendtian. Whatever Winch-inspired arguments we may wish to buy into about the incommensurability of different cultures, the fact is that the Central Europeans have believed themselves to be, and have been, part of a cosmopolitan tradition of humanistic values with roots in the European Renaissance and Enlightenment. They are, in other words, participants in a common European culture that is the intellectual basis of contemporary political theory. Cultural alienation, in short, cannot be a legitimate reason for the avoidance practiced by American political theorists.

[3] Another explanation presents itself, one that I have in fact frequently encountered—that the Central European literature of revolt may be historically or politically significant but it is not especially innovative or genuinely theoretical. Havel and Konrad may be brilliant and evocative writers but they raise and discuss no deep issues, so there is no reason to incorporate what they have written into our theoretical discussions in scholarly journals.

How wonderfully ironic is such a position in light of the widespread—and largely beneficial—relaxing of what constitutes theory that has been abetted by postmodern modes of political theory. As a result of the powerful influence of Jacques Derrida and Richard Rorty, we now have a fairly liberal—generous, relaxed, tolerant—view of what constitutes a text.[9] The hierarchical divisions between "authentic theory" and mere writing are in pervasive disrepute, and a deep suspicion of epistemological foundations is au courant. How, then, could the writings of important dramatists, artists, politicians, and public intellectuals be so easily dismissed? How can such powerful social criticism be discarded without reinstating a completely untenable, Platonic, "essentialist" conception of theory as a higher-order activity?

Further, even if we accept the distinction between deep or compelling theoretical issues and writing that is casual, uninteresting, *unphilosophical*, is it even true that no deep issues are raised by the Central European democrats? An examination of the essays of Vaclav Havel, for example, will reveal serious reflections on the banality of mass society and the ill effects of technology and instrumental rationality on modern life, reflections that mirror the concerns of such familiar writers as Heidegger and Arendt and yet are enriched by their author's experience of persecution and marginalization and his participation in a vital democratic movement, Charter 77. The writings—essays, plays, dramas—of celebrated authors such as Havel, Konrad, and Michnik, but also the more general pamphlet literature of the Central European movements, contained numerous arguments about the ethical and strategic prospects of different forms of resistance, the nature of democratic citizenship, and the importance of civil society. It is true that most of the authors of these texts were not professional philosophers or academic political theorists. But the fact that these writers brazenly defy political and disciplinary frontiers should make them even more compelling to a field increasingly preoccupied with the transgression of boundaries.

[4] But perhaps I am affording the democratic oppositionists too much credit. Perhaps the plain truth is that they have not received attention because they warrant no special attention, because they simply are unoriginal, revisiting the themes and concerns of a nineteenth-century democratic liberalism with which we are all familiar. Perhaps it is not that we believe them to be insufficiently deep, but rather consider them simply anachronistic and old hat. This is certainly the most powerful reason that can be adduced to account for our problem. Unfortunately, it suffers from a basic difficulty—it is untrue. The writings of Havel, Konrad, Michnik, and others offer pioneering treatments of important contemporary problems—the nature of civil, nonviolent resistance to post-totalitarian dictatorship, the character of self-limiting radicalism in a post-Marxist age, the importance of civil society, the role of the intellectual in the modern world.[10]

But even if it were true that these writers were wholly unoriginal and their politics entirely derivative, this claim could be established only on the basis of a serious engagement with their writings and their politics. It would constitute an *interpretation* of the revolutions of 1989, an *argument* that could be supported by evidence and might be debated.[11] What is most striking about recent American political theory is not that it lacks sufficient admiration for these revolutions but that it seems bereft of any interpretation or argument whatsoever.

And absence of originality, the rearticulation of anachronistic themes, in any case, can hardly be considered a reason for dismissal by a discipline marked by a preoccupation with historical texts. Have we stopped writing about Mill because he is a historical figure whose views are no longer modish, his conceptions of subjectivity surpassed by the latest Paris fashions about the constitution of the self? Do we ignore Locke because he is derivative of Hobbes, or Rousseau because he is derivative of Locke? As we of course all know and commonly acknowledge, no theory is wholly original, all theory is derivative, building upon prior idioms, expanding, enriching, reconstituting languages and themes already a part of the cultural and political landscape. So even if the revolutions of 1989 simply reinstated earlier idioms of democratic liberalism, this history would be a reason not to ignore them but to explore their links with earlier idioms and the reasons for them. What are the connections, for example, between Michnik's fascinating writings on the role of the Church in the Polish movement toward democracy and the thinking of early liberal tolerationists such as Locke and Voltaire?[12] What are the linkages between the rhetoric and practices of cosmopolitan federalism being advocated by figures such as Havel and the writings of Montesquieu, Jefferson, or Madison?

The writings of the Central European democrats are deeply relevant to the condition of humans in late modernity. But even if they were merely rearticulations of familiar modernist themes, this fact would present us with all the more incentive to examine *how* they rearticulate familiar themes, and why these themes have assumed such profound importance in parts of our world.

It is the apparent indifference to any such inquiry that constitutes the most serious abdication of contemporary political theory. If this indifference cannot be accounted for in any of the above ways, what *can* account for it? A number of possibilities quickly suggest themselves, possibilities that disturb the reassuring sense many political theorists have about the inherently innovative and critical character of political theory in contrast to the conventionalism of mainstream political science. They suggest that perhaps political theory has constituted itself as a mainstream unto itself.

[1] American political theory has become a thoroughly professionalized academic subdiscipline, where even the intellectual "subversives" are insulated, academicized, their intellectual practices routinized and normalized. Too many political theorists speak only to themselves, preferring esoteric languages to plain expression, seemingly profound formulations to common sense. In the late 1960s and early 1970s, Thomas Kuhn's *Structure of Scientific Revolutions* acquired widespread prominence as an account of the development of "normal science." Many practitioners of mainstream behavioral political science took Kuhn's description as a model to be emulated, seeking truly to normalize the American science of politics.[13] Others, including many of those active in the shaping of American political theory and the establishment of the journal *Political Theory*, dissented from this normalization. They saw political theory as a more open-ended, engaged, humanistic enterprise, fixated less on method than on relevance and meaning.[14] They may be seen as the founders of a revolution in inquiry. It is sad, but perhaps not surprising, how quickly the revolution has had its Thermidor.

American political theorists have become ensnared in their various disciplinary matrices. Preoccupied with situating ourselves vis-à-vis the writings of

Strauss and Arendt, Adorno and Lyotard, we have become puzzle solvers of the problems of others, focusing on approved topics, following academic conventions. As Kuhn observed, "perhaps the most striking feature of the normal research problems . . . is how little they aim to produce major novelties . . . the range of anticipated, and thus of assimilable, results is always small compared with the range that imagination can conceive."[15] It might be unsurprising to consider this an accurate description of some of the more traditional orientations in political theory. But, ironically, it seems true even of many self-proclaimed Nietzscheans, who have managed to constitute a thoroughly normalized discourse of "subversion," whereby theoretical puzzles—the problematics of identity, the effectivity of desire, the transgression of boundaries—get worked out in connection with Plato, Augustine, Machiavelli, Arendt, ad infinitum. The same theorists—Nietzsche, Foucault—establish the terms of reference, the same vocabularies and metaphors are deployed and redeployed, the same texts continually cited. There is certainly nothing particularly insidious about this; it is the way of most kinds of political theory, and of political science more generally. And it produces certain clear advantages, as Kuhn recognized, stabilizing inquiry, abetting the development of scholarly communities, institutions, hierarchies of accomplishment, and advancing the growth of specialized knowledges. These conventionalized and stylized modes of inquiry often produce insight. But they also engender intellectual conformity and inhibit more engaged, colloquial, *relevant* kinds of inquiry.

[2] Deriving from this academic conventionalism is a surprising preoccupation with "great works" that affects even the most avant-garde theorists. It has been more than a quarter-century since Quentin Skinner's path-breaking essay "Meaning and Understanding in the History of Ideas" heralded the deconstruction of the "myth of the tradition" in Anglo-American political theory.[16] The writings of Quentin Skinner, John Pocock, John Dunn, but also Michel Foucault and others have rather effectively undermined any notion that there is a body of political theory that constitutes some privileged or canonical repository of wisdom.[17] With the exception of some holdouts, primarily epigones of Leo Strauss, most political theorists will admit that political writing is a thoroughly historical and contextual activity, that in some sense wherever there is politics there is political theory, wherever there is political language there is something worth interpreting and explaining. And yet if one looks at what political theorists actually write about, one finds that they are still wedded to a canon of—mostly dead—po-

litical writers, to whom they continually recur. Since 1989, for example, 48 of
108 articles in *Political Theory*—45 percent—were on fairly conventional historical figures, commentaries on Aristotle, Locke, Hegel, et al. Even "critical" theorists committed to the deconstruction of such a canon as a canon seem magneti-
cally drawn to it.[18] Such historical figures constitute the core of what most of us
teach our undergraduates; they represent a secure reference point for our political thinking. It is easy, but also resourceful and sometimes ingenious, for us to
conduct our political conversations with reference to these key figures and texts
with which we are all familiar. Such a canon has a truly enabling function, and I
do not mean to suggest that we should—or can—discard historical tradition. But
such tradition can also easily become a dead weight that hinders us from moving
forward, a cloak—what Burke called a decent drapery (see how powerful is this
temptation!)—that conceals and obstructs political reality and our ability to experience it and interrogate it.

[3] Contemporary political theory is plagued by an aversion to first-order
questions in the name of theoretical depth. It seems almost beneath us to examine mundane, practical political problems located in space and time, in particular places with particular histories. These inquiries, we apparently reason, can
safely be left to historians and political scientists. How much more edifying,
rigorous, hip, or virtuous it is to discuss the constitution of the self, the nature
of community, the proper way to read an old book, or the epistemological foundations or lack thereof that are involved in examining mundane political
problems.[19]

Fred Dallmayr, for instance, begins his essay "Postmetaphysics and Democracy" by observing that "ours is an age of endings and beginnings." Talk of
"posthistory" and "postmodernity" takes place alongside a dramatic upsurge of
democratic politics across the globe. "How," he asks, "can one make sense of
this conjuncture of farewells and new initiatives, of denials and dramatic en-
dorsements?"[20] One might imagine that an answer to this question would involve a discussion of the ways in which old forms of politics constructed along
ideological lines have failed, an account of the political agendas being advanced
by talk of posthistory or postmodernity, or perhaps an analysis of the convictions
and political visions linking together—and separating—various democratic
movements in the world today. But instead Dallmayr seeks to explore "the secret
code or passageway that subterraneously links these disparate phenomena and
events."

What is this secret subterranean passageway? What Dallmayr calls "the paradox of revealment and seclusion," by which he seems to mean the fact that the democratic ideal supports the effort to institute certain egalitarian norms in the name of the civic body and at the same time withholds from any institution its unqualified imprimatur. This paradox, which has long been acknowledged by theorists as diverse as John Dewey, Hannah Arendt, and Claude Lefort, introduces an interesting dialectic of construction and contestation into democratic politics, one that might profitably be discussed in connection with long-standing images of radical politics, as Lefort has done, or with reference to actual political problems such as constitution-making, as Bruce Ackerman has attempted to do.[21] But Dallmayr forswears such inquiries. Instead, "enlisting the aid of prominent political theorists and philosophers," he offers an extended exegesis of some of the writings of Eric Voegelin, Lefort, and Martin Heidegger. These writers may aid Dallmayr in his pursuit of secret codes of revealment and seclusion; his essay surely contains interesting textual insights. But the dramatic political denials and affirmations that he mentions in his first paragraph—which these philosophic luminaries are purportedly invoked to illuminate—are never again mentioned.

This aversion to first-order inquiry affects even genealogical theorists, who most avow suspicion of abstract philosophizing. In "The Politics of Territorial Democracy," for example, William Connolly discusses the way a Foucauldian genealogy of identity might help to "relax" the principle of national sovereignty and its institutionalization of rigid national boundaries. While the actual problem with which he begins—the problem of sovereignty and its effects—is a pressing one, and his effort to draw insight from Foucault is beyond reproach, Connolly's discussion is pitched entirely at the metatheoretical level. He concludes by suggesting that "perhaps disparate and discrete phenomena such as Amnesty International, Greenpeace, the consolidation of international corporations, divestment movements aimed at global corporations doing business with states that trample on human rights, the series of movements to assist 'boat people,' Palestinians, and others residing outside the protection of territorial states, and non-state movements like the 'nuclear freeze' to foster arms reduction between states might provide reflection in this area with more specific exemplifications from which to proceed."[22] This suggestion is promising; but one can redeem it and get at the meaning of these phenomena only by engaging them through concrete, empirical, historical inquiry. While Connolly offers interesting and suggestive reflections on "identity" and "boundaries," reflections that might help to illuminate a serious investigation of global politics, he makes no effort to undertake such an investigation.

Indeed, his very language typifies the aversion to first-order questions that is so pervasive among political theorists—these disparate phenomena are treated as possible "exemplifications" of "reflection in this area." The area in question is "nonterritorial democratization" as this is constructed by genealogical theory. The disciplinary matrix or paradigm, if you will, is genealogy; and how it relates to international relations is the puzzle we are invited to solve, just as we might puzzle out the genealogical implications of media institutions or gender relations or homelessness in American cities. The intellectual-political project here is the fleshing out of genealogy. Instead of theory serving as a conceptual means of coming to grips with actual political phenomena, these phenomena serve as "exemplifications" of remote theoretical constructs. Instead of being shown how genealogy might illuminate contemporary movements, we are offered a suggestion about how such movements might give credence to—might validate—genealogy as a mode of scholarly and professional activity. What undoubtedly began as a means of understanding—geneaological theory—is thus converted into an end in itself. In his oft-quoted essay "Nietzsche, Genealogy, History," Foucault writes that genealogy is "grey, meticulous, and patiently documentary."[23] Yet too much political theory, even when influenced by Foucault, is impatient, forswearing documentary evidence, intent on producing metatheoretical insights at the expense of sustained engagement with empirical reality.

I mention Connolly's essay along with Dallmayr's because they are in some ways exemplary pieces of political theory as it is generally practiced, resting on a seductively appealing form of exegesis and containing genuine insight. Connolly's genealogical reflections in particular have helped to spawn important lines of inquiry into the politics of identity.[24] Yet they both also typify the general tendency of political theory to gesture at empirical reference and historical relevance without cashing in on the promise, to be more concerned with puzzling out existing paradigms and proliferating textual commentaries than with confronting political reality.

Let me be clear here. I am not suggesting that theoretical reflection, abstract conceptualization, and generalization are somehow illicit or to be condemned. They are indispensable to serious inquiry of any kind, and it is certainly impossible to imagine anything called political theory that abjures them. I am not claiming that political theorists should become activists or journalists or empirical political scientists, however we might define these complex and equally problematic identities. But I am saying that we political theorists investigate the same political world addressed by these other interpreters, and not—of course!—some superior, transcendent, esoteric, or Platonic reality. It is thus incumbent upon us to acknowledge this world as a source of intellectual and practical problems, to engage it in all of its empirical and historical messiness, to demonstrate that our categories help to illuminate this political reality and even, dare I say, to improve it in however modest a fashion.[25] Articles such as "Constitutionalism in Habermas," for example, and "Locke on Constitutional Government" clarify problems of constitutionalism in only the most remote and mediated way, typically devoting most of their energy to a critique of the existing exegetical literature, presenting some textual commentary of their own and offering little direct insight into substantive political concerns. While there is surely nothing wrong with such inquiries, they should more often be linked to the project of understanding constitutionalism, not simply the project of understanding Habermas or Locke. Real political problems ought not to be the pretext for scholarly investigations of other things; they should be what drives our inquiries. Such a linkage of historical and textual commentary with a broader enterprise of understanding actual political movements, struggles, and possibilities may not be the only "task" of political theory, and I share the postmodern suspicion of anyone who pretends to lay down a single model of inquiry to which all must adhere. But it is surely an important task, one that has been almost entirely marginalized by political theory in the American academy today.

[4] This fixation with the metatheoretical is abetted by the disturbing tendency to reinforce an ironically sharp distinction between theory and writing, a distinction that is surely anachronistic in our postmodern age, but one that is practically sustained by even the most postmodern among us. American political theorists too often tend to write journal articles rather than expository essays, to promote specialized languages rather than clear, plain English, and to direct themselves to a specialized, professionalized audience rather than a general readership. This tendency is part of the normal process of disciplinary professionalization, but it has surely been abetted by the hypertheoretical style of certain French and German idioms that have acquired prominence in the American academy.[26] As a consequence the kind of writing that receives validation as

"serious" and "scholarly" tends to place a premium on academic conventions—the careful and relentless citation of recent scholarship, a remoteness from collo-quial expression, and, most fatefully, an avoidance of directly political themes and positions—at the expense of originality or relevance. We are by now all well acquainted with the idea that language is not a medium of transparent commu-nication, that it secretes power and mobilizes biases. Yet this does not license ver-bal obscurity, poor writing, or unintelligibility. In his famous essay "Politics and the English Language," George Orwell argues that political language has come to consist "largely of euphemism, question-begging, and sheer cloudy vagueness."[27] While he surely saw the rise of propaganda techniques as the pri-mary cause of this corruption of language, he also documented how poor writ-ing aided and abetted this process by "anesthetizing" the mind, inhibiting clear thinking and honest communication. If we wish to understand the strange si-lence of political theory, part of the explanation seems to lie in the modes of ex-pression that have come to dominate our field, modes of expression that encour-age indirectness rather than directness, and that seem particularly ill equipped to identify with and relate to the kind of direct public expression and literary en-gagement that characterized the Central European democratic opposition.

[5] But the above explanations perhaps place too much emphasis on distinc-tively academic factors. Perhaps the fact is that the silence of American political theory is due to an insularity that characterizes American society as a whole. It certainly seems that British, French, and German theorists have paid more at-tention to recent events in Central Europe than have their American counter-parts. America has always been apart from the Old World, separated by thou-sands of miles of ocean, but also by a distinctive political history. While certainly fractious and violent in its own right, American history has always lacked the kind of ideological polarization that has characterized Europe. Our shores and our unique constitutional history have spared us two world wars, the ascen-dency of totalitarianism, fifty years in which half of Europe was dominated by Communist dictatorship and all of Europe threatened to become a nuclear bat-tlefield. Americans are far removed from and in some ways blithely indifferent to what is currently going on in Europe.

Daniel Boorstin has suggested that the peculiar genius of America is that it lacks any political theory, that Americans have been able to live liberal democ-racy while others have had to argue about it.[28] This is of course a controversial and in many ways flawed thesis, but it also highlights a truth, one discerned long ago by Tocqueville. The American Revolution was dramatically unlike the French Revolution that followed it, and American political history has thus been spared the trials and tribulations of having to struggle with the legacies of Jacobinism and anti-Jacobinism that have dominated modern European politics. In this sense American intellectual life has lacked the ideological anchoring so powerful across the Atlantic.

As Emerson, William James, and Dewey noted, this lack has been in many ways a blessing, creating opportunities for forms of eclectic, experimental, *pragmatic* political thought unencumbered by ideological orthodoxy.[29] And yet, through a strange twist of fate, this opportunity has largely been squandered. This is a complex matter. Part of the explanation surely lies in the bureaucratic model of university life, imported from Germany in the early part of the twentieth century, which helped to stifle creativity and promote intellectual professionalization.[30] Part of the explanation lies in the intellectual habits of mind that have acquired prominence among American political theorists. One thing is clear: the most dramatic development of contemporary history has been the defeat of the Jacobin revolutionary model by the revolutions of 1989. The Central European democrats have turned for guidance to the United States, to its history of federalism and political pluralism, and to writers, including Tocqueville and Arendt, who have emphasized the unique virtues of American democratic traditions and American forms of political improvisation. And yet, irony of ironies, American political theorists seem transfixed by the French and German philosophical *reactions* to the Jacobin model and its failure. While exciting and also portentous political upheavals proceed in Central Europe, many American theorists remain curiously caught in the orbit of Heidegger and Habermas, Foucault and Derrida, working through the offshoots of a critique of a Marxism that is now for all practical purposes dead. Others remain wedded to a monumental history of ideas that has its roots in German Romanticism, while few remain attentive to political developments taking place before their very eyes.[31]

Almost forty years ago C. Wright Mills published a book, called *The Sociological Imagination*, about the failure of social science to present intelligible and powerful accounts of the intersections between personal experience and political history. Mills demonstrated a variety of ways in which the intellectual habits of modern American academics—hyperempiricism and hyperabstraction, conceptual grandiosity, the use of jargon, the dismissal of historical materials—obstructed clear thinking about politics and abetted the evasion of significant political issues and relations. He argued that social science needed a new vision of intellectual craftsmanship and political vocation, a vision that attended to what was significant, and whose standards of significance transcended the narrow boundaries of academic and professional respectability and convention. In the spirit of Deweyan pragmatism, perhaps the richest idiom of distinctively American theory, Mills endorsed modes of inquiry that illuminated the historical experiences of our time in intellectually serious and morally *relevant* ways.[32]

Postwar American political theory was born in a revolt against many of the academic conventions Mills criticized, yet political theory today is susceptible to much the same criticism.[33] It lacks what we might call a political imagination, a sense of what is significant and a commitment to addressing it in illuminating and accessible ways. In some respects Sheldon Wolin's *Politics and Vision*, published in 1960, clarifies such an imagination, especially in its view of theory as a way of grappling with pressing political issues. But in other ways Wolin's seminal book is the forerunner of today's academicized political theory. For its vision of "the political" is too highly mediated not by positivistic methodologies but by a series of reflections on classic political thinkers and their contribution to a distinctive vocation of political theory with its own distinctive pedagogy. The result is a high-minded view of theory as a nobler kind of inquiry into an especially virtuous reality, a view that is one of the chief causes of the irrelevance that motivates my discussion.[34]

Wolin's book was perhaps the most important contribution to the effort to establish and defend a distinctive identity for political theory at a time of impending encroachment by behavioral political science. As I see it, the problem with political theory today is exactly the opposite—not that it lacks its own identity but that it is too wedded to its identity as a distinctive, *profound* enterprise, that it values theoretical ingenuity and philosophical declamation over empirical insight or historical relevance.[35]

The world is witnessing drastic and dramatic changes, promising hope but also danger and disaster. The "end of history" loudly proclaimed in 1989 has given way to a decade of bitter ethno-national conflicts. Political theorists ought to address these changes and to make them intelligible. Just as the American and French revolutions inaugurated an age of democratic reform and conservative counterrevolution, the developments known as the revolutions of 1989 have posed the possibility of new forms of democratic citizenship and new forms of authoritarian reaction. The failure of political theory to address these possibilities represents a missed opportunity for important intellectual work, and indeed belies the field's claim to do serious *political* theory. It also constitutes a grave ethical abdication. For current events present serious choices regarding moral responsibility, political membership, and constitutional foundations, choices that political theory might truly help to illuminate. The nondecisions of political theorists in this matter—the decisions to attend to other things—do have ethical consequences. Political theory fiddles while the fire of freedom spreads, and perhaps the world burns.

Having argued for more "relevant" and "engaged" kinds of inquiry, however, I must be frank. The challenges facing us at the dawn of a new century are truly daunting, and the political world is in many ways impervious to the kind of critical reason that political theory at its best seeks to promote. The kind of illumination that political theory might provide is hardly likely to be widely disseminated or to be politically influential. The age of Enlightenment is over. The reasons for its demise are the same reasons that account for the professionalization and normalization of intellectual life that I have been criticizing.

So what's the point of the criticism? What difference can political theory make? The answer, I think, is probably little difference. Surely political theory is not likely to make the kind of difference that self-styled progressive intellectuals once imagined. The idea of theory as the inspiration or the "head" of a transformative political subject, an idea stated so forcefully by Marx in his early essays and reiterated in different ways by John Dewey and Antonio Gramsci, is a myth whose time has passed. There is no such political subject. And even if there were, we live in a world in which intellectual values have little currency, in which the video frame has replaced the printed page, and the books that get published and distributed and bought are produced by such philosophic luminaries as Howard Stern and Dennis Rodman; a world, in short, in which political illiteracy and public attention deficit disorder are pandemic.[36] In such a world the prospects for meaningful public debate informed by democratic values and critical reason are dim. Political theorists interested in making sense of the pressing ethical challenges before us, and in seeking to make a difference through their thinking, their teaching, and their writing, confront serious and perhaps insurmountable obstacles.

And yet I think this is no reason to give up trying. For to give up is to succumb to the very forces of privatism and cynicism that pervade our social universe. It is to abandon the promise of intellectual inquiry. It is also to foreclose on those real possibilities for intelligent criticism and improvement, however modest, that do exist in our political world. An engaged political theory must be a modest political theory. It must frankly acknowledge the dim prospects of its own impact. It must acknowledge the very real pressures and attractions that lead many scholars to prefer a more "normal" occupation, an occupation that, however creative, ingenious, and authentically self-expressive, treats the work as its own reward, and concerns itself with little more. And, finally, an engaged political theory must frankly acknowledge the many forms engagement itself may take. We are past the point where we can in good faith imagine that there is a single method of inquiry or a single issue of political concern. We cannot read the agenda of History, for there is none. Yet having said this, I also maintain that we are not past the point of distinguishing between kinds of political theory that attempt in some way to understand and to explain important practical concerns, and kinds of inquiry that forswear such efforts. A political theory that is engaged but modest is different from a political theory that is immodestly disengaged.

In his influential essay "The Power of the Powerless," Havel writes about the "autototality" of mass society. While each individual possesses the capacity for independence, "each person somehow succumbs to a profane trivialization of his or her inherent humanity, and to utilitarianism. In everyone there is some willingness to merge with the anonymous crowd and to flow comfortably along with it down the river of pseudo-life."[37] There is nothing insidious about this, Havel maintains. Through laziness, but also because of genuine advantages, individuals adapt to the requirements of their careers and occupations and become creatures of routine, locked within the narrow horizons of their jobs and private lives. Too many American political theorists have in spite of ourselves succumbed to such an autototality, flowing down the river of pseudo-intellectual life. We are active, but active as generic beings, conforming to the stupidity of mechanics, snared in the intellectual confines of reigning paradigms and professional expectations.

"Books," Emerson wrote, "are for the scholar's idle times. When he can read God directly, the hour is too precious to be wasted in other men's transcripts of their readings."[38] Political theory has professionally arrived. Political theorists have demonstrated their ability to produce and sustain an inventive and sometimes insightful conversation among themselves, a conversation principally centered on their own transcripts and the transcripts of other theorists who have preceded them. There is much to be said for this way of doing political theory. It can be academically rewarding and often intellectually challenging. Yet at a time when we can "read God directly," the hour is too precious to limit ourselves to these insular pursuits. We need to open ourselves up to the dramatic political experiences of our time, and to think for ourselves about them in innovative and serious ways. If we fail to do so, we may continue to achieve professional success, but at the price of intellectual obscurity and political irrelevance.

3

> The trick in living seems to me precisely to reject all complete and
> well-rounded solutions and to live in a continual state of tension and
> contradictions, which reflects the real nature of man's existence.
>
> DWIGHT MACDONALD, "The Root Is Man"

Hannah Arendt is an enigmatic figure. One of the principal shapers of postwar academic political philosophy, she is known primarily as a classical thinker whose conception of politics is drawn from the ancient Greeks and Romans. Yet she was wholly a creature of the twentieth century, preoccupied with the problems of totalitarianism, revolution, and mass politics.[1] Intellectual historians of the Cold War have properly situated Arendt amidst those "New York intellectuals" who journeyed from anti-Stalinist radicalism to liberal anticommunism after World War II. The consensus among these historians is that Arendt's books "became the canonic texts of American exceptionalism and a new liberal anticommunist reaction," that "Arendt's arguments became the philosophical cement which firmly set this new view of political realities."[2] Even Alan Wald, who acknowledges that Arendt was a "maverick thinker of considerable creativity," writes that Arendt's *Origins of Totalitarianism* "may have performed a conservatizing role" by likening the Communist Soviet Union to Nazi Germany, thus dissolving "the difference between revolutionary anti-Stalinism and simple anticommunism."[3]

Arendt herself abjured all such political labels. Once asked what her "position" was on contemporary politics, she replied: "I really don't know and I've never known. And I suppose I never had any such position. You know the left think that I am conservative, and the conservatives sometimes think that I am left or I am a maverick or God knows what. And I must say I couldn't care less. I don't think that the real questions of this century will get any kind of illumination by this kind of thing."[4] One of the tragedies of the Cold War was that it rendered such sentiments difficult to sustain. Albert Camus once wrote that "nothing is true that compels us to make it exclusive."[5] During the Cold War

anticommunist liberalism and antiliberal communism claimed just such exclu-
sivity. As Irving Howe observed in 1954: "the Zeitgeist presses down upon us
with a greater insistence than at any other moment of the century . . . established
power and dominant intellectual tendencies have come together in a harmony
[that] makes the temptations of conformism all the more acute.[6]"

As a consequence, iconoclastic perspectives were either incorporated into
reigning molds, marginalized, or ignored altogether. In Arendt's case, some of
her insights about totalitarianism were appropriated by liberals without any attention to the place of these insights in her broader understanding of modern
politics. But the end of the Cold War makes possible a truer appreciation of critical potentialities submerged by Cold War orthodoxy. Hannah Arendt was a radical political thinker who rejected the terms of the Cold War. Like others of her
generation—Albert Camus and Dwight Macdonald spring to mind—she was an
independent thinker with anarchist leanings, who had seen totalitarianism at
firsthand and hoped that the resistance to it might presage a new, more humane
and democratic politics.[7] She was averse to all totalizing ideological visions, including "liberal anticommunism."

Yet neither did she fit easily into the mold of a "dissenting intellectual." Unlike the *Monthly Review* circle, C. Wright Mills, or even "revisionist" historians
such as William Appleman Williams, she resisted the attraction of an "anti-
imperialist" politics whose legitimate criticism of the American imperium
often obscured the dangers of revolutionary authoritarianism.[8] Unlike the social democratic writers associated with *Dissent*, she was attached to no programmatic politics, anchored to no labor movement or political party or even any de-
terminate historical tradition.[9]

Arendt was a strange radical indeed, inspired by Nietzsche and Heidegger as
well as Jefferson and Kant, a passionate critic of Marxism who nonetheless declared that the revolutionary workers' movements represented the primary
agencies of freedom in the modern world. An iconoclast, she argued with liberals, social democrats, and New Left radicals, yet she abjured these labels and refused these secure identities. Her elusiveness is frustrating to the theorist and
the activist. But as we confront a world in which existing ideological commitments seem increasingly hollow, it is also a source of much richness and vitality.
Arendt's refusal of settled forms of political thought, her brazen defiance of any
forms of political correctness, I suggest, is an appropriate model for the dissenting intellectual in our times. I hasten to add that I say "an appropriate

model" rather than "*the* appropriate model" quite deliberately. Arendt was not
the virtuous if misunderstood "true" dissident of our times. Her attitude toward the nitty-gritty realities of politics was often disturbingly aloof. In some
cases, most notoriously her criticism of school desegregation in Little Rock, Ar-
kansas, her thinking was encumbered by unwieldy and untenable philosophical
distinctions—such as "the social" versus "the political"—that clouded her judgment, whatever their intention or merit.[10] Yet even here her thinking is instructive, for it courageously defied conventional wisdoms, going against fashionable
intellectual currents that moved toward integrationism, and presciently dis-
cerning limits to this liberal strategy.[11] It is above all this brave effort to clear a
new path for thinking about politics that needs to be retrieved in our post–Cold
War age, in which the political energies mobilized by liberal anticommunism
have abated, and the ideological simplicities of that era have been replaced by
new and equally disturbing forms of thoughtlessness.

Totalitarianism and Modernity

It is widely held that the idea of totalitarianism was a weapon in the arsenal of
Cold War liberalism.[12] The fact that Arendt's *Origins of Totalitarianism*, published in 1951, was the most influential study of totalitarianism has thus been an
important source of evidence for the view of Arendt as Cold War liberal. There
is no denying that in the 1950s the discourse of totalitarianism versus Western
freedom served the ends of U.S. foreign policy and of liberalism more generally.
Yet it is a historical error to associate the idea of totalitarianism with the era in
which the idea was conscripted to serve reasons of state.[13]

The idea emerged not in the 1950s but the 1930s, when a traumatic series of
rapid-fire events—the rise of Hitler, the defeat of the Spanish Republic, the Mos-
cow trials, and the onset of World War II—provoked radical rethinking across
the political spectrum. Liberals such as Hans Kohn, Elie Halévy, and Raymond
Aron; Marxists including Victor Serge and Rudolf Hilferding; and independent
leftists, among them George Orwell, Arthur Koestler, and Ignazio Silone, all
converged upon the idea that Nazi Germany and Stalin's Soviet Union were both
"totalitarian" states based on unprecedented brutality and ideological indoctri-
nation. Far from being "establishment" intellectuals, most of these writers were
pariahs, exiles, their lives thrown into disarray by the rise of totalitarianism.[14]
Leon Trotsky himself—hardly a Cold Warrior—suggested, in his 1939 essay
"The USSR in War," that the coming war, if it did not lead to world revolution,

would lead to the triumph of "a totalitarian regime" in which "a new minimum program would be required—for the defense of the interests of the slaves of the totalitarian bureaucratic society."[15]

Arendt's *Origins of Totalitarianism* emerged from this context. Though published in 1951, it was composed of materials written throughout the 1940s, concerned primarily with Nazism and the extermination of the Jewish people.[16] Arendt's thesis is not the identity but the *essential similarity* of Soviet communism under Stalin and Nazism in respect of the totalism of their power and the nihilisitc manner in which it is exercised to commit bureaucratic mass murder. The book does not offer predictions either about the future of totalitarianism or about world politics, nor does it offer apocalyptic warnings about the need for "Western" vigilance. Indeed, the language of West versus East is entirely absent from the text, which is concerned primarily with the potential for destruction and evil latent in modernity.

The book is above all a critique of the "superfluousness of modern man" engendered by massifying economic and political forces, and of the "decline of the nation-state and the end of the rights of man" produced by national sovereignty in an age of imperialism. Arendt's 1951 preface to the first edition is hardly a celebration of American imperium. Traumatized by two world wars and horrified by the potential for future devastation and suffering presented by the postwar situation, Arendt observes: "Under the most diverse conditions and disparate circumstances, we watch the development of the same phenomena—homelessness on an unprecedented scale, rootlessness to an unprecedented depth . . . Never has our future been more unpredictable, never have we depended so much on political forces that cannot be trusted to follow the rules of common sense and self-interest . . . the essential structure of all civilizations is at the breaking point."[17] The themes sounded here—the death of hope, the dreadful unpredictability of the future, the anticipation of world war, the inadequacy of all political ideologies—are not inconsistent with the "hard liberalism" expounded by Arthur Schlesinger and Reinhold Niebuhr. And yet they are not compensated for by the faith in liberal reform, "modernization," and "postindustrial" technology so often articulated by postwar liberals.[18]

Any doubts about the distance separating *The Origins of Totalitarianism* from postwar liberal orthodoxy can be dispelled by a perusal of Arendt's 1953 essay "Ideology and Terror: A New Form of Government," later published as the final chapter of the 1958 edition of *Origins*. In it Arendt writes:

If it is true that the elements of totalitarianism can be found by retracing the history and analyzing the political implications of what we usually call the crisis of our century, then the conclusion is unavoidable that this crisis is no mere threat from the outside, no mere result of some aggressive foreign policy of either Germany or Russia, and that it will no more disappear with the death of Stalin than it disappeared with the fall of Nazi Germany. It may even be that the true predicaments of our time will assume their authentic form—though not necessarily the cruelest—only when totalitarianism has become a thing of the past. (*Origins of Totalitarianism*, p. 460)

Arendt makes two crucial points in this passage. The first is that totalitarianism is a product of "the crisis of our century" and is not explicable in terms of the machinations of subversives in league with an "evil empire." Indeed, she is quite clear that the emergence of the Soviet empire was a consequence rather than a cause of this crisis. Only the last third of *Origins* actually discusses totalitarianism. Part I discusses anti-Semitism and its ties to the political economy of the modern nation-state. Part II discusses European imperialism and the decline of parliaments and of the bourgeois public sphere in general, culminating in the catastrophic explosion of 1914, which "seems to have touched off a chain reaction in which we have been caught ever since." As Arendt writes:

Before totalitarian politics consciously attacked and partially destroyed the very structure of European civilization, the explosion of 1914 and its severe consequences of instability had sufficiently shattered the facade of Europe's political system to lay bare its hidden frame. Such visible exposures were the sufferings of more and more groups of people to whom suddenly the rules of the world around them had ceased to apply. (p. 267)

A long history of corruption and indifference to hidden suffering thus laid the basis for totalitarianism. Arendt makes clear that the issues she raises go much deeper than anticommunism; indeed, in her 1966 preface she warned that "we have inherited from the cold-war period an official 'counter-ideology,' anti-Communism, which also tends to become global in aspiration and tempts us into constructing a fiction of our own" (p. xviii).

Her second point follows from this—the soil from which totalitarianism sprang, the political terrain that we in many ways still occupy, poses problems that are no less disturbing because they are less atrocious than totalitarianism itself. Particularly troubling to her is "the decline of the nation-state and the end of the rights of man." A main subtext of *The Origins of Totalitarianism* is that state sovereignty is incapable of handling the problems of dislocation and degradation characteristic of our world. As she puts it, in the contemporary age "the very phrase 'human rights' became for all concerned—victims, persecutors, and onlookers alike—the evidence of hopeless idealism or fumbling feeble-minded hypocrisy" (p. 269). She concludes that any adequate response to the horrors of totalitarianism must include a new conception of human justice and solidarity, that "human dignity needs a new guarantee which can be found only in a new political principle, in a new law on earth, whose validity this time must comprehend the whole of humanity while its power must remain strictly limited, rooted in and controlled by newly defined territorial entities" (p. ix). The implication is clear: far from justifying a new American imperium, the experience of totalitarianism calls for a fundamental rethinking of the institutions of national sovereignty and a promotion of human dignity more vigorous, and more innovative, than the practices engendered by the even the most liberal system of nation-states.

Beyond the Cold War

If Arendt had been a supporter of Cold War liberalism, one would have expected her to hold what were at the time predictably liberal views with respect to the major issues of the Cold War—loud denunciation of communism and barely audible criticism of the persecutory ethos that eventuated in McCarthyism, enthusiastic support for NATO, and backing for U.S. counterinsurgency in the Third World. But on each of these scores Arendt's views were unfashionable.

Arendt clearly opposed communism both as a form of politics as it was practiced in the Soviet Union, China, and Eastern Europe and as an ideology that sought to transform the world according to a conception of an end to history. And yet she numbered Marx among the greatest of modern thinkers. Far from considering Marxist ideas anathema, or treating them as incipient rationales for communist despotism, Arendt engaged Marxist thought in a serious dialogue from which she gained much insight, and she openly acknowledged her debt.[19] Indeed, it is hard to think of any contemporary American philosopher of her stature who during this period so freely cited such Marxist notables as V. I. Lenin, Rudolf Hilferding, and Rosa Luxemburg. It is clear from her political and theoretical writings that Arendt strongly criticized Marxism in all of its forms; and yet she refused to join the ever-louder anti-Marxist chorus to which so many of her academic and literary colleagues had been recruited.

This refusal was more than a methodological commitment to intellectual openness, for it was linked to her equally unorthodox opposition to McCarthyism and the anticommunist hysteria more generally. Her private correspondence of the 1950s testifies to a growing fear that "Americanism" might become a new quasi-totalitarian ideology.[20] Arendt articulated these fears publicly in her 1953 *Commonweal* essay "The Ex-Communists," which proceeds from a critique of Whitaker Chambers to a scathing portrait of the "ex-Communist," whose anticommunism is governed by the same Manichean logic as the communism he once supported and now denounces. The ex-Communists, she insists, are not simply former Communists; they are "Communists turned upside down." For them as for the Communists, there are only saints and heretics. They exhibit the same contempt for allies as for opponents, and the same faith in history. "Since they have divided the world into two, they can account for the disturbing variety and plurality of the world we all live in only by either discounting it as irrelevant altogether or by stating that it is due to lack of consistency and character." Revolted by this mentality, Arendt offers a vigorous defense of civil liberties and American constitutional government against American reactionaries, especially Chambers and Joseph McCarthy, whose anticommunism threatened the very freedom it purported to defend.[21] Paralleling the arguments of Henry Steele Commager, the premier American intellectual to speak out in defense of civil liberties during this period, Arendt concludes that

> America, this republic, the democracy in which we are, is a living thing which cannot be contemplated or categorized, like the image of a thing which I can make; it cannot be fabricated. It is not and never will be perfect because the standard of perfection does not apply here. Dissent belongs to this living matter as much as consent does . . . If you try to "make America more American" or a model of a democracy according to any preconceived idea, you can only destroy it. Your methods, finally, are the justified methods of the police, and only of the police.[22]

Arendt, a refugee from Hitler, was frightened by the nativist spirit of McCarthyism. Deeply touched by the plight of stateless peoples, she was particularly disturbed by the McCarran-Walters Act, which threatened to exclude or deport general categories of "alien subversives." Elisabeth Young-Bruehl has com-

mented on the discrepancy between Arendt's "careful, reasonable public statements" about McCarthyism and the more passionate indignation expressed in
her private correspondence, attributing it in part to her fear of the repercussions
on her unnaturalized ex-Communist husband. Yet during this period Arendt
supported the National Committee for an Effective Congress, an anti-McCarthy
group, and was part of an abortive effort to found a civil liberties journal called
Critic.[23]

Arendt was a lukewarm supporter of an active American role in Europe. She
believed that massive U.S. economic assistance was necessary for European reconstruction and to support the containment of Soviet hegemony in Europe, yet
her support was mixed with despair about the Allied Reconstruction effort in
Germany, which in her view failed in the task of denazification. Unlike many
theorists of totalitarianism, Arendt never overlooked the fact that Germany, its
NATO membership notwithstanding, had been the site of the first and most barbarous totalitarian regime. Her 1950 essay "The Aftermath of Nazi Rule" offers
a somber portrait of postwar German politics and society. At the moment in
which this essay was published, West Germany was the front line of the heightening Cold War.[24] Yet while many Western liberals were celebrating the "freedom" of West Germany, Arendt bemoaned its conformity, regretting that a
militarized Germany was being established instead of the "federated Europe"
which alone might aid in the reconstruction of European politics as well as
economics.[25]

For Arendt the pressing concerns of human freedom and indeed human survival were best served by detaching them from the dualistic framework of Cold
War thinking. She criticized European anti-Americans for failing to recognize
the advantages of the Marshall Plan. Yet she was equally critical of "certain current 'Americanistic' attitudes and ideologies in the United States," which
sought to force everything into the terms of Cold War discourse.[26] While critical
of Communist and fellow-traveling leftists, such as Maurice Merleau-Ponty and
Jean-Paul Sartre, whose anticapitalism blinded them to the dangers of Soviet
communism, Arendt resisted that frame of mind which read any criticism of
either capitalism or the United States as a form of "extremism."[27] While she criticized those who laid all of the blame for the emerging arms race on the United
States, she was horrified by the atomic bomb. Like her mentor, Karl Jaspers, she
maintained that these weapons could never be used, and that the appearance of
atomic weapons means nothing less then that "the whole political and moral vo-

cabulary in which we are accustomed to discuss" war and peace has become "for all practical purposes meaningless." Atomic weapons threaten humankind and human posterity. They present a problem for civilization as a whole, and implicate "the intimate connection between modern warfare and a technicalized society." There is only one viewpoint that is more sharply criticized than "anti-Americanism," and that is "the conviction that it is better to be dead than to be a slave."[28]

Finally, Arendt opposed all forms of imperialism. She most clearly articulated this opposition in her contribution to a *Partisan Review* exchange, "The Cold War and the West." Asked by the editors to assess "the position of the West in the Cold War" and to discuss whether the United States should support the forces of radical change or of conservatism throughout the world, Arendt offers a critique of the Cold War itself. First, she insists that the conditions of modern warfare have rendered wars "politically, though not yet biologically, a matter of life and death." "Only if we succeed in ruling out war from politics altogether," she maintains, "can we hope to achieve that minimum of stability and permanence without which no political life and no political change are possible." Second, she holds that the nuclear age discloses even further dangers, whose awareness is foreclosed by the prevailing terms of political debate, which present only two choices, communism and anticommunism. Arendt maintains that no plausible answer can be decided "within the closed circle of this preposterous alternative," for within it both sides display a "reckless optimism"—"on one side, the readiness to count the losses in the tens and hundreds of millions . . . on the other side, the readiness to forget the concentration—and extermination—camps and with them the terrible prospect of freedom vanishing from the earth forever." She rejects the cynical dialectic that would force her to choose between hanging and firing squad, for both choices take refuge in a doctrine, foreclosing our own agency and responsibility. Arendt prefers to stake her faith on the creativity of human beings.[29]

That faith leads Arendt to her most important point—that the futile superpower confrontation has diverted our attention from the more politically significant phenomenon of contemporary revolution. Arendt chastises both Marxism and liberalism for their "conspicuous inability to comprehend the revolutionary spirit." Likening the 1956 Soviet suppression of the Hungarian uprising to the American Bay of Pigs fiasco in Cuba, Arendt criticizes the counterrevolutionary character of American foreign policy. "We have not understood," she insists, "what it means when a poverty-stricken people in a backward country where corruption has been rampant for a very long time is suddenly released from the obscurity of their farms and houses, permitted to show their misery and invited into the streets of the country's capital they never saw before."[30] If we did understand this, she suggests, we would recognize that in the Third World the only alternative to Bolshevik-style revolution is republican revolution, supported by a vigorous American policy of political and economic assistance. For Arendt such revolutions represent moments of freedom to be prized and nurtured rather than suppressed or manipulated—a far cry from the doctrine of "counterinsurgency" soon to become so popular among American liberals.

On Revolution

The main arguments of Arendt's book *On Revolution* are discernible in her *Partisan Review* essay—an endorsement of political rather than social revolution, and of the American rather than the Jacobin/Bolshevik model of revolutionary politics. *On Revolution* is a peculiar book. Because of its loud banishment of "the social question" from politics, and because its praise of a distinctively American politics seems to echo the postwar liberal doctrine of American exceptionalism, many commentators have seen it as the epitome of Arendt's Cold War liberalism. Yet this view is deeply mistaken.

Arendt's rejection of revolutionary Marxism rested on incisive criticisms—of Marxism's reliance on an untenable narrative of historical progress, its devaluation of problems of political judgment, and its utopian synthesis of utilitarianism and romantic individualism. Similar objections can be found in the writings of people as diverse as Macdonald, Camus, Theodor Adorno, and Max Horkheimer. Far from criticizing Marxism in the name of "the vital center," Arendt was motivated by a fear that "the whole radical movement of our time was destroyed through identification with and usurpation by the Russian Revolution."[31] In short, she sought to retrieve an authentically radical tradition, a "lost treasure" that had been submerged by Marxist ideology and by liberal counterideology. In this effort at retrieval she draws on many sources beyond the American experience—the libertarian Marxism of Rosa Luxemburg, the anarchosyndicalism of Russian and East European workers, and the resistance to totalitarianism in France, Denmark, and Hungary. Ironically, while Daniel Boorstin and others were arguing that "the genius of American politics" was precisely its distinctively antitheoretical character, Arendt retrieves the American revolutionary experience precisely because of the lucidity and cogency with which its protagonists self-consciously reflected upon—and theorized about—the creative possibilities of political action.[32] The writings of the American revolutionaries—Thomas Jefferson, James Wilson, even, strangely enough, John Adams—present, for her, a vision of a vibrant, contentious, open, revisable, democratic politics.

Arendt's way of thinking, to be sure, represents a sharp rupture with conventional "left" or "progressive" thinking on politics. Traumatized by the experience of the Weimar Republic, she is highly critical of parliamentary institutions and of political parties in general. She acknowledges that, in comparison with revolutionary Leninist party dictatorships, representative government offers some personal security and civil liberty. But Arendt is suspicious of any political projects that seek state power, especially those based on mass mobilization, and for this reason she is harshly critical of electoral politics even in constitutional democracies. Believing mass politics to be inherently disempowering and corrupt, she favors a robust civil society of voluntary associations that spring to life as the occasion arises, offering space for vigorous political particiation but presenting no ideological vision or programmatic, globalizing policy.[33]

This radical republican vision was hardly complacent about contemporary American politics. In *On Revolution*, Arendt argues that the statist institutions established by the Constitution have eviscerated vibrant experiments in participatory citizenship. In her subsequent writings of the 1960s, many of which were collected in *Crises of the Republic*, Arendt's social criticism becomes more pointed. In "Lying in Politics," a review of *The Pentagon Papers*, she disparages the national security managers responsible for American foreign policy. Capable of calculation but possessing no common sense, these bureaucrats deceived themselves and the American public, all in the name of an unjust and unwise war in Southeast Asia. Arendt also criticizes the more visionary "ideologists of the Cold War" whose "comprehensive ideology" was responsible for a situation in which "sheer ignorance of all pertinent facts and deliberate neglect of postwar developments became the hallmark of established doctrine within the establishment."[34] For her the Vietnam debacle epitomizes the lack of judgment and moderation characteristic of contemporary politics.

These themes are also sounded in "On Violence," a blistering attack on the celebration of revolutionary violence found in the writings of Jean-Paul Sartre and Frantz Fanon. Arendt has sympathy with revolutionaries struggling against colonial oppression, but she refuses to lionize them. Criticizing Sartre's pronouncements likening national liberation movements to Marx's missionary proletariat, Arendt insists that "to think . . . that there is such a thing as a 'Unity of the Third World,' to which one could address the new slogan in the era of decolonization, 'Natives of all underdeveloped countries unite!' (Sartre), is to repeat Marx's worst illusions on a greatly enlarged scale and with considerably less justification. The Third World is not a reality but an ideology."[35] Arendt of course would not deny that there is a Third World, if we mean by the term a set of countries that have a common set of postcolonial problems. But she rejects the effort to ideologize this reality, to offer a grand historical scheme in terms of which all postcolonial struggles make sense, and all political agents can be deemed "progressive" or "reactionary." Like any grand ideology, Third Worldism grossly oversimplifies political reality, and it offers its proponents a false comfort about their own righteousness. The connection between such righteousness and an authoritarian attitude toward dissent and disagreement is not accidental.[36]

But if Arendt criticizes the glorification of revolutionary violence she is equally harsh toward the perhaps more subtle deployments of violence characteristic of liberal democracies. "On Violence" begins by calling attention to "the obvious insanity" of a nuclear balance of terror. Citing Noam Chomsky, Arendt delivers a sweeping indictment of the "military-industrial-labor complex" that has dominated postwar American society and placed military definitions of reality at the center of political life. She proceeds to defend student radicals for their courage in opposing such a system. Here too her comments are nuanced. She praises the students' "astounding will to action, and . . . no less astounding confidence in the possibility of change," yet also criticizes their theatricality, arguing that often their enthusiasm is not supported by a sound analysis or by convincing proposals. The essays in *Crises of the Republic* make clear that Arendt believed that the Cold War had laid the foundations for nothing less than a "constitutional crisis" of liberal politics, marginalizing dissent and closing off "all institutions that permitted the citizens' actual participation."[37]

Arendtian Politics

These criticisms of American politics were consistent with the dissenting space that Arendt had fashioned for herself since the end of World War II. Throughout this period Arendt had challenged the closed-mindedness and hypocrisy of Cold

War liberalism. Underlying this dissenting posture was a coherent vision of politics. For Arendt the human condition is inescapably a condition of natality and mortality, creativity and frailty. The greatest danger of modern ideologies—whether fascist, communist, liberal, or ethno-nationalist—is that they seek to compensate for the partiality and provisionality of human existence by presenting oversimplified, grandiose conceptions of social unity and unquestioning conceptions of political identity. These ideologies worship different deities—*Volk*, History, Technology—but they share a refusal to take into account the recalcitrance of the world, the fact that there is more to the universe than is dreamt of in their philosophies. They lack a healthy sense of moderation.

Arendt's model of politics is thus anti-ideological in its rejection of totalizing visions of political organization or transformation. But it is visionary, indeed utopian, nonetheless. Arendt argued consistently for open, revisable, contestable political associations and communities, for a flourishing of praxis, the human ability to intervene creatively, to disturb the normal flow of events, to create new forms of solidarity and new ways of being. She supported an inclusive, participatory politics, yet not on the model of mass suffrage. Her most notorious account of such a politics appears in *On Revolution*, where she criticizes the principle of universal suffrage not because it includes those who should be excluded but because it homogenizes and eventually evaporates political energies. She proposes instead an "aristocratic" elite "that is chosen by no one but constitutes itself," who will drive a politics based upon voluntary associations, "islands in the sea" of mass politics.[38] Many have been rightly troubled by Arendt's account, more for what it leaves out than for what it says.[39] But two things seem clear. First, Arendt does not believe that this politics of elites can, will, or should completely supplant universal suffrage and representative government so much as she hopes that it may energize and complement more "normal" forms of modern politics. Second, Arendt's "elites" are not conventional elites at all: they are accorded no special privilege; they draw their power from nothing other than their decision to act in concert with their fellows; they are completely self-selecting. As she puts it, we need "a completely different principle of organization, which begins from below, continues upward, and finally leads to a parliament . . . since the country is too big for all of us to come together and determine our fate, we need a number of public spaces within it."[40] Here, as I argue in Chapters 5 and 7, she comes close to articulating a conception of "civil society" with deep affinities to the ideas of Vaclav Havel and George Konrad. For Arendt as for these writers, the principle of freedom extends upward beyond the boundaries of states to encompass new forms of federation and new forms of international responsibility, solidarity, and accountability.

This model of politics is "communitarian" insofar as it endorses multiple forms of public participation and empowerment that challenge the privatism and indifference so typical of modern society. But insofar as these forms are irreducibly multiple, Arendt's vision leaves room for things that often get short shrift in communitarian accounts, such as antagonism, conflict, even violence. Arendtian politics is thus fractious and agonistic even as it supports efforts to establish broader forms of public identity and power. Arendtian politics is also "existential" insofar as it seeks to multiply the opportunities for individuals to enrich their lives through public "performances" in concert with others, and to create themselves anew through their commitments and their deeds. And yet it is not a politics of "authenticity," if by this we mean an effort to find our "true selves," to manifest our deepest individual longings, to surpass our "alienation."

For Arendt to act politically—indeed, to act at all, in any capacity and in any circumstance—is to enter a complex web of interrelationships, conventions that antedate our action and often elude our understanding, and consequences that invariably escape our control. Political life, while it affords us empowerment, is thus a profoundly partial form of existence which can provide no ultimate satisfaction or validation. Politics is indeed characterized above all by difference and dissonance, by the presence of others, with alternative understandings and competing projects, from whom one cannot escape and with whom one must share the world. To ignore this imperative to share the world with others is to suffer from hubris, to imagine that politics can offer the kind of total identification or satisfaction that perhaps can be found only in death. To recognize it is to see that otherness and the respect for it are central to any decent and free politics. This is why Arendt endorses the idea of "representative thinking"—the idea that "the more people's standpoints I have present in my mind while I am pondering a given issue, and the better I can imagine how I would think and feel if I were in their place . . . the more valid my conclusions, my opinion."[41]

Here we return to the guiding thread of Arendt's dissenting attitude—a refusal of a monologic politics that is incapable of projecting beyond the subject, whether Nation, Class, Party, or Race, and an equally insistent refusal of its outgrowth—a polarizing politics in which the Other simply becomes a projection of one's own obsessions and fears, a silent interlocutor in a contest whose outcome can only be stasis or contending ruin. In place of such a politics, epitomized by the mutual balance of terror and conformity that until yesterday held the world in its grip for almost five decades, Arendt offers the vision of a politics always alive to difference, novelty, and particularity, one that refuses to force issues into the straitjackets of ideological labels, and that vigorously supports the freedom to be different from the way such labels demand that we be, at the same time that it seeks to promote new forms of solidarity and commonality.

This vision is as relevant now as it was during Arendt's lifetime. We are no longer caught in the ideological deep freeze of the Cold War, and we confront a situation in many ways more open and more hopeful than the moment in which Arendt wrote. But we face our own dogmas, exclusive truths no less disturbing because they lack the poignancy associated with Mutually Assured Destruction. Indeed, the post–Cold War moment in which we live seems to be a time of proliferating antagonisms and competing monologues, whether they be the certainties associated with resurgent racism and nativism, with Afrocentrism and militant religious fundamentalism, or with a belief in a postindustrial, postideological utopia of global markets and global communications. In such a world, pulled apart by the competing (and often reinforcing) logics of meanness and marketization, the iconoclastic vision presented in Arendt's political writings is both an inspiration and a resource for our own efforts to reconsider what it means to think politically.

4

Human Dignity and the Politics of Human Rights

> Human dignity needs a new guarantee which can be found
> only in a new political principle, in a new law on earth, whose
> validity this time must comprehend the whole of humanity
> while its power must remain strictly limited, rooted in
> and controlled by newly defined territorial entities.
> HANNAH ARENDT, *The Origins of Totalitarianism*

Hannah Arendt is perhaps the most widely studied political philosopher of the twentieth century. And yet little attention is paid to her views on human rights. While this omission is strange, it is not inexplicable, for in her constructive works she studiously avoided the vocabulary of rights, preferring instead to speak of "freedom" or "praxis." In terms made famous by Isaiah Berlin, Arendt was a theorist of "positive" rather than "negative" liberty, one for whom problems of political participation and civic agency occupied center stage, and for whom the juridical strategies for limiting state power typically favored by liberals were not central. She also drew inspiration from classical models of the ancient polis that had scant concern for human rights, models that advanced a conception of republican citizenship and patriotism that left little room for any conception of the human as such. These models exercised a powerful hold on Arendt's political imagination, particularly in those philosophical works—*The Human Condition, Between Past and Future*, and to a lesser extent *On Revolution*—that are most commonly interpreted by academic political theorists.

And yet the problem of human rights—understanding their intellectual foundations, securing their respect—was central to everything Arendt wrote. It was the subtext of *The Origins of Totalitarianism*, and the pretext of *Eichmann in Jerusalem*, the two books most widely known outside the circle of professional political philosophers. It motivated her critique of nuclear politics in her essays on the Cold War, her dissent from maximalist Zionism, and her opposition to the Vietnam War. In all of these instances she criticized forms of official propaganda and hubris that obscured palpable threats to the rights of civilians, refugees, national minorities, disobedients—those groups most powerless before the imperatives of national sovereignty.[1] On a more practical level, a concern with human rights was the source of some of Arendt's most notable political involvements—as a worker for Youth Aliyah in the 1930s, in which capacity she personally transported Jewish refugee children to Palestine; as a supporter of aid to Spanish refugees in the 1940s; and as an active member of PEN and Amnesty International.[2]

While Arendt presented her political theory as an effort to restore an almost completely eclipsed public world, this effort was motivated in large part by the distinctively modern problems of displacement and degradation—what she called "worldlessness." In countering this wordlessness, she addressed issues central to the problem of human rights: the incompatibility of national sovereignty with human dignity and civic responsibility; the need to rethink the ethical foundations of human rights at a time when liberal pieties about natural rights had lost all credibility; and the need for new forms of politics—international jurisprudence, regional and global forms of confederalism, unofficial forms of civic initiative—that would afford political empowerment to ordinary citizens and ground a commitment to human dignity.

Her lack of explicit attention to distinctively moral arguments of the kind to be found in more recent, standard classics of political philosophy, such as John Rawls's *Theory of Justice*, has led many people to overlook Arendt's concern with human rights; and this gap in her writing may well constitute a limitation of her thinking. While she does write favorably of Kant, perhaps she should have done more directly to engage the concerns of moral philosophers in the Kantian tradition of analytic reasoning. But she had her reasons for refusing to do so. She believed that human rights were not a problem of moral speculation or legal philosophy so much as a problem of *politics*, a matter of mobilizing new and effective forms of solidarity and concern. Her political theory hardly offers an exhaustive account of the moral and legal issues involved in human rights. But it contains an indispensable insight that cannot be found in those more prominent works of moral philosophy that focus more centrally on the elaboration of human rights—that the problem of rightlessness that has plagued our world since 1914 can be remedied only by a reconstitution of political identities and the formation of new forms of community that challenge the hegemony of the nation-state. In her distinctively political approach to the problem. Arendt's contribution, often overlooked, remains unsurpassed.

Totalitarianism and Modern Worldlessness

"Human dignity needs a new guarantee."[3] It is no accident that Arendt should introduce her analysis of totalitarianism with this thought. For the problem of human rights—the extent to which human rights is a profound problem, requiring new understandings and new practices—is the central concern of *The Origins of Totalitarianism*. Arendt offers a well-known morphology of the "elements" of totalitarianism. But this account is lodged in a much broader analysis of the circumstances that made genocide possible. While Arendt emphatically rejects the idea that totalitarianism is the necessary outgrowth of modern humanism, she views it as the terrifying apotheosis of certain tendencies of modern politics that render large numbers of people powerless and vulnerable to dangerous and often violent social and political forces.[4]

This is the main theme of Part II of *The Origins of Totalitarianism*, "Imperialism." Arendt's analysis of imperialism draws from Rosa Luxemburg, J. A. Hobson, and other turn-of-the-century theorists who argued that imperialism is a form of expansionist politics driven by domestic surpluses of capital. But she extends this analysis in important ways. First, she focuses, in hindsight, less on the causes than on the consequences of imperialism—a series of geopolitical conflicts that set in motion the two world wars that produced totalitarianism in Germany and the Soviet Union. Second, she treats imperialism as part of a dramatic transformation of European politics, creating kinds of human suffering experienced in extreme form by the victims of totalitarianism. As she notes: "Perhaps it may even be that the true predicaments of our time will assume their authentic form—though not necessarily the cruelest—only when totalitarianism has become a thing of the past" (p. 460).

The "true predicament" of our time ushered in by the age of imperialism is the "superfluity" of large numbers of ordinary people, "the masses." The masses—a recent historical formation—are superfluous in the sense that their active participation becomes increasingly dispensable in economic and political life. This dispensability is produced in part by the processes of capital accumulation, which result in continual expropriations, occupational and demographic shifts, and unemployment.[5] It is also created by the concentration of political power within bureaucratic structures, and the ascendancy of "state employed administrators of violence" who become increasingly remote from ordinary citizens and from representative institutions, and increasingly indispensable to the operation of an imperial foreign policy (p. 137). The result of such processes is the disempowerment and deracination of increasingly larger numbers of people. In such circumstances the ties of citizenship and class begin to lose their force, and nationalism becomes "a precious cement for binding together a centralized state and an atomized society" (p. 231).

But this cement was to prove itself increasingly noxious, indeed fatal, to both peace and human security. While nationalism had been an important ingredient in the republican revolutions of the mid–nineteenth century, by the turn of the twentieth century it began to assume antirepublican, often proto-fascist forms. The first indication of this noxious nationalism was the Dreyfus affair, in which French nationalism was mobilized against the Jewish Alfred Dreyfus, cast as un-French, anti-French, Other. Against this anti-Semitic surge stood Georges Clemenceau, one of the few "heroes" identified in *The Origins of Totalitarianism*, who articulated "the stern Jacobin concept of the nation based on human rights—that republican view of communal life which asserts that (in the words of Clemenceau) by infringing on the rights of one you infringe on the rights of all" (p. 106). Clemenceau's appeal to universal principles wore thin at the turn of the century; by the onset of the next its utter bankruptcy would clearly be demonstrated.

In France—an early nationalizer with a strong republican tradition—the ideology of nationalism was put toward increasingly antirepublican purposes, supporting centralized power, geopolitical intrigue, and a conception of patriotism with often authoritarian implications. In Germany—a later nationalizer with a weak republican tradition—antirepublicanism was even more pronounced. And in Central Europe yet more tribalistic, exclusivist forms of national identity appeared "as the nationalism of those people who had not participated in national emancipation and had not achieved the sovereignty of a nation-state" (p. 227). The fact that these nationalisms defied existing state boundaries made them irredentist as well. As a consequence, Europe became a tinder box of increasingly exclusivist and increasingly competitive nationalist claims. On August 4, 1914, the tinder box exploded, setting off "a chain reaction in which we have been caught ever since and which nobody seems to be able to stop" (p. 267).

According to Arendt, World War I "shattered the facade of Europe's political system to lay bare its hidden frame"—the sufferings of vast numbers of people "to whom the rules of the world around them had suddenly ceased to apply" (p. 267). In one of her most powerful chapters, "The Decline of the Nation-State and the End of the Rights of Man," Arendt argues that the war underscored the contradiction between the nation-state and the principle of human rights. In the name of the national interest the leaders of Europe had wreaked havoc upon their continent. The war produced millions of casualties and dislocated millions more. Effacing the distinction between combatant and civilian, it demonstrated that in the face of modern warfare and the nationalistic imperatives that propel it, ordinary people had no safe haven.

While the postwar settlements—the Versailles Treaty, the League of Nations, the Minority Treaties—sought to heal some of the wounds of war, Arendt argues that these were hopeless efforts to solve the problem without addressing its fundamental cause, the principle of national sovereignty: "No paradox of contemporary politics is filled with more poignant irony than the discrepancy between the efforts of well-meaning idealists who stubbornly insist on regarding as 'inalienable' those human rights which are enjoyed only by the citizens of the most prosperous and civilized countries, and the situation of the rightless themselves" (p. 274). Despite their good intentions, humanitarian reformers were doomed to failure as long as they refused to see that the principle of national sovereignty, by imperiously asserting the identity of nationality, citizenship, and state—and denying any other principle of global or human responsibility and authority— was at bottom what made the sufferings of so many people possible.[6]

Arendt writes with great passion, no doubt informed by her own experience as a refugee, about the mass denationalizations of Central Europeans after the war, which produced a veritable epidemic of displaced and stateless peoples.[7] She notes that national laws of asylum and naturalization exclude these peoples, that international law is unable to secure even the most basic rights for them, and indeed its principal enforcement organ—Interpol—operates by controlling, regulating, and policing "aliens" in the name of legality. The only substitute for a home that is offered by the regime of nation-states is, Arendt allows, the internment camp, a site of prolonged homelessness, an institutionalized limbo.[8] In this regard World War I not simply precipitated but prefigured World War II; and the crimes against humanity committed by the totalitarian regimes were the most brutal, extreme examples of an indifference—and often hostility—to human rights that is inscribed in the very logic of national sovereignty.

According to Arendt, these events demonstrate conclusively the emptiness and ineffectuality of the discourse of natural rights that heralded the modern republican nation-state. The plight of the refugees, and even more the sufferings of the victims of totalitarian genocide, make clear that "the Rights of Man, supposedly inalienable, proved to be unenforceable . . . whenever people appeared who were no longer citizens of any sovereign state." Deprived of citizenship, the stateless were deprived of more than their home, property, and political status; they were subjected to "the most fundamental deprivation," the loss of "a place in the world which makes opinions significant and actions effective" (pp. 293, 296). They were deprived, in short, of their basic human dignity, of their ability to function as moral and political agents, enjoying security and freedom among their fellows, experiencing the mutual recognition that only citizenship confers. According to Arendt, such deprivations, and the miseries and barbarities they engendered, offer ironic, bitter confirmation of Edmund Burke's critique of the French Declaration of the Rights of Man and Citizen. The survivors of the death camps attest that "the abstract nakedness of being nothing but human was their greatest danger" (p. 330). Shorn of law and convention, treated as a purely "natural" creature—a beast—man was left naked and shivering, a vulnerable, miserable creature, prey to hostile forces.

Arendt insists that human dignity needs a new guarantee because its old guarantee—the nineteenth-century Kantian idea of a cosmopolis of peaceful republics respecting the natural rights of man—has been destroyed.[9] Its faith in human moral agency was shattered by the complicity of so many in the evils of the century, and the indifference of so many more to these evils. Its confidence in the republican nation-state as the repository of the rights of man was undermined by three decades during which the most civilized nations on earth destroyed cultures and peoples in the name of their sovereignty, and then ignored the plight of the suffering in the name of a concern with "their own."[10] The political world had now become *the world*—the earth itself rather than that small part of it known as Europe—and in many ways the relevant community had now become humanity itself. In such circumstances the Kantian ideal had been revealed as narrow and parochial, its universalist convictions undermined by its commitment to the principle of national sovereignty, a principle that supported not peaceful cosmopolitanism and moral respect but imperial expansion, geopolitical intrigue, enormous violence, and, perhaps most troubling of all, a pervasive indifference to human suffering outside the confines of the nation.[11]

Arendt reflected on the Nazi policy of genocide in a 1944 essay titled "Organized Guilt and Universal Responsibility" and wrote of "the terror of the idea of humanity." While the architects of modernity had associated a growing awareness of humanity with progress, civility, and peace, from the perspective of the mid–twentieth century such optimism was no longer possible. For the two world wars had ferociously demonstrated a truth that the reigning political ideologies had long denied—"how great a burden mankind is for man."[12] The scientific power of humanity had issued in technologies of mass destruction and global annihilation. The economic power of humanity had produced a truly global economy, incorporating the entire species into an intricate, productive, and volatile web of interrelationships, governed by forces blind to problems of human security and dignity. The political power of humanity had produced a world of competitive nation-states concentrating human allegiances and mobilizing enormous human energies into causes that were all too often exclusivist and hostile. In the face of these terrific, terrifying feats of human initiative, what seemed most obvious and most disturbing was less the power than the *frailty* of humankind, the vulnerability of humans, who have created an enormously complex, interdependent world and now must learn to assume responsibility for living together in it.

Human Rights and the Human Condition

For Arendt human rights are not natural. *Pace* Locke and Paine, they are not inscribed in the nature of human existence, discernible principles of reason that normal creatures cannot help but respect. *Pace* Smith and Hutcheson, they are not secured by a "moral sense" implanted in the human heart. *Pace* Kant, they are not necessitated by the conscious reasoning of all humans as free subjects. For Arendt human rights are conventions, forms of recognition produced by human agreement, fragile artifacts of human living together. As conventions they require more than the ineffectual if well-intentioned lip service often paid to them by well-meaning liberals. But Arendt is not willing to go all the way with Burke. She acknowledges the "pragmatic soundness" of Burke's insistence that human existence as such confers no moral entitlements, that all such entitlements rely upon authoritative forms of recognition that can be found only in definite communities. But she cannot agree that one's moral status is determined *exclusively* by one's local habitus, is wholly "the offspring of convention," for if this were the case there would be little ground on which to condemn the suffering and disempowerment of those stateless, homeless, marginal persons who fall between the cracks of national or other authoritative political identities, and outside of officially recognized categories of membership.[13] And there would be just as little basis for the defense of the principle of human dignity, an emphatically *universalist* principle, one that Arendt insists must—the imperative is ethical—find a new guarantee.[14]

Arendt does not explicitly develop a theory of human rights as such. But her political theory centers on the problems engendered by the failure of human rights to secure human dignity. She seeks, in other words, to *reframe* human rights. As Julia Kristeva puts it, she sees that we must maintain "the requirement of a human, trans-historical dignity, whose content nevertheless needs to be made more complex, beyond the eighteenth century's optimistic naivety."[15] By a transhistorical dignity Kristeva means a dignity that applies to humans as such, one that is universally valid and not appropriate only for certain individuals or societies. Yet such a dignity cannot rely upon naive claims about human nature of the sort contained in the natural rights arguments that the twentieth century has proved unsound and Arendt, following Burke, has criticized. How does Arendt develop an account more nuanced and complex? The answer is contained in a place where few have found it, in *The Human Condition*.

This book is about the boundary conditions of being human, conditions that frame human existence without absolutely determining it. It presents, in other words, a theory of human existence. Arendt seeks to retrieve the distinctively human capacity for creative, transfigurative action, and to reclaim the practices of citizenship to which this capacity is related. This emphasis on citizenship is perfectly consistent with the Burkean argument of *The Origins of Totalitarianism*. In both cases what distinguishes humans is the capacity for membership and participation that is grounded in their autonomy and intersubjectivity. In both cases humans, when stripped of such membership and participation, are naked and shivering creatures, undignified, unfree, vulnerable, less than fully human.

And yet while the upshot of *The Origins of Totalitarianism* is that some other foundation for human dignity is necessary, many interpreters have read *The Human Condition* as a book about the baseness of the merely human in comparison with the grandeur of the superhuman, virtuous, courageous citizen. George Kateb presents the most extreme version of this view, proposing that there is "a dark underside" to Arendt's conception of praxis, "a barely indicated sense that wherever the threat of death is missing, political action is not truly present."

Without the risk of death, Kateb suggests, citizenship would lack the honor and greatness essential for Arendt.[16] Credence is given to this interpretation by Arendt's notorious assertion that "the politically most pernicious doctrine of the modern age" is that "life is the highest good," a point elaborated at length in Arendt's famous chapter on labor in *The Human Condition*.[17] It might seem, then, that in her political philosophy Arendt articulated a profound animus toward the very idea of basic human rights or an elemental human dignity, preferring instead a kind of heroism appropriate only to an elite unconcerned with the mundane problems of human living and human suffering. While there are grounds for this interpretation, I suggest an alternative reading. Although Arendt does not present her constructive political theory as a theory of human rights as such, her account of *praxis* is intended to highlight atrophied potentials whose realization might alone secure human dignity for all.[18] Indeed, Arendt's account of these conditions can be read as an answer to the problem of human rights set out in *The Origins of Totalitarianism*.

For Arendt the human condition is an inherently limited condition, since life is bounded by birth and death. She builds her argument on the twin concepts of natality and mortality. *Natality* corresponds to the experience of birth or beginning, which she connects with the possibility of human initiative or freedom. This capacity to begin is closely linked to the human capacity for speech, which allows us both to represent and to transfigure our common world, a point of course first made by Aristotle.[19] *Mortality* is the ultimate limit of human existence—finitude and eventual death. Mortality poses problems of subsistence and survival, to which work, and preeminently labor, are attempts at solution. But for Arendt there are no ultimate solutions to this problem. All human efforts to deal with the fact of mortality are provisional and, as far as human reason can comprehend, futile. In this sense "man is compelled to assent to a Being which he has never created and to which he is essentially alien."[20]

Influenced by the "existenz philosophy" of her teacher Karl Jaspers, Arendt goes only halfway with Burke. She agrees that humans are fragile creatures. Beneath the drapery of human conventions she sees vulnerability and mortality. *But she also sees creativity and power.* For Burke the "super-added ideas" and practices of human communities are almost providentially sustained havens in a heartless world.[21] Humans, naked and shivering, if they are fortunate and find themselves clothed in such "decent drapery," are thus redeemed; as the beneficiaries of this legacy they can take comfort in a wardrobe they took no part in furnishing. But Arendt takes a more Enlightened view; for her, human communities are themselves the products of human agreement, actualizations of the human capacity to infuse the world with meaning and imperfectly to shape it in accordance with this meaning, a process accomplished in concert with those others with whom one shares the world. Labor, work, and action all involve this effort to humanize the world, to make it our own. Each is productive but also limited. Labor secures subsistence, but it suffers from a Sisyphean futility. Work produces relatively imperishable creations, but they are only *relatively* imperishable. They are fragile artifacts, produced through a violence upon nature with often malignant consequences (a point also developed by the Frankfurt school). And action involves us in a seamless and boundless web of interrelationships; our deeds, enormously productive, often escape us in surprising, often grotesque ways that we neither intend nor even imagine.

The Human Condition, then, presents us with the generic features of being human—human power and human limit. In the light of the terrible human catastrophe recounted in *The Origins of Totalitarianism*, it is clear why action is so central for Arendt. It is because action is the distinctive human capacity to reflect upon, communicate about, and actively shape our common human condition of vulnerability and power in ways that promote dignity and freedom. It is only in concert, on the basis of claims that are mutually recognized and agreed to, that human dignity can be secured and continually resecured in a recalcitrant world.[22] If we fail to act, we will simply be acted upon. Given the forces at work in the modern world, such a course is unlikely to afford either security or freedom.

Action, then, represents a kind of civic initiative, by which humans resist degradation and assert their dignity. When we act, we define ourselves *for* ourselves, and in so doing we inscribe the world as *our* world.[23] This observation sheds a different light on why Arendt laments the "politically pernicious doctrine" that life is the highest good. It is not because she devalues life but precisely because she values *living freely*—both terms are important here—that she places so much emphasis on the capacity to begin anew, the basis of courageous civic initiative. A careful reading of the chapter on labor in *The Human Condition* reveals that the "philosophy of life" that Arendt deplores is not really a strong conviction about the dignity of the human personality or the sanctity of human life; it is the ethos of consumption that she associates with modern mass society, the idea that the essence of life is the appropriation of material objects, and that human productivity is the preeminent criterion of human well-being. It is this idea that she re-

sists. Yet she is careful not to dismiss categorically the emphasis on basic material thriving that is the product of the Enlightenment. She describes it as
politically rather than *humanly* pernicious. Why? Perhaps because she does not
wish completely to deny the value of such an ethos, but only to caution against its
hegemony. The emphasis on basic human needs that has informed so much of
modern moral philosophy has helped to advance the idea of an elemental, universal humanity, an idea that Arendt does not reject but cannot embrace. For the
irony is that the modern age, which proclaims the value of life above all else, is
also the age of genocidal mass murder. This irony was surely not lost on Arendt.
I suggest, then, that when she places action over life, she is endorsing not a mys-
tique of heroic sacrifice or the existential confrontation with death but rather a
conception of civic initiative that alone can affirm basic human rights and digni-
ties. She wants to resist the enormous brutality and suffering characteristic of
the twentieth century. But she does so not by appealing to a doctrine of natural
rights before which men are passive recipients, but by emphasizing the *activity*
of human beings, who can achieve their dignity only by *doing something about it*.
In a world filled with cruelty, mendacity, and callous indifference, such activity
will surely often involve danger, and the person who acts will be a person of courage, willing to endure sacrifice and perhaps risk death in the name of a higher
value. But the risk is endured in the name of a higher value—human dignity—
and not out of an existential attraction to limit-situations.

What Arendt has in mind can perhaps be clarified by a consideration of the actions of Vaclav Havel, who, in his 1975 open "Letter to Dr. Gustav Husak," de-
nounced the Czech Communist regime for promoting "the principle of out-
ward adaptation," whereby the citizen is offered all the benefits befitting "an
obedient member of a consumer herd" in exchange for political quiescence. "All
the evidence suggests that the authorities are applying a method quite adequate
for dealing with a creature whose only aim is self-preservation. Seeking the path
of least resistance, they completely ignore the price that must be paid—the harsh
assault on human integrity, the brutal castration of the humanity of men."[24] It
could be said that Havel underestimates the moral significance of a regime that
can offer relative security and prosperity to its people, and that his criticism im-
plicates some classical or Nietzschean conception of heroic virtue. But, of
course, Havel was at this time a persecuted dissident on behalf of *human rights*,
and the regime that he opposed, while it offered comfort in exchange for quiescence, offered no security for such rights, either to him or to the more ordinary

Czechs whose comfort was utterly contingent on the unpredictable policies of
an authoritarian regime. It alone ruled as guardian, and the citizens were expected to submit like sheep. He denounces "a creature whose only aim is self-
preservation" not out of a dismissiveness about security and civil liberty but in
their very name. His point is that in order for Czechs to secure their basic liberties and rights they need to develop and sustain a commitment to those rights,
and to take initiative on their behalf.[25]

As I read Arendt's criticism of "life," she is making much the same point. I
suggest that when she writes of "life" she is thinking about all of those who sat
idly by during the interwar years, living in security and comfort and indifferent
to the impending political crisis and to the suffering and degradation it could
cause. And when she writes of "praxis" she is thinking of those Danish resisters
during World War II who at great risk to themselves refused to comply with the
Nazis' efforts to deport the Jews.[26] Arendt does not disparage the desire to lead a
normal life. But she does believe that in the dark times of the twentieth century
one must have courage and be willing to take risks—one must *act*—in order to
secure such a life. Praxis, then, is preeminently a way of being that is essential to
basic human dignity in late modernity.[27]

The theme of dignity is highlighted in Arendt's 1946 essay on existentialism,
in which she invokes Kant's idea that "in every single individual humanity can
be debased or exalted." In this spirit she recommends the philosophy of Jaspers,
which "sounds the appeal to my freedom [which arises] through communication with others, who as my fellows and through the appeal to our common reason guarantee the universal." Jaspers retains Kant's cosmopolitan ideal. But instead of grounding it on rational necessity, he bases it on the *efforts* of feeling,
thinking, speaking human beings. Further, by maintaining, according to
Arendt, that man inhabits "islands of freedom" in a "discordant" universe, Jaspers sees that human dignity can be realized only in partial, limited ways, in a
world that we can never master. This is why the spaces of freedom and dignity—
note the plural—are islands in a tumultuous sea and do not cover the entirety of
the earth.[28]

Isonomy—"neither to rule nor to be ruled"—is for Arendt the ideal form of
political relationship, because this arrangement corresponds to the generic
qualities of humans as such, as beings who thrive and who suffer, who are capable of forming limited attachments in a world of many such attachments. Another way of saying this is that our world is what we make of it, that our rights and

our dignity can be ensured only by our own efforts and agreements. Arendt sees that our condition does not entail or necessitate human dignity; her argument in no way falls prey to the so-called naturalistic fallacy. She recognizes that our limited condition can bring forth one of two possibilities—either we can work out our anxiety and vulnerability by seeking to demean and oppress others or we can seek to develop arrangements that support the security and freedom of all. She supports the latter because she sees that the former is nothing but a recipe for suffering and mutual recrimination, as the history of conflict in our century has shown. Isonomy is her ideal because it is true to the facts of our common human condition, because it refuses to privilege any special ethnos, class, or nation, and because, acknowledging the elemental humanity of all humans and the irreducible plurality of the human world, it allows matters to be settled "through words and persuasion and not through force and violence."[29]

While Arendt does not frame her discussion in terms of a theory of human rights, she does make clear what she considers to be the most significant *wrongs* of our century—mass murder, torture, displacement; the suppression or persecution of difference; the silencing of individuals; political disenfranchisement. What these wrongs have in common is the organization of human affairs through force and violence rather than through persuasion. To the extent that words are used, they are spoken in a monologue, by a *dictator*, who treats those below as objects of rather than participants in political power. The clearest account of these wrongs is presented in *The Origins of Totalitarianism*. What, Arendt asks, does the loss of human rights suffered by "the rightless" mean? First, it means the loss of the homes, of the (of course fragile) security of existence and the familiarity provided by "the entire social texture into which they were born." Second, it means "the loss of government protection," the complete deprivation of legal status and the civil liberties and political freedoms that are based on one's legal standing. Finally, it means the loss of one's very humanity, the lack of any recognition whatsoever, the reduction of human beings to disposable, dispensable *creatures*. "The fundamental deprivation of human rights is manifested," Arendt writes, "first and above all in the deprivation of a place in the world which makes opinions significant and actions effective . . . This extremity . . . is the situation of people deprived of human rights. They are deprived, not of the right to freedom, but of the right to action; not of the right to think whatever they please, but of the right of opinion. Privileges in some cases, injustices in most, blessings and doom are meted out to them according to accident and without any relation whatsoever to what they do, did, or may do."[30] Totalitarianism represents the apotheosis of such rightlessness, in which the deprivation of humanity is enacted through a policy of genocide.

A perusal of Arendt's corpus can leave no doubt that her political theory represented a revolt against such wrongs, an effort to think through what it might take to guard against them. It is clear what values she sought to advance: the safety and bodily integrity of individuals; security of home and place from invasion and deportation; the ability to articulate one's concerns and to be heard, not simply to speak to oneself; the freedom to associate and to participate in public discourse. The loss of rights by so many millions of people represented a failure to protect those things. A new guarantee of human dignity would be a way to validate them.

Arendt does not develop this theme in terms of an elaborated theory of human rights. She never lists the above values and calls for their protection. But it is wrong to conclude that she is hostile or indifferent toward human rights. Their very *loss* is what drives her theory. She is quite clear about this in *The Origins of Totalitarianism*. "We became aware of the existence of the right to have rights (and that means to live in a framework where one is judged by one's actions and opinions) and a right to belong to some kind of organized community," she writes, "only when millions of people emerged who had lost and could not regain these rights because of the new global situation."[31] We—she includes herself—became aware of the right to have rights only *after* the decline of the rights of man. The right to have rights was an unspecified, and thus unrecognized, presupposition of the rights of man proclaimed in the eighteenth century. By treating one's basic humanity as springing immediately from the nature of man, the philosophes and their heirs failed to see just how fragile this status is, how much it relies on forms of human artifice. The nation-state was the form of artifice that made it possible for them to think this human status natural. But the nation-state has now failed, and in the wake of world war it has become clear that the humanity of individuals needs a new guarantee. The question, she avers, is whether "the right to have rights, or the right of every individual to belong to humanity, should be guaranteed by humanity itself." "It is by no means certain," she allows, "whether this is possible." But there is no doubt that she considers it desirable, indeed imperative.

In *The Origins of Totalitarianism* Arendt uses the language of rights—the right to have rights—in order to speak about a new guarantee for human dignity. In some of her more philosophical works she develops a different vocabulary, of "praxis" or "public freedom," but she does so in order to confront the same problem—the need to redress the rightlessness prevalent in the late modern world. The theme of dignity remains constant, a reminder of the Kantian problem that grounds her political theorizing.

Is Arendt then a theorist of human rights? No. But she is a theorist of the *politics* made necessary by a world that despoils human rights. The "right to have rights," she believes, can be secured only by politics, by the civic initiative of people vulnerable to the vagaries of world politics and those in solidarity with them. Perhaps the reason Arendt refuses to articulate her constructive political theory in terms of human rights is that she believes such rights have been specified often enough. What has been lacking is an understanding of how such rights might be rendered valid. Arendt's principal point is that such rights do not speak for themselves; nor do weighty declarations of intent speak for them. Such rights are mute and invisible unless spoken for, unless made actionable.[32] They cannot exist without a politics to back them up. Arendt's theory of politics—her conception of action, her emphasis on citizenship and the power that derives from concerted action—represents an effort to help back them up. It does so by emphasizing those generic features of human existence which make possible an elemental human dignity, which, paradoxically, can be realized only in partial communities, forms of national, ethnic, and other identity that are not all-encompassing, and that rest on political commitment and artifice rather than anything given in the human condition.

Human Rights and International Politics

Arendt is fully aware of the paradox in her argument. As she puts it, it requires "a new law on earth, whose validity this time must comprehend the whole of humanity while its power remains strictly limited." As heirs to Hobbes and Rousseau, we are accustomed to equating "validity" with "power," and to equating both with the principle of sovereignty. While Grotius, Locke, and Kant imagined the existence of valid principles of universal right, they too saw the state as the unproblematic vehicle of such principles; politically speaking, the only source of positive law, of validation, was the sovereign state. Arendt's paradoxical formulation seeks to shake us out of this habit. She insists that, somehow, universal principles might have validity—might be *effective*, backed up, enforced, in a way they are not at present—amidst a world of limited, bounded communities. In some of her more political writings she suggests how political institutions might validate such universal principles.

One such institution is constitutional government itself. A recurrent theme of Arendt's writing is the importance of limits in political life. While not a liberal, she shared the liberal view that constitutional limits on state power are indispensable to political freedom. This sentiment is developed in the conclusion of *The Origins of Totalitarianism*, where Arendt writes of the functioning of laws as "fences" that establish boundaries between men and protect "essential freedoms" (pp. 465–66). It is also developed in her much later book, *On Revolution*, in which she contrasts the French Revolutionary naiveté about rights with the seriousness with which the Americans treated the "legal personality" of the individual, a seriousness demonstrated by the Bill of Rights of the U.S. Constitution.[33] Perhaps Arendt's strongest statement of this theme appears in a 1953 criticism of McCarthyism, in which she vigorously defends the First Amendment's guarantee of freedom of speech: "Dissent belongs to this living matter [the republic] as much as consent does. The limitations on dissent are the Constitution and the Bill of Rights and no one else. If you try to 'make America more American' . . . you can only destroy it. Your methods, finally, are the methods of the police, and only of the police."[34]

The protection of civil liberties afforded by a constitutional republic represents a crucial hedge against the kind of "rightlessness" Arendt fears. But in a world governed by the logic of national sovereignty Arendt believed such a hedge to be doubly limited. One crucial challenge to constitutionalism is provided by the logic of "national security," which functioned, especially during the Cold War, to create a climate of fear and to empower unaccountable, in some ways extraconstitutional police and military agencies, "national security managers" unconcerned with civil liberties. This is a major theme of one of Arendt's later collections of essays, *Crises of the Republic*, though she first developed it in the 1950s. The second limit of constitutionalism is presented by the exclusionary character of even the most constitutionally oriented nation-state. The problem, in short, is that constitutionally based civil liberties are valid only for people who fall under the "jurisdiction" of the nation-state and are considered "full members" of it. The stateless, the refugee, and the citizen of a dictatorship beyond the bounds of the constitutional state are thus removed from its protections.[35]

While the constitutional republic is thus something of great value, it is not up to the task of remedying the crisis of human rights. As a nation-state in a system of national sovereignties, it is indeed part of the problem.

This is why Arendt saw more *global* institutions as being necessary. One such institution is an effective system of international jurisprudence capable of adjudicating violations of human rights. This is a major concern of *Eichmann in Jerusalem*. Most commentators have focused on Arendt's treatment of Eichmann's "banality," but the last quarter of the essay deals in great detail with the legalities surrounding Eichmann's trial. Arendt argues that Eichmann's crime poses profound challenges to traditional standards of jurisprudence. Whereas the traditional categories for handling war crimes—"acts of state" and "on superior orders"—consider these crimes as deviations from the general proscription against murder assumed to be recognized among all civilized nations, the Nazi genocide presents the case of "a state founded upon criminal principles." The Nazi policy of extermination presents a kind of normalized criminality, with global aspirations, unanticipated by traditional jurisprudence. The postwar Nuremberg Charter and trials, which distinguished among "crimes against peace," "war crimes," and "crimes against humanity," marked a recognition of the need for a supranational conception of humanity and human rights. Genocide, Arendt avers, is "an attack upon human diversity as such, that is, upon a characteristic of the 'human status' without which the very words 'mankind' and 'humanity' would be devoid of meaning." In the wake of genocide, she insists, it is necessary to find a new way of protecting this diversity, of giving some "validity" to humanity. She thus reproaches the Jerusalem court for charging Eichmann only with war crimes against the Jewish people and for not facing squarely the challenge posed by this new type of crime: "the supreme crime it [the court] was confronted with, the physical extermination of the Jewish people, was a crime against humanity, perpetrated upon the body of the Jewish people" (pp. 255, 268–69).

Yet Arendt sees that the Israelis were hardly unique in their narrow interpretation of the Nazi crimes. The Israeli trial, she maintains against its critics, was no different from the successor trials held in Poland, Yugoslavia, and elsewhere in Europe to deal with crimes against nations. All of these trials, unfortunately, remained trapped in the framework of national sovereignty, focused exclusively on the crimes committed against their particular nationals. They thus passed over the chance to rethink the legal principles of human order and state sovereignty.

That is, they used the trials to consolidate the nation-state rather than as an opportunity to rethink it.

In this light Arendt recommends the Genocide Convention adopted by the U.N. General Assembly in 1948, which provided that "persons charged with genocide . . . shall be tried by a competent tribunal of the States in the territory of which the act was committed or by such international penal tribunal as may have jurisdiction." She argues that this convention, when interpreted in light of the crimes committed by the Nazis against the Jewish people, had radical implications. The most significant implication is the possibility that the territorial principle might be reformulated in such a way that it applied to Israel, a political community which, of course, had not been in existence at the time of the Nazi genocide. Regarding this possibility, Arendt holds that "no State of Israel would ever have come into being if the Jewish people had not created and maintained its own in-between space throughout the long centuries of dispersion, that is, prior to the seizure of its old territory" (pp. 262–63). The Jewish people, in other words, had until recently been a dispersed historical nation detached from any state or sovereignty. As such they had been perennially vulnerable to persecution and unable confidently to claim the rights afforded to fully national citizens. Insofar as the Jewish people had lacked a state, they had lacked the recognition afforded to sovereign nations by international law. Thus individual Jews lacked the security and freedom that could be provided only by membership in a recognized sovereign nation. For jurisprudence to recognize, even retroactively, the crimes committed against the Jews, and to sanction adjudication of those crimes by Jewish authorities, would represent nothing less than "a new political principle"—the principle that peoples might have authority in the absence of sovereignty, and that their members might have recognizable rights in spite of their minority status within existing states. The principle of human rights, a principle of universal validity, would thus be sanctioned by authorities "rooted in and controlled by newly defined territorial entities."

Of course this conception of newly defined entities raises a thicket of practical problems regarding competing jurisdictions. To say that Israel, as the new political authority of the Jewish people, had jurisdiction over Eichmann for crimes committed against Jews is not easy to reconcile with equally plausible claims: (1) that other nations, including Poles but also Gypsies, equally without a state, could claim similar jurisdiction over Eichmann; and (2) that an international body analogous to the Nuremberg court might claim jurisdiction over crimes

against humanity. Arendt does not explore these difficulties in any detail. But before one leaps too quickly to the conclusion that her suggestions are impractical,
it is important to consider what they are designed to accomplish—the relaxation
of the principle of sovereignty and modification of the idea that there is any neat
correspondence between territorial residence, community membership, and legal responsibility.

The important principle that she establishes is that individuals may have in-
ternationally recognized rights even when they are members of national minorities that lack any territorially based sovereignty. While the implementation of
this principle does raise difficult questions, the institutions to which Arendt
seems committed attempt to resolve them. In fact, the major constructive argument of *Eichmann in Jerusalem* is not a defense of a redefinition of the territorial
principle that would enable disenfranchised national minorities to adjudicate
crimes committed against their people. It is the endorsement of a "permanent
international criminal court" based on the Nuremberg principles, something
also called for by her teacher Karl Jaspers.[36] Such a court would have the power
to hear human rights cases brought by aggrieved individuals and groups and to
render verdicts in those cases. Such verdicts would have the force of reason behind them. They would stand as symbols of justice, and the court would serve as
a kind of moral conscience of the world.[37] But it might also have a more potent
political sanction if a more *federal* system of global politics could be constituted.

Arendt does not propose new forms of legal authority as mere adjuncts to existing national sovereignties. She offers them as alternatives to the exclusive
claims of such sovereignties. She spells out her position on this matter most
clearly in "Karl Jaspers: Citizen of the World." This essay, published in 1968,
more than a decade after the publication of *The Human Condition*, demonstrates
Arendt's continuous and consistent concern with the problems of human dignity delineated in *The Origins of Totalitarianism*. Arendt tells us that she seeks to
rehabilitate the Kantian cosmopolitan ideal in a world in which "the most potent
symbol of the unity of mankind is the remote possibility that atomic weapons
used by one country . . . might ultimately come to be the end of all human life on
earth." She argues that the common vulnerability of humans should lead to a
new "global responsibility . . . a process of mutual understanding and progress-
ing self-clarification on a gigantic scale."[38]

How might such understanding come about? Arendt argues that it cannot be
on the basis of "a universal agreement upon one religion, one philosophy, or

form of government"; given the diversity of cultures in the world, such a unity could be achieved only by force, at the cost of enormous bloodshed and cruelty. She thus rejects world government as an invidiously utopian ideal that ignores the real differences of nationality, culture, and political identity that constitute the world. Instead she recommends the principle of federation, a principle consistent with both the diversity of communities and the need to relax the political energies and tensions bound up with national sovereignty. A federal arrangement would require "the renunciation, not of one's own tradition and national past, but of the binding authority which tradition and past have always claimed."[39] Arendt supports what Jürgen Habermas has more recently called a "post-traditional national identity," a political identity capable of renouncing any kind of chauvinism and reflexively acknowledging its own partiality in a world of many nations and communities.[40] She also calls for the establishment of new regional and international forms of cooperation that might override the centralizing tendencies of state forms, and might encourage new forms of regional and international identity and moral responsibility. In such a world the verdicts of international tribunals might appear not as infringements of a national sovereignty that is treated as absolute but as statements of higher principles that are commonly acknowledged. In a world in which the principle of national sovereignty and its corollary principle of justice—one nation, one army— gave way to other forms of collective security, such verdicts might even have the force of arms. And in such a world new forms of national and regional autonomy short of sovereignty might be imaginable.

Arendt had hoped such new forms might come into existence in the postwar Middle East. Her writings on this subject provide the clearest picture of how the practice of human rights might function amidst new forms of international politics. For Arendt the greatest tragedy of the Arab-Jewish conflict that broke out into full-scale war in May 1948 was that each side confronted the other with claims "which are nationalistic because they make sense only in the closed framework of one's own people and history, and legalistic because they discount the concrete factors of the situation."[41] In the face of such absolutist claims she insisted that the only way to save lives and to preserve the integrity of the peoples involved was to establish a binational, confederal state, based on forms of local self-government and Jewish-Arab economic cooperation. Rejecting national sovereignty as a recipe for disaster, she envisioned a political community with multiple and overlapping levels of authority, in which national identities would be respected but in which they would not be the exclusive bases of political power and citizenship.[42]

Lest this vision of regional and global federation be viewed as too "idealistic," it is important to see that for Arendt it was *anti-utopian* in at least two senses. For Arendt it was precisely the existence of profound differences and antagonisms between and among individuals, communities, nations, and states that made federation superior to world government. It is world government—a politics based upon a naive vision of global citizenship and unmediated human identity—that is idealistic.[43] It could never be effective, because it could never sustain a significant level of commitment and civic initiative in a world of deep and irremediable differences and antagonisms. These same differences and antagonisms, which had erupted in bloody conflict and demonstrated such callous inhumanity in our century, also made federation preferable to the laissez-faire principle of national sovereignty. For laissez-faire is simply a recipe for doing nothing, for allowing world politics to proceed as usual, while the millions who are refugees and national minorities remain displaced and disenfranchised, and the rest remain subject to increasingly remote and irresponsible sovereign states. Federation, in other words, was for Arendt an arrangement made practically necessary by the failures of political responsibility in the twentieth century, a responsibility made imperative by the serious problems besetting us. Far from imagining an end to such problems, Arendt proposes federation as a way of managing them, of regulating national differences, and of securing human rights in a world in which the need for such efforts has no terminus.

The Praxis of Human Rights

Just as Arendt saw global federalism as a form of politics, a process of resolving differences, she saw such institutions as themselves always relying upon more elementary forms of politics. Federalism is not a blueprint, much less a panacea. It is a possibility intimated by certain forms of existing politics, an always-uncompleted project animated by vigorous political agencies. Arendt's political theory was not only driven by the distinctively modern problems of superfluity, displacement, and homelessness; it was also inspired by contemporary forms of political action. The defense of Alfred Dreyfus spearheaded by Clemenceau and Jean Jaurès; the French and Danish resistance to the Nazis; the Ihud group of binationalist Zionists led by her friend Judah Magnes; the U.S. civil rights and antiwar movements; Amnesty International and PEN—these efforts all exemplify a politics of resistance to state actions that displace and degrade human beings in the name of oppressive ideologies. While they can be viewed as altruistic or humanitarian attempts to relieve human suffering, they are also forms of concerted action and political empowerment. The Danes who assisted Jews under the Nazi occupation, for example, were not simply acting out of altruistic concern for others. They were also acknowledging a connection with the Jews, the connection of a common subjection to Nazi power as well as a common humanity. And in acting on this acknowledgment they asserted their dignity in the face of oppression and danger. Thus their humanitarianism, if you will, was transformed through their common opinions and their collective action into a *politics*.[44]

Such examples of political praxis illustrate two of the most important features of Arendt's vision of the politics of human dignity. The first is that the most important locus of such a politics is neither the nation-state nor the international covenant or tribunal. These are of course crucial loci of power. The nation-state is still the preeminent political actor on the world scene. Constitutional limitations on the exercise of state power, forms of federated authority, and international legal codes—each a way of placing a kind of constraint upon state sovereignty—are all necessary if the rights of minorities, refugees, and dissenters are to be secured. But the primary impetus for such rights will always come from elsewhere, from the praxis of citizens who insist upon these rights and who are prepared to back up this insistence through political means. The words of Albert Camus are apposite: "little is to be expected from present-day governments, since these live and act according to a murderous code. Hope remains only in the most difficult task of all: to reconsider everything from the ground up, so as to shape a living society inside a dying society. Men must therefore, as individuals, draw up among themselves, within frontiers and across them, a new social contract, which will unite them according to more reasonable principles."[45]

Arendt's essays "Civil Disobedience" and *On Revolution* take up this very theme of a new social contract. Both deal with the subject of resistance to moribund and oppressive power, and treat this resistance as a prefiguration of a new politics that is centered on voluntary associations and council forms rather than formal or official state institutions. The "lost treasure" of the revolutionary tradition is, for Arendt, the model of an associational politics that exists beneath and across frontiers, shaking up the boundaries of the political and articulating alternative forms of allegiance, accountability, and citizenship. Echoing Camus,

Arendt writes that if there exists an alternative to national sovereignty, it is such an associational politics, which works according to "a completely different principle of organization, which begins from below, continues upward, and finally leads to a parliament." She quickly adds that the details of such a politics are less important than its civic *spirit*, a spirit that resists the deracinating tendencies of modern political life.[46] That such a politics runs against the principle of sovereignty is for Arendt one of its strengths. As many commentators have observed, there is a deep pathos to Arendt's treatment of revolution, which is for her a glorious, empowering, and yet evanescent phenomenon, a fire that burns brightly but soon dies.[47] Arendt recognized the paradox of rebellion in the modern world—that powerful associational impulses would be co-opted by more official forms of politics. And yet this can be viewed as the great virtue of this kind of politics—that it challenges the status quo and calls attention to itself in ways that demand redress and incorporation. Put another way, such forms of resistance invigorate formal politics and keep it true to the spirit of human dignity. Their vigilant insistence gives force to the support for human rights that is proclaimed by more authoritative domestic and international bodies but often honored in the breach.

The second point that follows from Arendt's argument is that there is no single community or single category of citizenship that can once and for all solve the problem of human rights in the late modern world. One arena of human rights praxis is clearly the state itself, and one kind of citizenship appropriate to it is clearly what we think of as "domestic" citizenship—membership in the nation-state, as an American or Italian or Croatian. But it should be clear that the idea of "domestic" is simply an adjunct of the idea of sovereignty; it denotes those matters that are contained within the boundaries of sovereign power and subject to that power. As such it encourages domesticity where vigor is also needed. For there is no reason to imagine that relevant human rights issues, or relevant communities, correspond to the boundaries of nation-states. Local, regional, and indeed global forms of citizenship are equally possible and equally real. One can speak about the rights of aborigines, for example, as a Mohawk, as a Canadian, as a North American, as a human. In these cases different forms of organization would be appropriate; the audiences one addressed would be different but not necessarily mutually exclusive. How human rights claims are articulated and mobilized can and will vary from case to case and from time to time, as political identities are transformed and new alliances forged.[48]

It would be equally mistaken to conflate ideas of community and citizenship with formal political organizations, be they states, nations, or confederations. In *On Revolution* Arendt writes about self-chosen "elites," groups of citizens distinguished by nothing but their deep interest and participation in specific public matters. She describes such elites as constituting, through their own efforts, "elementary republics." On the Arendtian view it is possible to imagine a multiplicity of overlapping "republics," sometimes in tension with one another, sometimes in support of one another. The kinds of international legal institutions and federated state arrangements that she endorses would constitute ineffective security for human rights were they not authorized, empowered, and invigorated by a robust civil society of such "republics."

The Helsinki Citizens' Assembly, formed in 1990 as an outgrowth of links formed between East European dissidents and West European peace activists after the Helsinki Accords in 1975, is an interesting example of what Arendt might have envisioned.[49] As Mary Kaldor, a cofounder, describes it, the assembly "is not addressed to governments except in so far as they are asked to guarantee freedom of travel and freedom of assembly so that citizens' groups can meet and communicate. It is a strategy of dialogue, an attempt to change society through the actions of citizens rather than governments . . . in short, to create a new political culture. In such a situation, the behavior of governments either changes or becomes less and less relevant."[50] The assembly has been described as a loose association of citizens acting together in self-organized associations, movements, and initiatives across national boundaries. It is hardly indifferent to the policies of governments; petitioning, demonstrating, and fostering debate about state policies regarding human rights have been central to its activities. But the power that its members have been able to constitute is an important force in its own right; indeed, it is only because of this power, an organizational *and* an ethical power, that it is capable of supporting more directly "political" efforts—legislation, for example—and to influence the course of state action. "We don't represent anyone except the movements and institutions in which we are involved," Kaldor writes. "In many cases, we represent no one but ourselves. And our power rests not on whom we represent but in what we do—in what we say, in our ideas, in our quest for truth, in the projects we undertake. It rests on our energy and commitment."[51]

Groups such as the Helsinki Citizens' Assembly, Médecins sans Frontières, and Amnesty International exemplify the kind of associational politics that is central to Arendt's conception of modern citizenship. They are forms of collective empowerment that might provide a new foundation for human dignity. They play an indispensable role in calling attention to human rights abuses, giving voice to the disenfranchised and persecuted, and empowering citizens to act in concert on behalf of the expansion of rights. They seek to alter state policies on matters of minority and refugee rights, for example, but also to offer their own, unofficial support for displaced or persecuted people. Spanish Refugee Aid, with which Arendt was involved, was no substitute for state policies hospitable to the rights of Spanish refugees, nor was it a substitute for diplomatic efforts to change a dictatorial regime; but the voluntary organization of relief efforts and forms of solidarity is itself an indispensable and preeminently political effort, without which more hospitable state policies would not be possible. Not a wholesale alternative to more inclusive or official forms of political community, such endeavors constitute vital forms of civic participation and empowerment. They can be viewed as "elementary republics" of citizens committed to human rights.

Our world is in many ways a different one from the world that Arendt described in her preface to the first edition of *The Origins of Totalitarianism*. Writing in 1951, with the recent experiences of world war and Holocaust seared into her memory, and another such conflict dangerously imminent, she noted that "this moment of anticipation is like the calm that settles after all hopes have died" (p. vii). From her perspective the world, still reeling after the traumatic shocks of totalitarianism and mass destruction, seemed to be hurtling toward other, no less disturbing forms of violence and human suffering.

We, on the other hand, are witnesses to the end of the Cold War. Our more optimistic contemporaries, invoking Hegel with apparent conviction, only yesterday proclaimed the end of history and the triumph of liberal democracy. And yet today few are sanguine about the state of the world. As I write, thousands of innocent civilians are starving in Rwanda and the Congo. Kurds in Iraq, Syria, and Turkey, Tamils in Sri Lanka, Palestinians in the West Bank and Gaza, Armenians in Nagorno-Karabakh, and countless other national minorities clamor for human rights. In the heart of Europe, the city of Sarajevo recovers from a protracted and destructive Serbian siege, and Bosnian Muslims fortunate enough to have survived suffer the aftereffects of a brutal, murderous campaign of "ethnic cleansing." German neo-Nazi youths vandalize and burn refugee hostels to the cheers of large crowds of sympathetic bystanders; and throughout Europe— in France, Italy, Germany—there are increasingly audible calls to exclude "foreigners" in the name of "real citizens," "true" Germans or French or Italians who do not wish to share their country with the others. Across the Atlantic Ocean things are no different; the Clinton Administration turned back Haitian refugees fleeing a brutal dictatorship, just as its predecessors had done before with refugees displaced by economic trauma and civil war in El Salvador and Guatemala.[52]

The *1992 Human Rights Watch World Report* notes that in the wake of the Cold War "respect for human rights faces a dangerous challenge in the rise of exclusionary ideologies . . . the quest for ethnic, linguistic or religious purity, pursued by growing numbers, lies behind much of today's bloodshed. By closing the community to diversity and stripping outsiders of essential rights, these dangerous visions of enforced conformity nourish a climate of often brutal intolerance."[53] Arendt, writing over forty years ago, observed that "under the most diverse conditions and disparate circumstances, we watch the development of the same phenomena—homelessness on an unprecedented scale, rootlessness to an unprecedented depth."[54] Such a vision sounds grimly familiar.

While Arendt is not a theorist well known for her reflections on human rights, her writing is an indispensable resource for thinking about the threats to human dignity in the late modern world. As Arendt recognized, human rights are not a given of human nature; they are the always tenuous results of a politics that seeks to establish them, a vigorous politics intent on constituting relatively secure spaces of human freedom and dignity. And as she saw, the nation-state, far from being the vehicle of the self-determination of individuals and peoples, is in many ways an obstacle to the dignity that individuals and communities seek. Those interested in human rights, who wish to provide a new guarantee for human dignity, have no alternative but to take responsibility upon themselves, to act *politically* as members of elementary republics, locally and globally, on behalf of a dignity that is in perpetual jeopardy in the world in which we live. As the *Human Rights Watch Report* makes chillingly clear, such a politics is hardly a matter of mere academic interest.

5

Hannah Arendt on Democratic Politics

> . . . they had taken the initiative upon themselves and therefore,
> without even noticing it, had begun to create that public space
> between themselves where freedom could appear.
>
> HANNAH ARENDT, *Between Past and Future*

When we consider the subject of democracy, the name of Hannah Arendt does not quickly spring to mind. Arendt's work is sometimes considered classical, sometimes Nietzschean, but almost always elitist, and thus antidemocratic. She argued strenuously in favor of a vigorous, participatory politics, and yet, as Sheldon Wolin has pointed out, in her many books she never systematically addressed the topic of democracy.[1] She surely was no "democratic theorist" as this term has usually been understood. In her most important work of relevance to the subject, *On Revolution*, in which she endorses spontaneous forms of political insurgency, she disparages representative government in favor of a politics conducted by an "aristocratic elite," drawing from, among others, John Adams, hardly renowned as a partisan of democracy.[2] These heresies of omission and commission have led many theorists to concur with Margaret Canovan, who has argued that there is a "deep and serious contradiction" between Arendt's elitist and democratic sides, a contradiction that severely limits the relevance of her thought to democratic concerns.[3]

I believe that this interpretation is mistaken, both about Arendt and about the subject of democracy. It would be foolhardy to insist upon a perfect fit between Arendt and democratic ideas, but for two reasons. The first, which scholars have often noted, concerns the ambivalences in Arendt's work. While not a nostalgic thinker, she was clearly drawn to certain features of ancient politics and revolted by many features of modernity, most notably its vast, impersonal character. Arendt disavowed all labels, including "democrat"; and her writings elude easy political classification. The second reason for the imperfect fit between Arendt and democracy has less frequently been noted. It is that there is no neat, consistent, and self-sufficient package called "democratic ideas" in connection with which Arendt's writings can be judged.

Democracy is a complex set of ideals and possibilities. The clear-cut association of democracy with liberal constitutional regimes is a fairly recent and problematic development.[4] Arendt was often elusive, to be sure, a source of continuing frustration for political theorists. But on the subject of democracy she was less elusive than scholars have believed. She refused the label "democrat" because she correctly saw that in the modern world this term has admitted of different, sometimes hostile interpretations. But this refusal did not make her an antidemocrat. To the contrary. While Arendt was quite clearly against mass democracy, she was *not* against democracy per se. Indeed, *On Revolution* advances a vision of grass-roots politics that is supremely democratic in its emphasis on the participation of ordinary people in their own governance. Even here things are more nuanced, for to say that she was against mass democracy is not to say that she anywhere proposed its wholesale transformation. Rather, she supported a kind of insurgent politics, rooted in civil society, that would invigorate rather than replace mass democratic politics.

While on the conventional view, Arendt reveals a tension or contradiction between her elitist and democratic sides, I believe that Arendt's unique contribution to thinking about democracy resides precisely in her argument in favor of elites. While most political theorists have sought to adapt democratic ideas to the requirements of mass politics, Arendt insisted on the extreme tension between mass behavior and meaningful citizenship. For this reason, she believed, citizenship must be insulated from the masses and made the province of elites if it is to embody democratic ideals.

Arendt's conception of grass-roots democracy bears reexamination, especially in light of the wave of "democratic revolution" that has overtaken us. I view her thoughts on democracy as a kind of lost treasure that needs to be retrieved. The effort to retrieve this treasure does not commit me to a wholesale defense of her political theory. I do not believe that Arendt presents a sufficient account of everything democrats need to consider. But I think she does present a necessary account of a kind of democratic politics that is too often ignored.

On Revolution and Democracy

On Revolution is a book intent on retrieving the lost treasure of modern revolution. According to Arendt, this treasure has been buried beneath the sands of liberalism and Marxism. Neither of these ideologies understands the distinction between liberation—the removal of impediments to action—and freedom—the exercise of capacities for participation in collective self-government. It is above all such participation, and the empowerment that it imparts to political agents, that Arendt wishes to rescue from a world overcome by a preoccupation with mass consumption and the ritualized spectacles of mass politics.

Arendt's lost treasure is less a tradition than an antitradition, a loose assortment of political visions, experiments, and institutions that includes the writings of Jefferson, Proudhon, and Bakunin, the innovations of the American and French revolutions, and the workers' councils that briefly flourished in Russia, Germany, and Hungary in the twentieth century.[5] What unites these phenomena is a revolt against the principle of concentrated state power and against the party institutions that seek to organize such power. They resist oppression and prize the spirit of political freedom. As such, they may seem supremely democratic. And yet Arendt's description of revolutionary politics strikes a paradoxical chord. On the one hand, she describes it as a "regeneration of democracy." Whereas representative institutions produce a professional political class, the councils institutionalized "the average citizen's capacity to act and to form his own opinion." Tragically, these political forms did not, perhaps could not, last. This failure is tragic, for, as Arendt insists, "whenever knowing and doing part company, freedom is lost." The councils incarnated a vigorous, participatory, and egalitarian politics. They represented "a new form of government that would permit every member of the modern egalitarian society to become a 'participator' in public affairs" (*On Revolution*, pp. 262–64).

On the other hand, Arendt maintains that such councils did not and could not accord with the democratic spirit of the egalitarian age. They were contrary to the typical institutions of modern democracy—political parties, competitive elections, representative government—because of the oligarchical character of such institutions. They also rejected the essential principle of modern democratic politics, the principle of mass politics itself, with its watery, fictive equality and its tendency to homogenize public affairs, reducing citizenship to infrequent forms of vicarious participation and public discourse to a kind of public relations game.[6] In one of the most notorious passages in the book, Arendt describes revolutionary forms as "islands in a sea or oases in a desert." Freedom, she avers, is possible only among equals, but equality is not a universally valid principle, and requires limits in order to operate. For this reason Arendt supports the idea that politics should be the province of elites, for "the political way of life has never been and will never be the way of life of the many" (p. 275). If the spirit of freedom is to be preserved, such elites must strive "to protect the island of freedom they have come to inhabit against the surrounding sea" of necessity and banality. Arendt's conclusion has chilled the hearts of many a democrat: "To be sure, such an 'aristocratic' form of government would spell the end of general suffrage as we understand it today; for only those who as voluntary members of an 'elementary republic' have demonstrated that they care for more than their private happiness and are concerned about the state of the world would have the right to be heard in the conduct of the business of the republic" (pp. 277–79). Arendt understands that her proposal is highly unconventional, but she allows that "it is not the revolutionary spirit but the democratic mentality of an egalitarian society that tends to deny the obvious inability and conspicuous lack of interest of large parts of the population in political matters as such" (p. 277). Only someone misled by the prejudices of a democratic mentality, she tells us, could fail to see the merit of her argument. This sounds antidemocratic indeed. And yet Arendt has earlier described her elementary republics as the *regeneration* of democracy. How can we explain this apparent contradiction?

The answer, I submit, is that Arendt recognizes two competing conceptions of democracy. Both derive from the same distinctively modern, egalitarian principles: that matters of public concern ought to be contestable rather than insulated from public debate; that forms of contestation should be opened up to all who wish to be heard rather than restricted to a privileged few; that "the average citizen's capacity to act and form his own opinion" must be recognized. She rejects the logic of mass democracy because, in spite of its inclusiveness, mass democracy is a form of oligarchical politics, in which political parties, through their monopoly on nominations and on public debate, serve "as very efficient instruments through which the power of the people is curtailed and controlled." In such a system public debate is characterized by an "obvious phoniness"; in spite of the rhetoric of popular will, "the voter can only consent or refuse to ratify a choice which . . . is made without him," a choice that is embellished by techniques of propaganda and political advertising "through which the relationship between representative and elector is transformed into that of a seller and a buyer." Arendt criticizes, then, precisely what defenders of democracy such as Joseph Schumpeter and Robert Dahl have presented as the cardinal features of modern democracy.

But she criticizes this system in the name of the regeneration of a grass-roots democracy. She celebrates the average citizen's ability to think, deliberate, and act. All of this clearly seems democratic. Yet Arendt paradoxically links such action with a system of elites, a system premised upon the insulation of politics from the masses. How can it then be democratic?

Consider first that the model here is not the so-called democratic elitist model. Arendt's elites are not selected by the electorate to rule over them. Arendt's elites select themselves. They represent none but themselves. And they rule over none but themselves. Arendt quite clearly rejects the common association of the term "elite" with "an oligarchical form of government, the domination of the many by the rule of the few" (p. 276). Her elites are distinguished by their insulation from the many, not by their rule over them. While Arendt acknowledges that some of her examples of revolutionary elites, such as the Russian soviets, did "determine the political destinies of the many," she maintains that this outcome was secondary to their principal concern, which was their own freedom to act according to their opinions. Furthermore, such elites are self-selected and self-constituted. Arendt is insistent on this point. Her elites are not authorized or privileged by a state or any other official political body; and they do not in principle exclude anyone. They are open, she insists, to "those few, from all walks of life, who have a taste for public freedom and cannot be 'happy' without it." To be more precise, there is a principle of exclusion, but it is a flexible one, not discriminating against particular kinds of people, certainly not barring ordinary people. The principle is the principle of interest. All you need to do to belong is to care about matters of common concern and to act on this concern in concert with others of similar opinion. A certain virtue or nobility is involved in such participation, but it is not necessary to accept Canovan's disparaging claim that for Arendt "political freedom, which is the all-important glory of human existence, is possible only among an aristocratic leisure class undisturbed by compassion for their serfs."[7] Arendt certainly does not make this argument. Her "aristocracy" is an aristocracy of civic-mindedness, not a hereditary elite based on access to wealth. Indeed, she insists that participation be open to all people, from all walks of life, who have a taste for freedom. Her most vivid examples of such an elite are modern workers' councils, hardly the organizations of a leisure class.[8] The virtues exhibited by the participants in these councils—the extraordinary courage of their convictions, a willingness to put one's reputation on the line, rhetorical and pedagogic skills—certainly distinguish them from those many others for whom participation exerts no appeal. But they are hardly the province of a privileged group.

Finally, Arendt does not speak of a single elite. Her language is decidedly pluralistic. She writes about voluntary participation in *"an* elementary republic," not *the* elementary republic. She clearly envisions many elementary republics and many levels of authority. This vision is perfectly consistent with her emphasis on plurality in *The Human Condition*. Difference, for Arendt, is an intrinsic feature of human existence. There is no reason to assume that she imagines that political virtue can be located in a single place.[9]

So Arendtian elites are not conventionally understood elites at all. If in one sense they are extraordinary, in another they are quite ordinary. They are not privileged, and they are open to all who wish to participate. It is their multiplicity and openness, their self-constitution and self-government that distinguish them, and it is no doubt for these reasons that Arendt considers them a regeneration of democracy, a new form of government that would permit every member of the modern egalitarian society to become a participator in public affairs.

But what about the masses? Even if it plausibly can be argued that Arendt's conception of vigorous participation has democratic features for the limited, exclusive, even if self-selected *demos*, what about the rest, the excluded, those too caught up in the everydayness of social life to take an interest in politics? Arendt's comment about the end of suffrage as we understand it today—she is talking here about universal suffrage—are quite vague, but it gives little succor to those democrats concerned about the condition of the masses, their rights, and the responsiveness of politics to their needs and demands. It also offers few clues about how her vision makes real the egalitarian promise of making participation available to every member of society. There are several answers here. While they are not explicitly developed by Arendt in the name of a democratic theory, it is possible to reconstruct them from her text. They can leave little doubt about her commitment to a plausible interpretation of democratic politics.

First, for Arendt the concept of the masses is a sociological category. It refers to the members of a mass society, to the kind of character that is produced by a society based on mass consumption. The member of the mass tends to be anonymous, and is treated as such by dominant corporate and state institutions. This person tends to be what Robert Dahl called a "homo civicus" rather than a "homo politicus," a privatized individual who participates only minimally in any kind of public discourse, and whose infrequent acts of voting are based on narrow constructions of private interest that are largely taken for granted—"subjective preferences," in the language of microeconomic theory.[10] Sheldon Wolin links Arendt's aversion to the masses with Nietzsche.[11] He might also have linked her with Heidegger, her teacher, for whom *das Mann* of modern society was a banal, mediocre, and pathetic creature overcome by forces beyond his control.[12] There can be no doubt that she was influenced by the totalistic critique of modernity offered by these thinkers.[13] But the critique of mass society need not have the kind of antidemocratic implications that Wolin attributes to it. Consider the words of John Dewey, who warned that democratic principles had been eclipsed by the scale of modern society and by the diversions from citizenship that modern society offers: "The confusion which has resulted from the size and ramifications of social activities has rendered men skeptical of the efficiency of political action."[14] Or consider C. Wright Mills, a contemporary of Arendt, who wrote about the "cheerful robots" of mass society, ordinary individuals caught up in disempowering, bureaucratic forces largely beyond their control. Such individuals become "adapted men." They gear their aspirations and their energies to the situation they are in; they become the consumers of products and images that the institutions of their society require them to be.[15] These writers were not antidemocrats; they were democratic social critics who sought to highlight the failure of modern societies to live up to democratic ideals. Arendt partakes of a similarly anti-authoritarian sensibility.[16] For her what distinguishes the masses is their tendency to conformity, a tendency engendered by the institutions of mass media, mass politics, corporate mass production and consumption. Arendt believes that in the face of these institutions it is futile to imagine that significant forms of popular empowerment and political participation are possible. Furthermore, to the extent that they are possible, they will be channeled not through these institutions but *in response* to them, against the conditions of impersonality and sameness that they promote. In this sense Arendt's elites are counterposed to the masses. But the counterposition is not between a privileged few and an incapable many. It is not between two classes or types of people so much as between two competing *attitudes*. All those who revolt against the conformity of modern society by that action constitute themselves as citizens of an elementary republic. In so doing they exhibit a kind of virtue typically in short supply. But this prescription is not a derogation of average people; it is an invitation, perhaps even an incitement, for them to surpass their ordinariness simply through their voluntary association and concerted action.

But again, what about the masses? What about those who, for whatever reasons, of which choice may simply be one, do not become politicized, do not associate with others in elementary republics? Once we see that "the masses" is not a psychological category intended to denigrate the capacities of ordinary men and women, and once we see that for Arendt there is not one but many elites, it becomes clear that who is a member of an elite and who is a member of the mass is not a question that can be answered once and for all. At different times and for different reasons, some people will become politicized in the face of the disengagement of most others. But there is no reason to imagine that the identity of these people never changes. The citizen is not, then, a higher type of person but an otherwise ordinary person who chooses, under specific circumstances, to throw caution to the wind, to disrupt the routines of mass society by acting against the grain of social routine. This definition helps to explain how it is possible for Arendt to consider modern labor movements—made up of ordinary proletarians distinguished only by their passionate commitment to justice—as exemplars of her political spirit, their activities constituting "one of the most glorious and probably the most promising chapter of recent history."[17]

Furthermore, those who at any time constitute the mass are not thereby subjected to any particular exclusion or degradation beyond those exclusions and degradations that characterize modern society itself. They remain just as they were before—large groups of anonymous individuals, incorporated into the same remote forms of mass politics, subjected to the same social and economic forces, assuming their assigned places in the social division of labor in exchange for the material benefits that accrue to those places. Arendt is not condemning this way of life, though it is one she clearly finds wanting. But she rejects the idea that it can meaningfully be considered a life of political freedom. And she also rejects the idea that it is possible to transcend such a society in the name of a "true democracy" based on meaningful forms of mass political participation. For her the ideas of mass and participation can have only the most metaphorical connection; she thus insists that only through more limited forms of participation is effective participation and empowerment possible.[18] The argument about insulating politics from the masses, then, is not antidemocratic, though it is unconventional. The point is not to exclude a class of people but to establish boundaries that keep out the impersonality and routine characteristic of mass society.[19] Such boundaries insulate the oases of civic engagement from the desert of mass politics. But they are no substitute for mass politics.

It is tempting to believe that Arendt's rejection of "general suffrage as we understand it today" requires wholesale abandonment of representative democracy. But this notion is also mistaken. It is true that some of her examples of elementary republics, such as the Russian revolutionary soviets, did claim to be alternatives to parliamentary institutions. But Arendt presents these as bearers of a certain political spirit rather than as literal examples to be emulated.[20] Nowhere does she advocate the revolutionary transformation of postwar liberal democracy. Indeed, the weight of her corpus leans heavily against such transformations. It is only with great circumspection, she holds, that we can undertake to construct political institutions, and even then we cannot proceed *ex nihilo*. The problem with modern ideologues is precisely their unbridled confidence in themselves and in their projects of wholesale transformation. "Firmly anchored in the tradition of the nation-state, they conceived of revolution as a means to seize state power, and they identified power with the monopoly of the means of violence."[21] Arendt's model of elites is not an alternative model of state power. Rather than envisioning a total structure of power that might replace the institutions of representative government, Arendt envisions the pluralization of political space. Instead of a single project of mass empowerment, as envisioned in different ways by Marxism and populism, she endorses the multiplication of forms of popular participation. One way of multiplying them is through a decentralization of political authority; and alternative institutions, such as the Jeffersonian wards, the council system, and confederal models of authority, play important roles in Arendt's thought.[22] But Arendt never puts forth these models as wholesale alternatives. It is likely that she considered the normal institutions of liberal democratic politics too entrenched to be undermined and replaced. And it seems certain that she recoiled from the prospect of such a total transformation in any case.

An overlooked passage in *On Revolution*, part of the same paragraph as the notorious comment about suffrage, serves to clarify her thought. Commenting on elementary republics, Arendt writes:

> It would be tempting to spin out further the potentialities of the councils, but it certainly is wiser to say with Jefferson, 'Begin them only for a single purpose; they will soon show for what others they are the best instru-

ments'—the best instruments, for example, for breaking up the modern
mass society, with its dangerous tendency toward the formation of pseudo-
political mass movements, or rather, the best, most natural way for interspersing it at the grass roots with an 'elite' that is chosen by no one but constitutes itself. (p. 279)

Arendt refuses to say too much about the councils. Instead of identifying them
with a grandiose program of transformation, she identifies them with nothing
more than the impulse toward empowerment. Yet while she refuses to turn the
councils into a counterideology, she does indicate their political significance.
They are instruments not for replacing but for *breaking up* mass society, countering its homogenizing tendencies, interspersing modern society at the grass
roots with forms of voluntary association. I think it is clear in these comments
that Arendt sees her elites not as alternatives to the formal institutions of representative government but as complements to them, reproaches to their tendency to treat people as subjects rather than citizens, consumers rather than
makers of their own destinies. As such her revolutionary elites represent an in-
vigoration of democracy; they take the democratic idea of citizenship seriously,
but see it being most appropriately applied in the domain of civil society rather
than directly in the sphere of the state itself.

Margaret Canovan is thus incorrect when she claims that Arendt failed to no-
tice the difference between normal and extraordinary politics, and mistakenly
desired "the replacement of parliamentary government by this council system."[23] In advocating the end of universal suffrage as we practice it today, Arendt
was not advocating the abolition of parliamentary institutions or urging a restricted franchise. She was arguing that we ought to cease treating these institutions as the essence of politics, the apotheosis of democracy, and that we should
deprive them of their sovereign status. She was advocating an opening up of political space, rejecting the presumption that only a professional class can act politically, and that citizenship is an identity more or less defined by the occasional
act of designating those who claim to act on your behalf. In Arendt's democracy,
it is reasonable to infer, there would still be elections and representative institutions. But there would also be alternative forms of activity, debate, and participation, alternative forms of membership and citizenship, ones more vital and empowering than the metaphorical equality of membership in the nation-state.
The extra-ordinary—that which stands outside the norm—would constitute a

form of empowerment in its own right. But it would also stand as a reproach to the political system as a whole, challenging the boundaries of acceptable discourse, keeping political parties honest and accountable, nurturing a healthy suspicion of constituted authority and a healthy respect for democratic values.

Parties, Elites, and Democratic Politics

Margaret Canovan considers it "baffling" that Arendt "should have thought such a utopian system obviously preferable to the system of representative democracy existing, for instance, in America."[24] George Kateb makes a similar point. Arendt, he argues, failed to appreciate the virtues of representative government, which preserves accountability of officials and, by institutionalizing partisan competition, generates public debate.[25] While Arendt did not offer a system in place of representative democracy, she was nonetheless a severe critic of it. But this is perfectly understandable when we place her criticisms in their appropriate historical context. Arendt was a German Jew who was forced to flee Hitler. She was the product of the failure of Weimar democracy. The experience of her generation was the failure of the parliamentary system. The disillusioned socialist Robert Michels, the critical theorists Otto Kirchheimer and Franz Neumann, and the fascist Carl Schmitt concurred that the institutions of mass democracy had failed effectively to mediate between the state and the citizenry; that they had become corrupt vehicles of entrenched corporate interests; and that the public debate that had been generated by parliamentary institutions during the early modern period had given way to the engineering of mass opinion by increasingly remote political elites.[26] This view was particularly influential among those who had experienced the breakdown of parliamentary democracy, but it was not limited to them. And it was not only in Europe that this view was articulated. It had an influential American supporter in John Dewey, whose book *The Public and Its Problems*, written in 1927, even before the downfall of Weimar, developed similar themes. Democracy, Dewey argued, was possible only with a flourishing of independent publics, groups of citizens bound together by an articulated common concern. But in the twentieth century such democratic publics had been eclipsed by the growth of a mass society. In such a system public debate had become corrupted and partisan competition ritualized; meaningful forms of civic politics had been rendered increasingly difficult to initiate, much less sustain.[27]

This critical perspective was current among American public intellectuals in the postwar period. For this group fears of a closure of parliamentary democracy were exacerbated by the emergence of a national security bureaucracy and the spirit of McCarthyism. Perhaps the most notable critic of the American system during this period was C. Wright Mills, whose book *The Power Elite* built upon Deweyan themes in criticizing the growth of large-scale, bureaucratic corporate and state institutions.[28] Arendt's political theory was developed in this intellectual milieu. As someone who had experienced the absence of constitutional government in Germany, she was well aware of its virtues. Her criticism of liberal democracy was not mindless or indiscriminate. Consider this text, written in 1953 in response to the McCarthyite witch hunts:

> America, this republic, the democracy in which we are, is a living thing which cannot be contemplated or categorized, like the image of a thing I can make . . . It is not and will never be perfect because the standard of perfection does not apply here. Dissent belongs to this living matter as much as consent does. The limitations on dissent are the Constitution and the Bill of Rights and no one else. If you try to "make America more American" or a model of democracy according to any preconceived idea, you can only destroy it. Your methods, finally, are the justified methods of the police, and only of the police.[29]

Note the conjunction of themes—a staunch commitment to civil liberties, praise for the Constitution as a framework of such liberties, and a vision of democracy as an inherently open-ended process, not to be identified with any formal political arrangements or any end state. Arendt's critique of McCarthyism points beyond normal constitutional politics in its emphasis on experimentation and dissent; but it also recognizes the value of such a normal politics.[30] Arendt never dismissed the importance of the constitutional "fences" established by liberal democratic regimes.[31] Yet events had instructed her that it was not in the parliamentary arena that democracy could most effectively be defended or deepened. The parliamentary experience in Europe and the closure of American domestic politics during the Cold War led her to conclude that it was through vigorous resistance and dissent, including forms of civil disobedience, that liberal democratic values could be preserved at the same time that more participatory forms of democracy could be experienced. Arendt's idea of "oases in the desert" was thus very much informed by the crises of representative government in our time, and by the need to go beyond normal forms of mass politics even to defend constitutional liberties, not to speak of developing more effective forms of empowerment.[32]

Critics have likened Arendt's conception of extraparliamentary civic action to neo-fascist views prevalent in late Weimar Germany.[33] Arendt, it is argued, like the so-called political existentialists, among whom Carl Schmitt was the most notable, rejected the liberal parliamentary state and sought more direct, unmediated forms of popular action. In the name of authenticity she thus repudiated modern democracy. These critics are right to note the presence of existential themes in Arendt's work, and also to establish the antiparliamentary context in which she wrote. But they are gravely mistaken to conclude that she can thus be linked with the antidemocratic sentiments of such thinkers.

It is worth underscoring again that for Arendt what distinguishes such elites is not simply that they affirm a sense of personal identity and worth but that they embody *democratic* ideals. They make real the possibility of participation of every member of society—though not at the same time—in public affairs. Such elites are clearly democratic in their own constitution. They are also democratic in a broader sense, as forms of popular empowerment that seek to open up existing forms of authority to questioning and to raise the possibility of their revision. The withdrawing of consent, the refusal any longer to submit to authoritative forms of power, is for Arendt a principal feature of a "revolutionary" politics.[34] Such a politics claims power for the powerless, but it does not seek to rule over anyone. Any politics that seeks to vilify, exclude, or rule over others, or to limit the scope of public debate, would seem plainly inconsistent with the spirit of Arendt's argument. While Arendtian citizenship seeks authenticity, it also recognizes the partiality of all political movements and the *plurality* of the world.[35] This chastened sense of empowerment is the direct antithesis of the romantic appeal to national homogeneity that characterized fascist ideology.

Fascism, after all, was antiparliamentary and fundamentally antidemocratic. It was above all else a form of mass mobilization intent on eliminating cultural and political diversity. Schmitt, for example, invoking Rousseau, writes chillingly about a homogeneous "people's will" that is mobilized by and organically linked to a dictator. In contrast to parliamentary democracy, he insists, such an "authentic democracy" involves the immediate rule of the people, conceived as an organic unity, a people seeking "elimination or eradication of heterogeneity."[36] Arendt's notion of citizenship is radically at odds with any such conception. Indeed, given her own experience as an "eliminated" Jew whose closest friends had been eradicated, it could not have been otherwise. In *On Revolution*, she explicitly rejects the conception of popular sovereignty traceable to Rousseau, which connotes "a mass that moves as one body and acts as though possessed by one will." In its stead she recommends the view of the early Americans: "The word people retained for them the meaning of manyness, of the endless variety of a multitude whose majesty resided in its very plurality." Instead of seeking unanimity, "they knew that the public realm of the republic was constituted by an exchange of opinion between equals . . . a multitude of voices and interests" (pp. 92–93). Arendt's critique of parliamentary democracy, then, is eminently democratic. The authentic citizen is one who acknowledges the limitations of even his most justifiable claims—acknowledges, in other words, the rights of others to press their claims as well.[37]

Her endorsement of small dedicated groups—elites—is no more antidemocratic. While the idea of democratic elites may seem oxymoronic, it is important to see that Arendt was not alone in thinking in these terms. Indeed, she was connected with a group of intellectuals, distinguished by their participation in the resistance to totalitarianism, whose democratic credentials can hardly be questioned.[38] These figures were radicals whose revolt against Leninism and indeed all forms of vanguardism led them to reconsider the possibility of meaningful forms of mass politics. Consider Dwight Macdonald, editor of *politics* magazine and Arendt's close friend, whose influential 1946 essay "The Root Is Man" offered a withering critique of mass parties for having failed as vehicles of democratic empowerment. "The only way, at present, of . . . acting," he writes, "seems to be through symbolic individual actions, based on one's personal insistence on his own values, and through the creation of small fraternal groups which will support such actions, keep alive a sense of our ultimate goals, and both act as a leavening in the dough of mass society and attract more and more of the alienated and frustrated members of that society."[39] Andrea Cafi, the Russian anarchist who was an important influence on the *politics* circle, concurred: "Today the multiplication of groups of friends, sharing the same anxieties and united by respect for the same values, would have much more importance than a huge propaganda machine. Such groups would not need any compulsory rule. They would not rely on [mass] collective action, but rather on personal initiative and effective solidarity, such as can be developed only by friends who know each other well."[40] C. Wright Mills, another *politics* associate, placed similar emphasis on the importance of local forms of dissent and resistance.[41] Perhaps the most influential articulation of this theme was Albert Camus's 1947 novel *The Plague*, an allegory of the resistance to Nazism. Dr. Rieux, a leader of the resistance, refuses any macropolitical program, preferring to work tirelessly with his small band of dedicated colleagues. "Salvation," he declares, "is just too big a word for me. I don't aim so high. I'm concerned with man's health; for me, his health comes first."[42]

Arendt was closely acquainted with this circle and their ideas. It is no mistake, then, that she closes *On Revolution* by memorializing René Char, the French poet who had participated actively in the resistance. This is one of several places where she quotes his aphorism that "our heritage was left to us by no testament," expanding upon the feeling of empowerment and authenticity that Char experienced during the resistance.[43] Arendt elsewhere writes that "without premonition and probably against their conscious inclinations, [the resisters] had come to constitute willy-nilly a public realm where—without the paraphernalia of officialdom and hidden from the eyes of friend and foe alike—all relevant business in the affairs of the country was transacted in deed and word." Her point is that the resisters had gone beyond resisting oppression in the way that Allied soldiers, for example, had resisted Nazism; they had *constituted themselves* as political agents. Drawn into the struggle against the Nazi occupation, they "had become challengers, they had taken the initiative upon themselves. and therefore, without even noticing it, had begun to create the public space between themselves where freedom could appear."[44] They had become citizens of an elementary republic and experienced the joy of inserting themselves, through their voluntary action, into the public realm.

There is no question that the experience of totalitarianism and the resistance to it had an enormous impact on Arendt's political thought. Her ideas about revolutionary elites were shaped by her reading of the tragic history of twentieth-century politics, but also by the ideas about the limits of mass politics and the importance of more local forms of resistance to oppression that were prevalent in her milieu. This milieu sheds a new light on Arendt's elitism. In such light Arendt's argument need not appear either baffling or antidemocratic. Instead, it can be seen as an argument about the importance of new forms of empowerment at a time when the more conventional forms of representative democracy seemed to be in eclipse.

Arendtian Democracy Assessed

Proving that Arendt's conception of revolutionary elites represents a coherent vision of democratic empowerment does not prove the merits of such a vision. Is it plausible? Is it practical? It is impossible to ignore these questions. The most commonly adduced charge against Arendt here is the charge of utopianism. Arendt, it is said, presents a vision that is contrary to the spirit of modern society. The kinds of spontaneous praxis she endorses are evanescent, insubstantial, pathetic glimmerings of long-ago glory.[45]

This charge of utopianism is, I think, unfair. It suggests that Arendt's vision exists nowhere, that it occupies no identifiable political terrain. But this is plainly untrue. Her argument was a self-conscious effort to capture the reality of a kind of insurgency and empowerment whose significance had been lost to mainstream political thought. Arendt's works furnish many examples of "elementary republics"—the French and Danish resistance to the Nazis; the Hungarian workers' councils set up in 1956; the Israeli kibbutzim; the American civil rights movement; Students for a Democratic Society, and the antiwar movement more generally. Each of these movements was a consequential form of resistance to unjust authority; each sought to open up, to *democratize*, the space for civic activity. Does Arendt romanticize these episodes? Perhaps she does. Clearly she fails sufficiently to explore the limits of these forms of resistance, or to explain their connection to more normal forms of democratic politics. But before we move too quickly to this criticism we might consider her vision in the light of the dissident movements for democracy that struggled against communism in Europe.

Among the most instructive of these movements was the Charter 77 movement, a human rights campaign that soon become the nucleus of a variety of independent initiatives aimed at the democratization of Czechoslovak society.[46] In the course of its evolution the members of the Czech democratic opposition converged on a conception of politics with remarkable affinities to Arendt's view.

Among the many parallels to Arendt, three stand out. First, the Czech democrats viewed politics in nonstrategic, though not antistrategic, terms. While they always sought particular objectives—indeed, in their revulsion against grandiose ideologies they turned particularity into a virtue—they had little aspiration to influence public policy directly. For them politics was primarily a way of being and acting so as palpably to experience one's power and affirm one's dignity. As Ivan Jirous wrote, the parallel polis "does not compete for power. Its aim is not to replace the powers that be with power of another kind, but rather under this power—or beside it—to create a structure that respects other laws and in which the voice of the ruling power is heard only as an insignificant echo from a world that is organized in an entirely different way." The "entirely different way" to which Jirous refers is the deadening and repressive mode of decaying totalitarianism. In the face of a political system whose power seems secure and beyond radical transformation, he insists on the necessity of creating independent poleis—elementary republics—beneath and beside it. Such republics do not principally direct themselves toward the state or the formal political system; the activities they sustain "are their own goals. In them, the intrinsic tendency of people to create things of value is realized. By giving meaning to their lives and the lives of those close to them, people are able to resist the futility that threatens to swallow them up."[47]

Ladislav Hejdanek sounded a similar theme:

Such a [democratic] regeneration is possible only in the form of free initiatives undertaken by individuals and small groups who are willing to sacrifice something in the interest of higher aims and values . . . The beginning of all independence is taking our lives seriously, deciding for something that is worth taking responsibility for, being prepared to devote our energy, our work, and our lives to something of value, or, more appropriately, to someone rather than something.[48]

The Arendtian resonances—creating value, resisting futility, regenerating democracy—are striking.

Equally remarkable is the metaphor with which the Chartists described their community—a "small island in a sea of apathy," the "visible tips of the iceberg" of discontent. For the Chartists the insularity of the parallel poleis was one of their prime virtues. Such insularity afforded protection from a repressive state, but also established protective walls around activities otherwise threatened with being "swallowed up" by the conformity and consumerism of modern industrial society. As Havel wrote:

It seems to me that all of us, East and West, face one fundamental task from which all else should follow. That task is one of resisting vigilantly, thoughtfully, and attentively, but at the same time with total dedication, at every step and everywhere, the irrational momentum of anonymous, impersonal and inhuman power—the power of ideologies, systems, apparat, bureaucracy, artificial languages, and political slogans.[49]

The islands of civic engagement and solidarity improvised by the Czech democrats represented for them the most effective way to practice such resistance. The courage and conviction exhibited by the citizens of such islands distinguished them from the mass surrounding them, threatening to engulf them. Their membership and their objective bound them together in ways that mass organizations could never hope to do. These citizens could see and hear their fellows. They could directly experience the results of their actions. They could personally be affirmed by their citizenship. Who were these citizens? Artists, writers, historians—persecuted, underemployed, insecure, to be sure—but also shopkeepers, housewives, students, even factory laborers. They came from all walks of life, and what distinguished them was their commitment to principle, not their origins or their social status.[50]

Charter 77 and its adjuncts were not elites in the conventional sense. They were elites only in the sense of people bound together by a common refusal to be swallowed up by the conformity that surrounded them. Their members lived in truth where most lived a lie. Where most lived as subjects, accepting the disempowering structure of society, performing rituals of obedience in spite of their misgivings, the Chartists lived as citizens who had the courage of their convictions. Yet the Chartists refused to consider themselves a higher type of person, just as they refused to consider more ordinary, conformist individuals to be inherently corrupt. As Vaclav Havel noted, it is impossible to distinguish categorically between the conforming member of society and the true, independent citizen, for the line separating the two "runs de facto through each person." Everyone is in some respects complicit in the ongoing structures of mass society, and no one is so utterly entrapped within them that he or she is incapable of some kind of independence on some occasion. The boundaries separating the islands and the seas are thus ever shifting. At the same time, the connections between islands and seas vary. As Havel maintains:

It is probably not true to say that there is a small enclave of "completely independent" people here in an ocean of "completely dependent people" with no interaction between them. There is an enclave of "relatively independent" ones who persistently, gradually, and inconspicuously enrich their "relatively dependent" surrounding through the spiritually liberating and morally challenging meaning of their own independence.[51]

In this way the elementary republics are not wholly self-absorbed in spite of their insularity. They point beyond themselves, having a "radiating effect" on their environment, an effect caused by the force of their example, by the embarrassment of those who failed to act, by the indirect moral pressure exerted on the regime. At the same time they discover the appropriate locus of political responsibility—the civic initiative of concrete human beings acting on their own behalf, thinking and speaking for themselves

There can be no denying that this conception of democratic praxis has proved itself to be enormously powerful, having inspired some of the most potent democratic movements of our time. But it might still be asked whether it has any relevance in a post-totalitarian world, where the problems of democracy no longer center on how to resist totalitarian rule but instead on the difficulties of orderly government.

As I will argue at greater length in Chapter 7, the answer is yes. In a post-totalitarian world resistance movements no longer have such an obvious antagonist. But the practice of resistance to unjust authority has hardly become a thing of the past. The problem of justice can never finally be solved; believing they could solve it was one of the most grotesque errors of the revolutionary Marxists. And as long as the problem of justice remains, political argument and contestation will go on. But isn't it precisely the virtue of liberal democracy that it institutionalizes such argument and contestation, as Kateb, for example, argues against Arendt ?[52] What can be the relevance of Arendt's vision of elementary republics to a post-totalitarian world in which liberal democracy has triumphed? The answer here must be twofold.

First, liberal democracy has *not* triumphed. It is in some sort of crisis in every post-totalitarian society. Is Austria the future of Central Europe, or is Bosnia-Herzegovina? The owl of Minerva cannot furnish an answer. It is precisely because liberal democracy has not triumphed that it is important to sustain the kinds of independent initiatives pioneered by the former anticommunist opposition, initiatives prefigured in the writings of Arendt. As Arendt saw, to achieve liberal democracy, liberal democratic means—parties, constitutional machineries—are not enough. Equally important are the democratic habits of mind that can be sustained only in civil society, in initiatives—publications, civic associations, social movements, forms of disobedience—undertaken at the grass roots.

Moreover, just as it would be mistaken to view liberal democracy as the future of the postcommunist states, it would be equally mistaken to view it as the riddle of history solved, the terminus at which we in the so-called West have fortunately arrived. Actually existing (as opposed to possibly emerging) liberal democracy has profound problems of its own, problems identified by Arendt in her critique. It seems unable to sustain high levels of political participation even in voting. It establishes a distance between citizens and their state that generates serious problems of legitimacy. Furthermore, the kinds of bargaining encouraged by liberal democratic political culture tend to produce a government colonized by special interests, impeding effective public policy and further alienating citizens. All of these defects in the functioning of liberal democracy are fairly well known, and have been common currency among political scientists for decades.[53] But as important as they are, none of them speaks to the *normative failings* of liberal democracy.

As I have argued, in the twentieth-century liberal political theorists inspired by Joseph Schumpeter attempted, with some success, to redefine the meaning of "democracy" in a way consistent with the factual realities of liberal democratic politics in the United States and Great Britain. These theorists were certainly correct in arguing that liberal democratic government, based on competitive elections, political bargaining, and a high degree of political passivity on the part of ordinary citizens, was the most realistic macropolitical system of government even remotely consistent with the idea of democracy. The existing macropolitical alternatives—fascism, communism, and various combinations of the two—had clearly proved themselves disasters. In the name of authentic people's democracy and unmediated popular rule they produced great misery and injustice. But the Schumpeterian redefinition of the term left a good deal—too much—of its meaning behind.[54] In the name of realism the idea of rule by the people became wholly metaphorical, meaning nothing more than the right of citizens occasionally to select candidates who appeared to offer them some of what they wanted from government. As Arendt put it, the relationship between politician and citizen was transformed into that of a seller and a buyer, under conditions of a seller's market. This reality is clearly wanting from the perspective of the democratic ideal of self-government. And simply redefining the term will hardly convince those who take this ideal seriously. Yet the great difficulty of

much so-called participatory democratic and communitarian criticism of liberal
democracy has been its imprecision.[55] The criticisms always seem to imply one
of two alternatives, either a reform of the system that leaves intact its bureaucratic features and makes its peace with the imperatives of mass society—as in
some variants of social democracy—or a romantic vision of direct and unmediated democracy, an alternative system of sovereignty that is left unspecified.[56] It
is not clear exactly how either alternative represents an advance in terms of democratic values, in the first case because democracy seems sacrificed to practicality, in the second because of its blitheness toward questions of practicality.

Arendt's conception of elementary republics enables us to refocus this debate.
Self-styled "political liberals" *and* social democrats are right—a wholesale democratic alternative to liberal democracy is inconceivable. At the level of the
nation-state the "rule of the people" must always be more or less metaphorical,
channeled, diluted, and corrupted by mass political organizations and bureaucratic structures. But partial alternatives to such a politics—elementary republics, parallel poleis—are not only conceivable. Such oases are a part of our political landscape, though an often ignored part. What do they look like? Among
their more dramatic forms are the Green movements in Europe; the civic initiatives, such as the Helsinki Citizens' Assembly, that continue to operate in Central Europe; feminist groups such as the National Abortion Rights Action
League and the many local chapters of Planned Parenthood; environmental activist groups such as Greenpeace. But the less dramatic forms are no less significant. I am thinking here of the many battered women's and rape-crisis shel-
ters; the many local environmental groups and coalitions that seek to clean up
their community or to resist the construction of toxic incinerators and hazardous waste dumps; local parent-teacher associations; the religious and social action committees of synagogues and churches; community development organizations; the list could easily be expanded.[57]

These more participatory forms of democratic citizenship are not alternatives
to mass democratic citizenship. They are complements to it.[58] As Arendt put it,
they break up modern mass society, interspersing its large-scale organizations
and imperatives with more grass-roots activities, and with concerns that cut
against the grain of ordinary politics centered on the sovereign nation-state. As
such they incarnate the spirit of association that may serve to invigorate the normal institutions of the liberal democratic state. But, it must be repeated, they are
not and cannot be alternatives to these normal institutions. It is scarcely conceiv-

able that members of modern society can experience any civil or political freedom worthy of the name in the absence of a constitutional system based on the
rule of law.[59] Furthermore, a system of competitive political parties to coordi-
nate social interests on a large scale is an indispensable condition of any meaningful democratic citizenship. Without such parties, as remote and bureaucratic
as they may be, political power will inevitably concentrate in even more centralized and bureaucratic institutions with even less accountability.[60] Finally, the
imperatives of advanced industrial society make some forms of state regulation
of economic and social life inevitable. Such conditions make reformist labor
movements and social democratic parties equally indispensable. For without
these organized political forces to articulate publicly questions of regulation and
justice through the liberal democratic process, such matters will surely be articulated in ways remote from any kind of civic oversight and further still from
meaningful participation.[61]

On all of these important matters Arendt's conception of a democratic politics
centering on a plurality of elementary republics has little to say. Because these
concerns rightly have preoccupied political theorists writing about democracy,
and because Arendt adamantly refused to address them directly, it has been common to consider her beyond the pale of democratic theory. But as democratic theorists wrestle with the legitimation problems that have long plagued liberal democracy, it is perhaps time to reopen the question of what democracy means in
the late twentieth century.

Arendt's work addresses an important dimension of this question that has until recently been ignored. For she recognized a paradox that democratic theorists
could do well to ponder—the effort to irrigate the deserts of liberal democratic
mass politics can draw only from the wellsprings of a robust civil society of elementary republics; and yet the effort fully to incorporate these oases can lead
only to their eventual evaporation. Parliaments, courts, and bureaucracies are
indispensable, but when civic associations are reduced to being the target constituencies of politicians and the supplicants of judges and bureaucrats, they are
on the road to ruin. Their collapse would deprive liberal democracy of its nour-
ishment. It would also end the most meaningful forms of democratic participation possible under modern conditions. For this reason Arendt insists that while
the oases of civic initiative may engage and invigorate the larger system, they
must always prize their own independence and insularity or else risk their own
demise. While such a politics would not necessarily be averse to broader strate-

gies of coalition and movement building, it would always be wary of the diluting—the corrupting—effects of such efforts. A tension between meaningful participation and strategic effectiveness is thus built into such a politics. Perhaps this tension between civic initiative and mass political organization is the terminal condition of modern democratic politics.

6

I've no more than the pride that's needed to keep me going. I have
no idea what's awaiting me, or what will happen when this all
ends. For the moment I know this; there are sick people and
they need curing. Later on, perhaps, they'll think things
over; and so shall I. But what's wanted now is to make
them well. I defend them as best I can, that's all.

ALBERT CAMUS, *The Plague*

In the crisis, this philosophy of intelligent control just
does not measure up to our needs.

RANDOLPH BOURNE,
"Twilight of Idols"

American democracy is at a watershed.

The so-called social contract that governed American politics ever since 1945
has broken down. The public policy arrangements that constituted this contract—a system of "universal" social security broadly construed, a more or less
orderly system of corporate labor relations, a co-optive and mildly reformist social policy designed to ameliorate racial antagonisms and urban problems—are
all in disrepair and disrepute. The political coalition that supported these arrangements—the politics of the "vital center," a largely bipartisan politics dominated by the Democratic party—is equally disrupted and demoralized. The consequences of this breakdown—social decay, incessant ideological posturing and
symbolic antagonism, and government immobility—have been widely acknowledged by commentators for years, and they are well summed up in the title
of E. J. Dionne Jr.'s 1991 book on the subject, *Why Americans Hate Politics*.[1]

Our most recent "social contract"—the Republican Contract With America—is both a symptom of and a reaction to this state of affairs. The Contract is
the product of the long-term decline of American liberalism and the equally
long-term rise of the New Right.[2] While the language of a "Republican Revolution" is surely hyperbolic, it is clear that the conservative Republican agenda has

significant political momentum, and that it seeks to effect a profound transformation of the infrastructure of postwar liberal democracy—a drastic retrench-
ment of federal social policy, an equally drastic reduction of the fiscal and policy
resources of the federal government, a dramatic restoration of political power to
state and local governments, and a decisive repudiation of the politics of social
reform. The conservative vision is deeply antiliberal—the term "liberal" has indeed been converted into an epithet of abuse—and it is equally anti-intellectual.
It rests on a rhetoric of pseudodemocratic populism that counterposes a mythic
America to an unsavory cast of characters—variously called "liberal elites," "the
Washington establishment," and "the counterculture"—who are purported to
rule the United States and to be responsible for the corruption of its economy
and, more ominously, its soul. It is no exaggeration to say that this vision represents nothing less than a repudiation of the spirit of liberal progressive social reform that prevailed in the United States for a century.

This assault on liberal politics, it bears emphasis, is the surface expression of
deeper difficulties confronting American liberal democracy. The party system,
long considered a means of efficiently channeling public opinion into public policy, is in disrepute, and public faith in and engagement with the political system
more generally has plummeted.[3] American political culture is deeply fractured
along racial lines and riven by intense "culture wars" that have badly damaged
the social consensus on which postwar liberalism rested, and these fractures
have helped to fuel the emergence of a potent, if small, movement of right-wing
extremists.[4] Accompanying the growth of this spirit of alienation and resentment, and no doubt in large measure responsible for it, is the breakdown of the
conditions of economic growth that helped to sustain liberalism in the postwar
period. America's industrial base has dramatically eroded as new forms of global
investment and "flexible accumulation" have created a new, "lean and mean"
economy in which relatively secure and high-paying employment increasingly
has given way to insecure low-wage jobs. The real wage of the average American
worker has been in decline since the 1970s, and inequalities in the distribution
of income and wealth have grown.[5]

These accumulated difficulties of liberalism have not gone unnoticed by liberal political theorists. One sign of their attention is a renewed emphasis on the
ideas of toleration and civility and a greatly diminished concern with questions
of distributive justice.[6] Another sign is growing interest among liberal theorists

in the problems of "deliberative democracy" and the need to enhance the quality
of liberal public discourse.[7] A third is the extraordinary outpouring of discussion about civil society as an intermediate sphere of public deliberation and association essential to the flourishing of democratic politics.[8]

Liberal democrats and those on what used to be called "the democratic left,"
then, sense that American liberalism is politically adrift. While academic political theorists have tended to treat this problem at one or two steps removed, a
powerful liberal response has emerged, powerful both because of the sense it
makes and because of the traditions from which it seeks to draw sustenance. Liberal democrats, it is argued, need to revive a "progressive" politics that is modeled on the Progressivism of the turn of the twentieth century.[9] Like the Americans of the 1890s, it is argued, we confront severe challenges that demand a new
spirit of progressive reform. Overwhelmed by our own interdependencies, we
need new forms of social intelligence and social planning.[10] Debilitated by an inflationary "rights revolution," we need a more pragmatic yet vigorous approach
to governmental regulation.[11] Beset by fragmentation and division, we need a
new "activist public policy," centered on the problems of a postindustrial economy and the decline of middle-class living standards, that may repair the social
fabric and restore "direction and coherence to national life."[12] The only alternative, progressives maintain, is to submit to the forces of reaction, to squander the
prospects for progress presented by new opportunities, and to resign our politics to a prolonged period of suffering, resentment, and antagonism.

This, in a nutshell, is the new progressive argument. While I find it compelling in many ways, I believe that it is anachronistic and impoverished, and that
those democrats who wish to resist the new conservative agenda and to address
the serious problems that confront American liberal democracy have to think
about such a politics in a different way. My argument is straightforward and in
some ways fairly simple: the conditions that made previous reform efforts possible no longer obtain, and the political world that we inhabit can support neither
the policies contemporary progressives envision nor the confidence in political agency that those policies presume. Democratic responses to our current
difficulties are certainly not impossible, but they need to be conceived more
modestly. A meaningful democratic politics for the new century must thus be
chastened in a way that the New Progressive arguments are not. While many
progressive aspirations are noble and some may well succeed in some fashion,

there is surely no reason to share the optimism of E. J. Dionne Jr., who predicts that progressives will dominate the next political era. At the very least, such a project is an aspiration rather than an achievement—an aspiration that confronts severe if not insuperable obstacles.

The New Progressivism

Emanating from the center to the center-left of the Democratic party, the new progressives have articulated overlapping tactical, strategic, and ideological perspectives. Some, such as Stanley Greenberg, have focused on the resurgence of the Democratic Party. Others, such as E. J. Dionne, Michael Lind, Jacob Weisberg, and John Judis, are interested in arresting the deterioration of public policy and public civility and promoting a coherent middle-class agenda. Democratic socialists such as Joel Rogers raise the prospect of a third party and seek to advance a long-term strategy—an updated version of the socialist hegemony pioneered by the Italian Marxist Antonio Gramsci—to transform American capitalism in a more social democratic direction.

There can be no doubt that this new progressivism was stirred in part by the results of the 1994 midterm congressional elections, which dealt a harsh blow to Democratic strategists and to whatever hopes had remained of "New Democratic" reforms of health, educational, or welfare policy under the leadership of Bill Clinton. Did 1994 represent a deep realignment of the electorate and the party system, as Republican pundits have liked to claim? Stanley Greenberg argues that the answer is an emphatic no. There is no doubt, he admits, that the electorate is deeply dissatisfied with politics as usual, and that this dissatisfaction was taken out on incumbent Democrats and the "big government" policies with which many were identified in 1994. Yet, Greenberg argues, most Americans do not support a wholesale assault on the welfare state, and they crave a more middle-class-oriented politics. He insists that "what is uncertain is whether Democrats and progressive organizations can mobilize popular opposition to this reign of conservative Republicanism. If they can give voice to the skepticism and offer something better, this volatile electorate is ready to shift loyalty once again. If they fail, we will see a deepening disaffection with government and politics, and not merely a surge of conservatism."[13] This is the central theme of Greenberg's book *Middle-Class Dreams*: that to regain its political credibility "the Democrats will have to engage in a profound renewal of the bottom-up idea . . . to forge a modern, middle-class-centered bottom-up party; a broad-based party encompassing the needs of the disadvantaged and working Americans and focusing on the values and interests of the middle-class."[14]

This refrain is common among those concerned about the future of the Democrats. Thus John Judis emphasizes "the importance of using economic issues to revive the class basis of the Democratic party."[15] The liberal Democrat Paul Wellstone, senator from Minnesota, claims that "a strong, progressive populist politics is in order. Progressive forces need to galvanize around, rally around, a strong opposition that offers alternatives that make a difference to ordinary people." And Vic Fingerhut, an influential Democratic political consultant, maintains, "The Republicans are framing everything very cleverly. They are stirring working and middle-income people against minorities, immigrants, and welfare mothers. American politics comes down to this: if working and middle-income people can be conned by Republicans into thinking that this is a fight against the undeserving poor, then the Republicans can win. But the Democrats can win if they focus attention on those elements that favor the rich and the irresponsible corporations and do not favor the working and middle-income people."[16]

Ruy Teixeira and Joel Rogers offer an interpretation of the 1994 electorate that supports Fingerhut's judgment: "Whatever the reasons for its current timidity, unless the Democratic Party embraces an alternative story and shows a broader willingness to contest business interests and encourage mobilization along class lines, Democrats will continue to be on the defensive and Republicans will continue to have the high ground."[17] Jeff Faux similarly argues that the Democratic Party has become too timid and too tied to a narrow legislative agenda, leaving its core constituencies to fend for themselves. "A liberal strategy for rebuilding the Democratic Party," he writes, "must begin with an understanding that the decline in real wages and living standards is at the heart of the anger and frustration being felt by the middle class." Democrats thus need to begin "a new conversation with the majority of Americans who work for a living . . . They have to be willing to name and attack their enemies . . . Exposed and unsheltered, the core constituencies of the party must regroup, reorganize, and pursue a disciplined, independent path . . . to revitalize themselves as a political force."[18]

These general themes have been sounded in a flurry of essays that make explicit the need to revive the project of social reform initiated by the turn-of-the-century Progressives. John Judis and Michael Lind's manifesto "For a New American Nationalism," the centerpiece of a March 1995 issue of *The New Re-*

public, helped to bring this argument to the foreground of discussion. Criticizing the incoherence of the Clinton administration and the "primitive anti-statism" of Gingrichite Republicanism, Judis and Lind called for a "new nationalism," inspired by the examples of Alexander Hamilton, Abraham Lincoln, and Theodore Roosevelt, a vision summed up in Herbert Croly's influential book *The Promise of American Life* (1909). They write:

> America today faces a situation roughly analogous to the one Roosevelt and the progressives faced. Workers are not threatening to man the barricades against capitalists, but society is divided into mutually hostile camps . . . the goal of a new nationalism today is to forestall these looming divisions in American society . . . Can we meet these challenges? In the decades between Lincoln and Theodore Roosevelt, the country floundered as badly as it has during the last few decades. Their mountebanks were no different from ours; their corruption was even more pervasive; and their sense of political paralysis even more profound. Still, they were able to think and act anew. As we prepare to enter the next century, we believe that we are on the verge of a similar era of national renewal.[19]

This theme is echoed in E. J. Dionne Jr.'s *They Only Look Dead*, whose subtitle aptly sums up its argument: *Why Progressives Will Dominate the Next Political Era.* The 1990s, Dionne argues, "most closely resembles the period 1870 to 1900, which led to the Progressive Era." Opening with an epigraph from Theodore Roosevelt, Dionne thus endorses a "New Progressivism," whose "task is to restore the legitimacy of public life by renewing the effectiveness of government and reforming the workings of politics."[20] Jacob Weisberg makes a strikingly similar argument, replete with allusions to Croly and Roosevelt, in *In Defense of Government: The Fall and Rise of Public Trust.*[21] It is a theme frequently sounded in the pages of important liberal journals of opinion such as *The New Republic* and *The American Prospect.*[22]

But surely the most emphatic endorsement of such a politics is to be found in Michael Lind's *Next American Nation.* Lind proposes nothing less than a periodization of the entire sweep of American history, in which we currently stand poised for economic and cultural renewal at the dawn of a "Fourth American Revolution." Lind proceeds from the impasse of post-1960s liberalism. Like most of the other "progressives" cited above, he views this impasse as the result of two reinforcing processes—the domination of American politics by a finan-

cial and economic elite and the cultural and especially racial polarization that
has helped to secure this elite domination by fragmenting the traditional constituencies of liberal democratic—and Democratic—governance and abetting
the rise of the New Right.[23] Lind's solution—a new "liberal nationalism" inspired by Hamilton and Roosevelt, which will pragmatically yet vigorously deploy the powers of the federal government in "an egalitarian assault on the unjust and inequitable political institutions" of American society. Such an assault
will require "a genuine democratization of our money-dominated political system and a commitment to the kind of social-democratic reforms" supported by
the New Deal alliance before its demise under the weight of inflationary racial
and cultural demands.[24]

Lind's book is the most programmatic expression of the new progressive revival. It outlines an elaborate set of social and economic policies designed to turn
back the deterioration in middle-class living standards and to cement a strong
reformist political coalition. Lind supports campaign finance reform; a pragmatic and flexible trade policy to replace indiscriminate free trade, based on a social tariff that discriminates against low-wage foreign labor; immigration reform; more progressive taxation; a policy of high-wage, technology-intensive
industrial growth based on tight labor markets; and strong national reform of
health care, education, and welfare. Such policies, he avers, can succeed only as
part of a "war on oligarchy" which seeks to make the accumulation of private
wealth compatible with overall national interests. This is an ambitious policy
agenda. But it is linked to an even more ambitious program of national renewal;
Lind proposes nothing less than a virtual cultural revolution, whereby Americans will come to see themselves as part of a "trans-racial" nation committed to
social justice, and the polarities of identity politics will give way before a new, in-
tegral sense of American national identity.

There are striking parallels between these reappropriations of liberal progressivism and arguments further to the left about the need to revive class politics in
America. Indeed, the rehabilitation of Croly among liberals is mirrored by the
revival of an almost Gramscian project of developing an emergent "progressive"
hegemony. Thus Michael Kazin suggested, in an essay titled "The Workers'
Party?" that "not since the Depression have conditions seemed so ripe for a true
class-based liberal movement. Real wages have fallen over the last two decades,
while income inequality has risen sharply. Employers shift manufacturing jobs
to whichever country offers the cheapest labor, and unions are too weak to stop

them. Meanwhile, corporate lobbyists help the Republican Congress draft bills that jeopardize occupational health and safety rules and cut back the earned-income tax credit for low-paid workers." We need, Kazin avers, a revival of "class warfare," which might move debate to the left and raise the level of pressure for serious reforms, just as the earlier Populist and Socialist movements were able to do.[25] Similarly Sidney Plotkin and William E. Scheuerman suggest that "perhaps the power elite's very indifference has created a strategic opening, a systematic vulnerability to a politics of democratic change. Perhaps mainstream politics has created a gap in responsiveness to concrete problems faced by most people in their everyday lives that action from below can yet fill." They thus urge working people to "find ways to channel their anger across the divide of sectarian identities and diverse movements," and to identify with a broad "national majority" that may institute meaningful social and economic reform.[26]

A more extensive argument to this effect has been advanced by Joel Rogers in essays written in support of the New Party, a left-wing grass-roots alternative to the Democrats.[27] Like Lind, Rogers sees the Democratic Party as hopelessly entrenched and captive to special interests. Like Lind, he believes that American politics needs a powerful counterweight to conservative Republicanism, and thinks that it can come only from a reenergized left. Yet Rogers distances himself from liberalism, which he claims is too technocratic, too suspicious of mass movements: "Without organized popular support, liberals cannot do the heavy lifting against entrenched and resourceful corporate actors required to enact desired policies. And without the monitoring, enforcement, and trust-inducing capacities of socially-rooted organizations, they commonly cannot administer those policies effectively." Rogers mirrors Lind in his insistence that the renewal of American democracy requires that the "social control of the economy" must be put "back on the table of American politics." But his project is even more ambitious, for it seeks a coherent and reformist national agenda based on an organized mass movement "challenging corporate power and mobilizing outside the state."[28]

In Gramscian fashion, Rogers argues that this project can be realized only if the left proves itself capable of "uniting the particular with the universal," and that such an integration is a matter of political strategy. In this light Rogers proposes a three-pronged strategy: (1) Democracy Now, a movement for citizen, worker, consumer, and taxpayer bills of rights designed to build on the pervasive alienation from American politics, and to aid the formation of progressive organizations; (2) Sustainable America, a high-wage industrial strategy, much like Lind's, based on a social tariff, full employment, and a shortened workweek; (3) the New Party, "a natural electoral vehicle for a more consolidated progressive movement—a movement that itself should be built in part through greater national coordination and presence, and in larger part, in terms of organizational strategy, from the ground up."[29]

Rogers sees how difficult such a political project is to achieve, how many obstacles such a revitalized left confronts. Yet he nonetheless endorses an optimism of the will, a concerted strategy designed to surmount these obstacles. "A modern Left (even more than the Left of old)," he writes, "needs to make investments in organizational infrastructure to facilitate its own coordination and impact." By the proper development of strategies and the proper deployment of resources, a coordinated left, it is argued, can arrest the deterioration of American democracy and project a genuinely forward-looking vision of the future.[30]

While Rogers's endorsement of a New Party strategy differs from the arguments presented by Lind, Judis, Weisberg, Dionne, and Greenberg, some themes are common to all of them: the so-called New Deal coalition has been shattered; the social democratic reforms of the postwar period supported by this coalition are under siege by a politically ascendant conservatism; and the only way to defend a reformist social policy and to address the social and economic problems plaguing American society is aggressively to rebuild a coherent liberal-left movement, and to fashion a partisan vehicle for this movement.

On the first two points it is impossible to dissent. The New Deal coalition that supported postwar liberalism *has* been shattered, and the social policies created by liberals *are* in jeopardy. Yet I believe that the conclusion that is drawn from these observations is mistaken. A new progressivism is not, I fear, the answer to these problems. Let me be clear. It is not that the prospect of a revitalized, organized left inspired by a progressive vision is objectionable. It is not objectionable. The policies most often supported by progressives—labor law reform and a corporatist industrial policy, a shortened workweek, health care reform, welfare reform, a social tariff, public investment—are good policies.[31] They would help to address American social problems and to remedy many injustices. The idea of unifying diverse constituencies—the women's movement, racial minorities, environmentalists, community organizations, and of course the working class—around such a program of social reform is appealing. And it is probably true that only such a progressive movement could support a meaningful program of social and economic reform. The problem with the new progressivism is not principally its desirability—though there are some serious problems here, to which I will return—but its practicality. The reforms and the movement-building strategy to which they are integrally connected are, quite simply, anachronistic. They constitute an effort to revive a politics—a politics of a unified "left"—under conditions that render this politics no longer symbolically compelling or politically feasible.[32]

The Fallacies of Progressivism

The new progressives are not simpleminded. They acknowledge that historical conditions change, and that today's progressivism cannot simply recapitulate the progressivism of the past. Michael Piore, for example, acknowledges that "the context in which we are resurrecting social policy today is new and different from the context in which it was pursued in the past, and the institutions through which it is implemented must be different as well, even if we call them by names borrowed from the past and charge them with functionally equivalent missions."[33] Yet I do not believe that progressives have taken the full measure of this changing context, and I question whether a meaningful response to the current challenges to democracy can so easily invoke the names and missions of the past. The progressive vision, I maintain, rests on fallacies or specious presumptions; and it is only by subscribing to these fallacies that it is possible to share the progressive vision.

/ / / THE MATERIALIST FALLACY. At the heart of the progressive revival are two beliefs: that the most significant facts about American politics today are the declining real wage, the growing inequality of income and wealth, and the prospects of deteriorating economic conditions for the majority of Americans; and that the principal cause of the conservative ascendancy has been the ability of the right to obscure these economic realities. Thus Jeff Faux maintains that the Republicans have succeeded in "diverting the economic question into a social one."[34] Vic Fingerhut insists that "if working and middle-income people can be conned by Republicans into thinking that this is a fight against the undeserving poor, then the Republicans can win."[35] This theme is sounded again and again in the progressive literature—public disaffection with liberalism is due to the "cleverness" of conservatives, who have "obscured" reality, "diverted attention" from the real issues of concern to Americans, and "conned" their way into governmental power. If only Americans can be awakened to the truth, it is argued, then a progressive agenda can be revitalized.

But the economy is not the only issue of concern to Americans, and there is no reason to think that the declining middle class is the central fact of life in the United States today. Important, yes; morally troubling, certainly; but politically central, no.

The most striking feature of the new progressive literature is its failure to attend to the cultural and symbolic sources of politics today. It is not that these factors are denied; it is that they are treated as somehow epiphenomenal, surface expressions of more profound issues. Faux's language is typical: these concerns are "distractions" from what is really important, the class issue. This belief is simply wrong. Acrimonious identity politics, racial antagonism, the resentment of the white middle class toward affirmative action and "welfare," religious fundamentalism and the phenomenal mobilization of the Christian Coalition— these political formations are not distractions from what is truly real; they are what is real, and effective, in American life, deeply embedded in our culture, in our media, and in the dynamics of our organized political life.[36] They cannot be dismissed, nor is there any self-evident way that can they be transcended. The idea that "it's the economy, stupid," is stupid, and also condescending. There is no reason to believe that somehow the economy will in the last instance prevail. At the very least we must acknowledge that nonclass identities are as important and effective as class identities. And in an age in which, as Rogers acknowledges, the "organic solidarities" of class have dissipated, it is impossible to presume that economic insecurity and the declining real wage occupy any privileged position in the range of concerns that motivate most ordinary Americans.

/ / / THE VOLUNTARIST FALLACY. Again, the new progressives are not simpleminded. They acknowledge the obstacles to the class politics they propose. Dionne's *Why Americans Hate Politics* and Lind's *Next American Nation* both offer brilliant accounts of the way the class-based politics of the postwar period broke down in the 1960s under the weight of a complex set of pressures— the rise of the New Left and of new social movements centered on race and gender, the (partial) co-optation of these movements by federal affirmative action policies, the crisis of Cold War liberalism presented by the Vietnam War—and how this fragmentation of postwar liberalism was accompanied by the slow but steady rise of the New Right. The new progressives do not deny any of these challenges. But their view of the political implications tends to be simplistic. The 1960s, with all that that decade represents, is acknowledged as a source of liberalism's difficulties. But it is viewed as a historical diversion that somehow needs to be averted. A revitalized progressivism, it is held, requires us to get back on track, to put the sources of cultural and symbolic division behind us and move forward with a class-based politics.

I call this belief a voluntarist fallacy because it fails to acknowledge the irreversibility of history. We cannot turn back the clock on thirty-odd years of political and cultural history. This history is a record of heady triumphs—a civil rights revolution, profound and beneficial changes in gender and sexual attitudes and relations, an inflationary discourse of rights that has advantaged previously marginalized groups but has also produced its own hypocrisies, injustices, and resentments. It is also a record of disturbing and sometimes devastating setbacks—the dramatic decline in the organized labor movement, the resurgence of new forms of white racism, the rise of anti-intellectualism and religious fundamentalism, and, most important, the ascent of the New Right, which has fed off both the triumphs and the tragedies of liberalism. These triumphs and tragedies are two sides of the same coin. They are the legacies of postwar liberalism broadly construed. The new progressives are voluntarists because they give no account of how we can transcend the manifold cultural and political forms these divisions have taken, how we can get beyond the legacies of the decades since the 1960s. Men and women may make history, but we are also made by history, and our history is one of profound barriers to the kind of class unity new progressives envision. The difficulties new progressives have on this score are seen in Todd Gitlin's book *The Twilight of Common Dreams: Why America Is Wracked by Culture Wars*, which shows how a fractious identity politics represents both a perversion and a natural outgrowth of the New Left. The unfortunate legacy of the New Left, Gitlin argues, is a fixation on race, gender, sexual and cultural identity, an inflationary rhetoric of victimization, and a proliferation of particularistic political commitments. This is not, to be sure, the only legacy of the New Left, but Gitlin is well aware of the ironic and tragic denouement of the New Left—a twilight of common dreams. Where, then, does Gitlin leave us? With a powerful moral appeal, but little else. "While the critics of identity politics are looting society," he concludes, "the politics of identity is silent on the deepest sources of social misery: the devastation of cities, the draining of resources away from the public and into the private hands of the few. It does not organize to re-

duce the sickening inequality between rich and poor. Instead . . . it distracts
what must be the natural constituencies of a Left if there is to be one: the poor,
those fearful of being poor, intellectuals with sympathies for the excluded."[37]

A left if there is to be one. The idea of such a left is not without appeal. But what
if there is not to be one? What if, given our culture wars, there can be no unified
left but only a diversity of lefts, perhaps congenitally weak lefts? The burden of
Gitlin's analysis is that old visions of a unified left have been wrecked by many
years of fragmentation and acrimony. His point about the consequences are telling. The poor and the disadvantaged are *not* well served by this state of affairs.
The decline of civility in American life *is* troubling. And Gitlin's closing injunction—"We ought to be building bridges"—is noble, and on the whole compelling. But it is hard to build solid bridges on shifting soil, especially when the
ground is fracturing in so many directions and the builders struggle against a
tidal wave of opposition. And it is even harder to build a single bridge on such
fractious moorings, no matter how ecumenical and flexible such a bridge might
be.[38] Gitlin's cultural analysis is more nuanced than that presented by many new
progressives, but he shares their generally voluntaristic attitude. We have been
diverted from our true path. We must extricate ourselves from "cultural" preoc-
cupations and rededicate ourselves to the task of building bridges along class
lines. The fragmentation of the left is, so to speak, the natural history of the pre-
ceding decades. The progressive clarion calls us to summon up the will to erase
the legacy of these decades and to move forward. The word "optimism" fails to
do justice to the willfulness of such a will.

/ / / THE RATIONALISTIC FALLACY. Once it is acknowledged that class does
not represent a more essential reality, and that class politics has been dealt devastating blows, it is still possible to call for a revitalization of class politics, to appeal
to people to make their economic interests a priority, and to join together on soli-
daristic grounds. Such an appeal is an expression of an optimism of the will; and
it seeks to nourish such an optimism and such a willfulness in others. But there
is nothing either morally objectionable or political impossible about such appeals. The devastation of the cities and the growing gap between rich and poor
are troubling, *are* unjust, and this point *should* be made. My problem with the
new progressives is not with the fact that they wish to make this point but with
the implications that they believe follow from doing so. The new progressivism
rests on the belief that these developments are (1) real and (2) unjust, and that
this reality and injustice, when proclaimed, asserted, and mobilized, will lead to

what Dionne calls a "politics of remedy."[39] The economic prognosis offered by progressives is by and large accurate. Their ethical and political objections to this state of affairs are equally compelling. But I question whether it follows that a revitalized, mass-based progressive politics of remedy is possible.

The belief that it is possible rests in large part on another fallacy. I call this the rationalistic fallacy because progressive strategies seem to rely on the belief that an accurate diagnosis of our ills furnishes the key to unlocking and solving them, that the active promotion of the "truth" about the causes of our deteriorating social, economic, and civic life will, in time, lead to "progressive," forward-looking, remedial change. Progressives believe, in other words, that the truth will set us free. This is a noble and powerful belief, traceable to the Enlightenment. There is nothing distinctively Marxist about the idea that humankind only presents itself with problems that it can solve, that rational diagnosis can and ought to be the basis of political prognosis and effective praxis. Yet this idea is, I fear, in large part mistaken, an anachronistic residue of a more optimistic and more genuinely "progressive" era.

The new progressivism, like all progressivisms before it, fails to take the full measure of the divorce of critical reason and effective political power, a split that has dramatically widened in our own time. By failing to see this split, progressivism vastly overstates the possibilities for the general public enlightenment that its political project presupposes. This divorce of reason and power is in different ways the theme of two of the most powerful and influential schools of social theory today, the "critical theory" of Jürgen Habermas and the "postmodern" approach generally associated with Michel Foucault and Jacques Derrida. This divorce has many dimensions, and its political implications can be variously interpreted. Let me simply identify two of the principal sources of this divorce.

The first is fairly straightforward and has been widely acknowledged—the insulation, professionalization, and global political irrelevance of the liberal professions in general and of intellectuals in particular.[40] There are, to put it simply, a limited number of venues for the promotion of the kinds of values and strategies favored by progressives. Michael Piore, for example, argues, I believe rightly, that innovative progressive policies would require both "a breakthrough in the social sciences that would clarify the underlying constraints upon policy" and a political agent capable of developing "a consensus around these newly generated theories."[41] It is not that there are no progressive think tanks or compelling progressive programs; these things do exist, though the competitive disadvantages they suffer due to funding difficulties and lack of access to media are severe. It is that there seems little hope of an effective vehicle for these ideas, and this is partly a function of the political marginalization of intellectuals and ideas in general and "progressive" intellectuals and ideas in particular.

More could and should be said about this problem, but it still might be replied that the only solution is to act more creatively in developing and disseminating ideas, in exactly the ways that writers such as Lind and Rogers propose. But the divorce of reason and power is only partly due to the marginalization of public intellectuals. Its more important cause has to do not with progressive intellectuals per se but with the broader world in which they live and that they seek to effect.

Let me be blunt. Progressives are realists. They believe that they can accurately depict the world, and that their accurate depictions can help them to alter the world. The problem is that in many ways the social world itself defies realism. The social world, to use a term coined by the French writer Jean Baudrillard, is hyperreal.[42] This judgment does not imply that there is no reality. The middle-class standard of living *has* declined. But it implies that the modes of communication and experience increasingly prevalent in American society, and in advanced capitalist societies more generally, efface this reality by juxtaposing it and combining it with other "realities," and by creating new "realities" that necessarily detract from it, and perhaps deny it. This is a complex subject, both sociologically and philosophically. But it can perhaps be clarified with an example. Sherry Turkle, in *Life on the Screen*, raises the following question: If a person spends four, six, or eight hours on the Internet every day, acting out various characters, participating in various "virtual" realities, is it possible to say that the identities that person adopts are any less real than the identities she adopts in "real" life, as an employee, a neighbor, and a citizen?[43] In many respects, especially in respects related to the person's sense of self and emotional energy, she may well *be* the identities she assumes in what we call "virtual reality." Virtual reality *is virtually real*: it is real for all intents and purposes; it has real effects on consciousness and behavior. Any parent whose children have become addicted to computer or video games will understand what I mean.

Now, let's extend this insight. The point is not that we have all become creatures of the Internet, though more of us are becoming so every day. It is that in other important ways the symbolic world we inhabit in the late modern age of mass communication and mass consumption is a virtual or hyperreal world, a world in which the difference between fact and fiction, truth and falsehood, appearance and reality is progressively—no pun intended—effaced. This is one of the central points of Benjamin Barber's book *Jihad vs. McWorld*. Barber points out that recent developments in mass communications—advertorials, infomercials, docudramas, soap-opera-style commercials, MTV and Nickelodeon "worlds," corporate advertising and the licensing of spin-off merchandising—work together to "blur the lines between domains once thought to be distinct," so that "the distinction between reality and virtual reality vanishes." As he tellingly writes:

> Distinctions of every kind are fudged: ABC places its news and sports departments under a single corporate division; television newsmagazines blend into entertainment programs, creating new teletabloids . . . ; films parade corporate logos (for a price), presidents play themselves in films . . . while dethroned governors (Cuomo and Richards) do Super Bowl commercials for snack food in which they joke about their electoral defeat, Hollywood stars run for office . . . and television pundits become practicing politicians . . . Politicians can do no right, celebrities can do no wrong—homicide included. Nothing is quite what it seems."[44]

Add the ethically anaesthetizing effect of hours of television watching, for adults and, even more fatefully, for their children, and the general debasement of public discourse abetted by the rise of talk radio and Geraldo-style live television talk shows.[45] The specific effects of the diverse mass media are a complex matter, but the point I wish to make here is a simple one: these and many other forces conspire to subject individuals to a range of contradictory images, impulses, and desires. They produce a general cynicism about and indifference to "reality"—we can always switch the channel by remote control, can't we?—and an affinity for episodic, fragmented modes of communication, like the video image frame (infinitely erasable) and the thirty-second sound bite. Mass communications, in other words, dull political sensibilities and help to create a mass social *irrealism*.

What, then, is more real, more palpable—Alfonse D'Amato the corrupt politician or Alfonse D'Amato the inquisitor of corrupt politicians? Pat Buchanan the affable talk show host or Pat Buchanan the Savaranola of talk show guests? Bill Clinton the advocate of school prayer or Bill Clinton the critic of school prayer? What is more real, the decline in our real wages, the decay of our cities, our racial or gender sensitivities, our religious fears, or our favorite television shows?

My point is not epistemological; it is sociological.[46] The kinds of concerns—principally economic concerns, leavened perhaps by a sense of justice—that progressives believe are latently central to Americans, and can and should be made more central to them, must compete with myriad other concerns that are no less pressing to most Americans, and that often are more so. In a hyperreal world there is economic suffering, and it is surely possible and desirable to call attention to it and to fight against it. But the facts, theories, and moral sensibilities to which progressives typically appeal necessarily fight a steep uphill battle—perhaps a Sisyphean task?—against the indifference, cynicism, and attention deficit disorder of American mass culture.

/ / / THE HISTORICIST FALLACY. On some level most progressives know how hard it is to get out the message, how hard it is to organize people.[47] Yet the pessimism of their intellects does not chasten their wills. This persistence is not due to stubbornness. It is due in part to a sincere and commendable commitment to egalitarian values and a conscientious belief that it is wrong to let injustice stand. But equally important, I think, is the historical vision on which they draw their sustenance, a vision indeed betokened by the very signifier "progressive."

Lowercase progressivism has a different lineage than Progressivism. On the left—that is, on the political formations traceable to the various socialist and communist movements of the early twentieth century—the term "progressive" was often a euphemism for socialist or Marxist, sometimes for fellow traveler; this euphemism was adopted during the Popular Front period, and it served a useful function during the dark days of McCarthyism and the Cold War. Progressivism with a capital P is a liberal reformist ideology traceable to the Progressives of the early twentieth century; its more recent ancestry includes those Cold War liberals that "progressives" have challenged. Yet in spite of the diverse genealogies, these identities converge—perhaps in part because they face together the problems presented by the New Right—and the term "progressive" in contemporary politics marks a clearly defined genealogy encompassing the liberal-left broadly construed.

Why "progressive?" To speak of progressivism is to invoke a philosophy of history, a way of thinking about the ordering of events, according to which the passage of time and the development of technological and organizational capacity is associated with human betterment, with "progress." Progressivism is optimistic about the future and about our ability to master it. On this score the liberal Croly and the Marxist Gramsci were as one. Current progressives share this faith in the future. They face adversity but they insist that adversity cannot last and that it must eventually give way to good fortune. This is a common refrain. Thus Piore insists that Republican economic policy, which promotes low corporate taxes and low wages, is "a prescription for a continuous decline in the standard of living, if not for the nation as a whole then definitely, and even more precipitously, for a sizable portion of the lower end of the income distribution. In such a situation the [current] social tensions . . . would only be the beginning of a series of upheavals that would eventually lead to revolt and rebellion, if not forestalled by legislative restrictions."[48] It is not Piore's prognosis that I question. If Republican policies are adopted—and there is a good chance that in some version they will be adopted, though perhaps by Democrats—then the standard of living of many Americans *will* decline further. But it does not follow that the immiseration that might occur would lead to widespread rebellion that could be forestalled only by coercive means. This judgment, I suggest, falls in the realm of prophecy. Suffering may lead to protest, but it may not, and in either case an enormous gulf separates discrete acts of protest from an accumulation of protests sufficient to provoke "legislative restrictions." Yet the rhetorical effect of Piore's formulation suggests that current trends can result in only one of two possibilities, either discontent and repression or progressive social reform, which alone can abate the grievances that will invariably accumulate. This is a common refrain among progressives. Thus Greenberg, too, sees only two possibilities: either progressives can tap "popular opposition" to conservatism or conservative policy will produce a further "deepening disaffection with government and politics."[49] On this view a continuation of the status quo can lead only to disaster, and only progressive reform can avert disaster.

The most explicit statement of this theme is provided by Mark Levinson in an essay titled "Looking Backward: The Republican Revolution." Evoking Edward Bellamy's utopian fiction, Levinson presents an imaginary dialogue between a reporter and an editor sometime in the early twenty-first century. The editor explains to the reporter why the Republican Revolution of the mid-1990s was a passing phenomenon that grew increasingly unpopular as the years passed, and he recounts how a growing mass movement, centered on a revitalized AFL-CIO, emerged to contest Republican policy and advance a program called Democracy 2000. The program of Levinson's imaginary Democracy 2000—public investment, the elimination of corporate subsidies, labor law reform, universal health care, a higher minimum wage, a worker-oriented trade policy—is the program of current progressives. In Levinson's account, "candidates signed on to it, and unions and community organizations ran grassroots campaigns of support. In a way, it was modeled on the Contract With America, but it had more popular support than the Contract." Levinson presents this scenario, of course, as a utopian fantasy, but he does so in all earnestness. His scenario is the one imagined by most current progressives, who reason that the status quo cannot work and can produce only unhappiness and resistance, and that only a progressive movement can remedy the political crisis bound to follow.

This is a highly unlikely scenario. And even were it to eventuate, it does not follow that a progressive movement would be able either to generate mass support, to acquire political power, or to use political power in a way that would solve pressing problems and abate social tensions. Indeed, at each step in this logic there are reasons to be deeply skeptical, and it is only on the basis of a leap of faith in historical progress that it is possible to pose the alternatives as starkly as most progressives currently do.

The progressive argument, then, recapitulates a common historical refrain that can be traced back to Marx and to Hegel before him—that a dynamic of change is built into the current order of things, that the contradictions, tensions, and unresolved difficulties of the present give history a progressive tendency or directionality.[50] There are many good reasons, historical and philosophical, to reject such a notion, but the most compelling reason has been stated by Michael Walzer, and it is eminently practical: "The various social catastrophes looming in the mind of the left—millions of men and women begging in the streets, the destruction of the black middle-class and the disappearance of black students from elite universities, massive environmental pollution, a surge in industrial accidents, and so on—are probably not going to happen, at least not on the expected scale. A long, dreary, and dispiriting decline in all these areas is more likely than a dramatic crash."[51] The historical pressures and forces that many progressives imagine will help revitalize the liberal left, then, will probably not be forthcoming.

///THE HISTORICAL FALLACY. What these various weaknesses in the new progressive view add up to is a seriously questionable, indeed anachronistic, reading of the historical moment. Many current progressives hark back to the earlier Progressive era; some hark back to the New Deal; and, as I have indicated, some draw sustenance from a Gramscian vision of hegemonic opposition to capitalism. What progressives fail to see is that these moments are unrecoverable, that the current moment is distinct and unique in that the historical conditions of serious, large-scale movement-building around social reform are largely absent. In previous eras it may have been possible to entertain progressive aspirations and to effect some of them. Today, I suggest, the aspirations ring hollow and the prospects for realizing them are dim at best.

Consider the Progressive era, which presents a model for many liberals today.[52] The Progressives undoubtedly instituted a series of important reforms, laying the foundation for the regulatory state.[53] More important, they effected a transformation of American liberalism, away from a neo-Jeffersonian distrust of state power toward an active reformism based on a robust federal government. There is much to admire here and to identify with. And yet if we pause for but a sketchy comparison between the Progressive era and our own, it will be clear how different the twenty-first century must be:

[1] Progressivism drew force from an active and ascendant liberal Protestantism; today the most politically mobilized religious force in the United States—the Christian Coalition—is on the far right.[54]

[2] Progressive public discourse was supported by an active, reformist, muckraking journalism for which there is simply no current analog, despite individual efforts; and the variety of mass media today function to deaden serious ethical conviction rather than to nourish it.[55]

[3] Progressive reforms were supported by a growing faith in the power of science—scientific management, administrative science, educational science—a faith connected to the emergence and ascendancy of the modern research university; yet neither science nor the university today has this kind of credibility or this kind of reformist ambition.

[4] Linked to the ascendancy of scientific reform and the bureaucratic university was the rise of the modern social sciences, committed to an ethos of professional social reform and what C. Wright Mills called "liberal practicality"; the social sciences today are thoroughly specialized, anaesthetized, and insulated from broader currents of political argument and social reform.[56]

[5] The age of Progressivism was the age of a growing labor movement; the labor movement today is in serious and possibly terminal decline.[57]

[6] As many historians have pointed out, Progressivism was above all a form of corporate liberalism suitable to the interests of an ascendant, national

corporate class imbued with a high degree of class consciousness. Progressive reforms were functionally compatible with, and in some sense required by, the form of corporate capitalism that was evolving at the turn of the twentieth century. Today capitalism is thoroughly global, and the interests once served by the national corporate form of regulation—what some Marxists, following Gramsci, call a "Fordist" regime of accumulation—have now transcended the boundaries of the nation-state. The form of "flexible accumulation" that is ascendant requires neither a strong collective bargaining agent—a union movement—nor the same kinds of social and economic regulation. In many ways, then, it is opposed to and destructive of progressive types of social and economic policy.[58]

[7] There is, finally, the matter of the general political scene. While Progressivism served certain "functional" needs of an emergent corporate capitalism, and while it was supported in part by capitalists concerned about these needs, to these factors we must add one more: the flourishing of a variety of radical, insurgent movements to the left of the Progressives—the IWW, the remnants of turn-of-the-century Populism, and a Socialist party that, under the leadership of Eugene V. Debs, had a significant electoral presence and an even more significant cultural presence. The Progressive movement and the reforms it instituted were in large part efforts to co-opt these political forces. There was, in other words, a powerful left pole in American politics that helped to pull politics to the left. American politics today is mobilized to the right rather than the left. There does not exist anything remotely resembling the kind of political pressure that gave impetus to earlier efforts at social reform. In some sense advocates of the New Party recognize this problem and seek, by force of organizational ingenuity and political will, to create such pressure. But they fail to recognize that current sociopolitical realities are no less hostile to a revitalized progressive left than they are to a revitalized progressive liberalism. Each requires the other; and, given the current state of affairs, neither seems to be forthcoming.

This is not to say that social movements are impossible or that specific reform efforts are futile. It is simply to say that there are no good reasons to believe that it is possible to recreate today an analog of earlier progressive movements. The historical moments in which these movements flourished are irrecoverable. And current conditions make the re-creation of a coherent, mass-based progressive movement of social reform highly unlikely, perhaps impossible.

What Is to Be Done?

What is to be done? The question is a compelling one, for postwar liberalism is in crisis and the New Right alternative offers little succor to those concerned about social justice and democratic equality. Surely something needs to be done to remedy the serious problems enveloping American society and to address the deteriorating legitimacy of its democratic political order. Yet I suggest that the question "What is to be done?" is an anachronism—a compelling query, indeed a noble incitement to action, but an anachronism nonetheless. It presumes a coherent or unified political subject to whom this question can be posed and for whom it may be answered; and it assumes that this subject can assemble a coherent set of possibilities into a single strategy for action. But who is the subject of a revitalized democratic politics? Is there a single identity that might be mobilized? Is there a coherent constituency for a revitalized "progressive" movement? I think the answer to both questions is no. There is no core issue around which a mass progressive constituency might readily take shape. And there is no way that the many problems confronting American society can be remedied through a single democratic agency. The progressive vision of a powerful national party at the head of a strong majoritarian movement for social change is thus, I believe, improbable, and the policies that progressives seek to enact— strong social legislation, a high-wage growth policy, a shortened work-week— are equally improbable.

At its heart the progressive vision suffers from a typically modernist faith in the powers of collective action, a faith shared by liberal progressives such as Croly and Marxist progressives such as Gramsci. This progressivism repudiates dogmas of social liberation through invisible hands or the dialectics of history and substitutes a belief in the importance of conscious social purpose. "In this country," as Croly insisted, "the solution of the social problem demands the substitution of conscious social ideal for the earlier instinctive homogeneity of the American nation" and "a vigorous and conscious assertion of the public as opposed to private and special interests." The Promise of American Life presents a powerful vision of a strong national government exercising public power for public purposes, regulating the economy and promoting a "national good faith" and collective purpose.[59] It expresses an infectious optimism about "human excellence" and offers a powerful antidote to the conservative Jeffersonianism that held back reform in the late nineteenth century and that threatens to destroy the reforms of the twentieth. And yet it is impossible to share this optimism. Think about the achievements it has produced—a robust if limited public sector, a reformed system of public education, an extraordinary physical infrastructure of railways, roads, sewers, and public utilities, and an equally impressive cultural infrastructure of schools, museums, and public parks. Think of the cities that owe their phenomenal growth in the twentieth century to this progressive reformism. They are truly an impressive legacy, even if they did not "solve" the social problem. But they are all in various stages of decomposition, increasingly the sources of our problems rather than means to their solution. And the spirit of progressive reform has given way to a spirit of cynicism not simply about the power of collective purpose but about its very meaning.

The progressive vision of conscious purpose, in short, seems to have reached its tragic denouement. It is not clear that there is any way beyond this state of affairs, and there is surely no reason for optimism of any sort.

On April 2, 1995, Robert Reich published an op-ed piece in the *New York Times* titled "Drowning in the Second Wave." A critique of the Republican Contract With America for its failure to offer public policy solutions to the dramatic economic displacements taking place in American society, the essay called for a renewed federal commitment to rebuild the "human capital" of American workers so that they could compete in the global marketplace. Only then, Reich insisted, would Americans be poised to ride the rising tide of "third wave" technologies and the opportunities those technologies present. Reich was at that point one of the few remaining "progressives" in the Clinton White House, and his argument epitomizes the progressive vision. On this view our challenges are nothing more than obstacles waiting to be surmounted and opportunities waiting to be exploited. Progressivism is Machiavellian in its confidence in the ability of conscious political agency to master fortune and to channel its powerful currents in beneficial, "progressive" ways. Reich's aspirations have come to naught, and it is likely that progressive aspirations more generally will come up equally short. The reason, it seems to me, is complex and yet simple. What if American society is not drowning in the second wave but *drowning in the third wave*? What if the tidal wave of profound and disorienting change that is currently taking place is overwhelming, if it presents multiple, severe challenges at the very moment when we are least capable of addressing them? What, in other words, if there is an unbridgeable disjuncture between our difficulties and the powers available to us for their remedy?

Shortly after the 1994 Republican congressional victory, I wrote that "the weakness of genuinely democratic agencies should lead us indeed to a pessimism of the intellect, but also to a tempering of the will. Only a more modest, localist democracy now makes sense in America."[60] By "localist democracy" I did not meant democracy centered on geographic localities. I meant the opposite of global democracy, the opposite of an overarching, globalist, totalizing strategy of social reform or transformation, the opposite of a new "hegemony," whether Lind's "progressive liberal nationalism" or Rogers's "progressive left."

This idea of localist democracy does draw on the same Jeffersonian imagery that captivates the New Right. It shares a suspicion of concentrated and bureaucratic power, and prefers forms of political activity and organization that promote the direct engagement of ordinary citizens and the sense of responsibility that only direct engagement can support. But its disavowal of social engineering approaches is not "neo-Bourbon" or reactionary, as Lind writes. First, there is nothing parochial about disavowing a global, hegemonic politics. To insist that democratic responses to the manifold problems confronting American society must be partial is perfectly consistent with a general, global understanding of how things fit together; and it is equally consistent with all kinds of regional, national, and even transnational forms of organization. It simply refuses to imagine that these organizations can or should be all-encompassing, or that their projects will eventually converge on a common program of social change. A localist democracy, then, is localist only in the metaphoric sense, not in the geographic one. Second, the reasons for localist democracy are pragmatic rather than dogmatic. It is not out of allegiance to the rhetoric of Thomas Jefferson or Andrew Jackson that localist democracy recommends itself, nor is it out of hostility toward effective reform, as is the case for the New Right; it is because the conditions that once supported progressive politics have been altered, and the prospects for a revitalization of progressivism are dim.

Neither is localist democracy complacent. I do not think that democrats can afford to throw up their hands and do nothing in response to the pressing problems before us. But neither do I think that there is any single strategy that might encompass the range of practical responses or that there is in American society today any basis for widespread agreement on such a strategy should one be advanced.

What, then, does this view of localist democracy mean in practice? I can only furnish some examples. They do not and cannot converge on a single overarching vision of social change. Neither do they constitute an exhaustive or even representative sampling of the possible forms that localist democracy might take. Yet each represents a viable form of democratic response to contemporary challenges.

[1] The Algebra Project, founded in 1982 by Robert Moses, former director of SNCC, seeks to help poor, at-risk students acquire math literacy and basic learning skills by creating a supportive network of parents, teachers, administrators, and community leaders. The project has been adopted by over one hundred schools across the country.[61] In *Reclaiming Democracy*, Meta Mendel-Reyes suggests that the Algebra Project represents an abandonment of Moses's earlier vision of "participatory democracy," and that its narrow focus on math education is inconsistent with broader themes of democratic empowerment.[62] Yet it is also possible to view the project as an eminently pragmatic approach to democratic empowerment: it attacks a specific problem, math illiteracy, through specific pedagogic solutions, and involves local communities in a way calculated to promote a sense of efficacy and to make a difference in children's lives.[63] Such activities address practical concerns, they resist the deteriorating conditions that beset the poor, and they promote loose networks of common concern and commitment. They are modest, but they are potentially effective.

[2] Community organizations such as ACORN (Association of Community Organizations for Reform Now), the Industrial Areas Foundation (IAF), and the Citizens' Action Coalition do not constitute a "backyard revolution" in the sense that they represent the seeds of a general and dramatic transformation of American society. But they are vital means for citizens to act collectively to address specific difficulties—urban decay, affordable housing, crime—by harnessing existing, albeit limited, community resources in effective and empowering ways.[64] Such groups help to organize local community development by promoting political skills, and they furnish national networks of organizers and activists that share information and strategy.[65] As Father Leo J. Penta, an IAF organizer, has said, such efforts seek "to establish islands of political community, spaces of action and freedom in the sea of bureaucrats, political image mongers and atomized consumers."[66]

[3] The movement for environmental justice began as a series of local responses to the problem of toxic waste disposal and blossomed into a broad-based movement, organized around issues of class, gender, and race, that has heightened public awareness about environmental concerns, raised the cost of corpo-

rate negligence, and created an extensive network of organizing and information sharing. The environmental justice movement has not transformed American capitalism or effected an overarching vision of progressive reform, but it has profoundly shaped public discourse and provided a variety of outlets for civic responsibility.[67]

[4] New economic networks have been organized—largely by unions—in response to the globalization of capital and the new system of "flexible accumulation." Such networks monitor national and transnational investment and its environmental impact, track wages and the human rights of workers, and provide solidarity and support across state and local boundaries. One such network is the coalition of groups in the United States, Mexico, and Canada that challenged the North American Free Trade Agreement (NAFTA). European groups include the Counter Information Service, the Foundation for Research into Multinationals, and the Transnational Information Exchange. Jobs With Justice has formed workers' rights boards in Cleveland, Boston, Buffalo, and Vermont to hear workers' complaints and to involve community, business, and labor leaders in an informal mediation process to resolve such grievances.[68] These networks do not constitute a wholesale alternative to corporate power. As Hilary Wainwright has argued, "They have been formed primarily as networks of resistance . . . [and] they exist only in the nooks and crannies of the capitalist edifice. Where they lack the support of some public institution or independent foundation they have a very precarious existence."[69] Yet they represent important forms of collective action and democratic empowerment. While they recognize the global economic sources of many pressing problems, and they abjure parochial solutions, they represent local, *partial* ways of addressing these problems, ways of resisting adversity without seeking fully to conquer it.

Hannah Arendt once described democratic forms of praxis as "islands in a sea or as oases in a desert."[70] What she meant was that in a world in many ways like a political desert—inhospitable to democratic awareness, agency, and empowerment—forms of civic engagement that do promote awareness, agency, and empowerment are like oases—rare and isolated, perpetually threatened by the encroachment of the political desert, in danger of being drained of life, or simply of being overwhelmed by the heat.

This, I think, is an apt metaphor for the future of democracy in the United States. The prevailing forces in our society and in our world are damaging to democracy, both in the advantages they distribute to a few and in the problems they distribute to most. And these problems are accumulating, just as the capacity to master them in a coherent way is diminishing. Democrats embarking on the twenty-first century confront, to use the language of Walter Lippmann, a world of drift that they cannot master. Difficulties and disorientation we have aplenty, but we find little constructive political energy and a surplus of ill will and resentment.

This is not a cause for despair, for there are democratic energies, and there are vehicles for them. It is just that these energies and their vehicles offer little hope for large-scale, progressive social reform. The progressive vision of social intelligence and social policy is simply too ambitious, too unrealistic. Elections can be won by "progressives," and local initiatives can have an accumulating impact on public awareness and public policy.[71] But the project of marshaling a new hegemony is anachronistic, and is not likely to succeed in constructing a new, effective regime of public policy or in mastering the problems confronting us. What I have called initiatives in localist democracy are surely insufficient to this task. They cannot help us to master our difficulties, and citizens who engage in them are bound to be frustrated. But it may well be that this task ought to be abandoned, that we ought to give up the hope of mastering our difficulties and settle simply for resisting them as best we can.[72]

In Albert Camus's acclaimed novel *The Plague*, an allegory of the European resistance to fascism, Dr. Rieux, the heroic leader of of the resistance, is asked what gives him the confidence to persist in his action. "I've no more," he responds, "than the pride that's needed to keep me going. I have no idea what's awaiting me, or what will happen when this all ends. For the moment I know this: there are sick people and they need curing." The world, he avers, is shaped by death; and our victories on behalf of life are always temporary, always fragile. Yet this "is no reason," he maintains, "for giving up the struggle."[73] American democracy faces severe challenges. I do not think that we can in good faith confront the twenty-first century with the same optimism and ambition with which Progressives confronted the twentieth. The kinds of democratic responses that are likely to be effective are bound to be partial, limiting, fractious, and in many ways unsatisfying. They are likely to disappoint us in our modernist quest for mastery and our progressive faith in the future. Yet it is the great virtue of democracy as a form of politics that it prizes contingency, and that it recognizes that politics is nothing else but the Sisyphean task of constructing provisional solutions to our unmasterable difficulties.

7

> History, as an entirety, could exist only in the eyes of an observer
> outside it and outside the world. History only exists, in the
> final analysis, for God.
>
> ALBERT CAMUS,
> *The Rebel*

> The historicist does not recognize that it is we who select and
> order the facts of history . . . Instead of recognizing that historical
> interpretation should answer a need arising out of the practical
> problems and decisions which face us, the historicist believes that
> . . . by contemplating history we may discover the secret, the essence
> of human destiny. Historicism is out to find The Path on which
> mankind is destined to walk; it is out to discover The Clue to History
> or The Meaning of History . . . [Yet] *history has no meaning.*
>
> KARL POPPER, *The Poverty of Historicism*

In 1789 the Ancien Régime fell, accompanied by the crash of collapsing ramparts. In an age of democratic revolution, the upheaval caught the attention of the world.[1] Immanuel Kant spoke for many "enlightened" thinkers when he observed: "The revolution of a gifted people which we have seen unfolding in our day may succeed or miscarry . . . this revolution, I say, nonetheless finds in the hearts of all spectators . . . a wishful participation that borders closely on enthusiasm."[2] Almost exactly two hundred years later ramparts again came crashing down, this time in the east of Europe. Symbolized so dramatically by the demolition of the Berlin Wall, the entire edifice of Communist rule—a truly immense superstructure weighing down upon its people—came tumbling down, and with it the Iron Curtain dividing Europe from itself, and democratic oppositions long subjected to persecution and marginality were swept into power.[3]

What is the significance of these events for the citizens of what used to be called Eastern Europe? What is their significance for democrats at the dawn of a new century? Intellectual history since 1789 proves that it is impossible to arrive at a single interpretation of events of such magnitude. For over two hundred years writers have argued about the meaning of the French Revolution. As we continually reassess ourselves, our political communities, and the problems facing them, we quite naturally reconsider those foundational episodes and events that have shaped our past and help to define our political identities. In this sense history has no absolute or final meaning; it is continually, *historically* interpreted and reinterpreted. On this most philosophers and historians would probably agree.

The events of 1989 are surely subject to a range of interpretations, yet a powerful consensus has taken shape around an avowedly liberal interpretation. The most famous, indeed notorious, exponent of this view is a writer who, intoxicated with Hegel, has clearly not yet properly learned the lessons of historicism taught by Popper and Camus. Francis Fukuyama, in an influential essay, "The End of History," and later in a book of the same name, proclaimed that we have reached "the end point of mankind's ideological evolution and the universalization of Western liberal democracy as the final form of human government."[4] Fukuyama was not alone in his enthusiasm. Marc Plattner, coeditor of the *Journal of Democracy*, seconded this view, declaring that we now find ourselves in "a world with one dominant principle of legitimacy, democracy."[5]

Such Hegelian optimism has been challenged by many liberal democrats. Jean-François Revel has cautioned against "an overhasty assumption that the movement toward democracy represented a sort of reverse millennium, the arrival of the eternal kingdom of history."[6] Perhaps the most serious statement of such skepticism has been articulated by Samuel P. Huntington. "To hope for a benign end to history," he writes, "is human. To expect it to happen is unrealistic. To plan on it happening is disastrous."[7] Yet one need not be Hegelian to hold that the revolutions of 1989 represent the triumph of liberalism. Indeed, Huntington's own sophisticated account of the current "third wave" of liberal democratic transformation is one of many efforts to develop more realistic, constructive policies to ensure the triumph of the liberal democracy that Fukuyama prematurely heralds.[8] In spite of significant disagreements, liberal analysts concur that the transition to liberal democracy is the principal issue on the agenda today.

While I believe that there is much merit to the liberal interpretation, I consider it both politically and morally flawed. It is politically flawed because it marginalizes or ignores important forms of politics that were practiced by the Central European democratic oppositions, forms not adequately covered by liberalism. It is morally flawed because, in doing so, it prematurely forecloses some very complex questions about the meanings and legacies of 1989, thereby precluding certain important avenues of political action. More specifically, it minimizes the importance of nonelectoral, nonparliamentary forms of political activity—the kinds of civic initiatives that played important roles in the resistance to communism—in opposing authoritarianism and constituting genuine spaces of democratic politics. While the "high politics" of normal liberal democratic institutions are important, they need to be supplemented by—and sometimes challenged by—more vigorous, grass-roots forms of citizenship. This need is particularly great at a time when masses of people experience economic difficulty and frustration, and the institutions of mass democratic politics cannot compensate for these sufferings and indeed are often viewed as part of the problem. The kind of liberal interpretation that I criticize fails to see this connection.

In criticizing this liberal interpretation I do not wish to indict liberalism as a whole. Liberal democratic theorists have developed criticisms of existing liberal democracy that overlap substantially with the democratic arguments I defend. It would be a serious mistake to lump all liberals together and declare them celebrants of existing liberal institutional arrangements. Yet the currently prevailing liberal viewpoint does celebrate such arrangements and seeks to incorporate the democratic revolutions of 1989 neatly within them. This version of liberalism is a monist liberalism if ever there was one, and it merits criticism.

In the spirit of Popper's critique of historicism, I reject the idea that 1989 has a single meaning. It has many meanings. While in some ways it suggests a triumph of liberalism, in other ways it presents more democratic and participatory possibilities. While it would be a mistake to overestimate these possibilities or their significance, it would be as great a mistake to ignore them. For at a time when liberal democracy is suffering from its own crisis of legitimacy, these more democratic possibilities have relevance for the future of democracy in the East and in the West.[9]

The Triumph of Liberalism?

Fukuyama's 1989 essay articulated a sense of liberal enthusiasm that was fairly widespread among politicians and media commentators,[10] and even liberal scholars who saw the weaknesses of his historicism did not fully dissent from his prognosis regarding the end of ideology. Stephen Holmes, for example, in his scathing review of Fukuyama's book, noted that "throughout the post-Communist world . . . we are observing waves of radical change that look so far like a liberal revolution." "Is liberal revolution," he asked rhetorically, "not the most significant fact of contemporary political life?"[11] Contra Fukuyama, liberalism is not eschatological; but it is stable, fair, open, and free. What is taking place, Holmes suggests, is surely a liberal transformation, one more complex and problematic than the triumph proclaimed by Fukuyama, but a vindication of liberalism nonetheless.

As Gale Stokes writes, the events in Central Europe constituted "not a revolution of total innovation, but rather the shucking off of a failed experiment in favor of an already existing model, pluralist democracy."[12] This is surely the dominant interpretation of 1989. Thus Bruce Ackerman identifies 1989 with "the return of revolutionary democratic liberalism," the revival of a political project inaugurated by the framers of the U.S. Constitution.[13] Ralph Dahrendorf writes: "At its core, the European revolution of 1989 is the rejection of an unbearable and, as we have seen, untenable reality, and by the same token it is a reaffirmation of old ideas. Democracy . . . pluralism . . . citizenship . . . are not exactly new ideas." What has triumphed, Dahrendorf insists, is nothing but the idea of an "open society," a liberal idea whose progenitors include Locke, Hume, Madison, Kant, and, more recently, Raymond Aron and Karl Popper.[14] This thesis has been stated most forcefully by Timothy Garton Ash, who maintains that the European revolutions "can offer no fundamentally new ideas on the big questions of politics, economics, law or international relations. The ideas whose time has come are old, familiar, well-tested ones"—liberal ideas about the rule of law, parliamentary government, and an independent judiciary.[15]

Those who subscribe to this view do not necessarily believe that the triumph of liberalism has yet been assured. Indeed, most believe no such thing. Valerie Bunce articulates a common concern when she notes that "the question foremost on the minds of people in the East and the West alike . . . is whether the new regimes in Eastern Europe will succeed in their desire to become genuine liberal democracies."[16] Because this *is* a question, liberal political scientists and constitutional theorists have turned their attention to matters of constitutional and political engineering. Stephen Holmes noted in 1992, in the inaugural issue of the *East European Constitutional Review*, the journal of the newly established Center for the Study of Constitutionalism in Eastern Europe at the University of Chicago Law School: "From Albania to the Baltics and, more recently, in Russia itself, attempts are being made to design liberal-democratic political institutions . . . Chances for a successful transition to liberal democracy vary from country to country . . . [but] institutional design will have important long-term consequences for the stability and effectiveness of democratic government."[17] Bruce Ackerman echoes this sentiment. At a time of enormous turbulence and uncertainty, he says, "the challenge for statecraft is to use these fleeting moments to build new and stronger foundations for liberal democracy."[18] Western analysts have turned their attention to this challenge of statecraft with a vengeance. A proliferation of books and scholarly articles debate the virtues and vices of alternative electoral schemes, the perils of the presidential or parliamentary system, the character of judicial review, and the logic of constitutionalism. New journals, such as the *Journal of Democracy* and the *East European Constitutional Review*, focus on how better to effect a transition to functioning and stable liberal democracy in Central Europe.

The view that 1989 set Central Europe on the path of liberal democratic transition is not simply the view of Western theorists; it is given credence by the reflections of Central Europeans themselves, including many who are quite famous for their roles in the democratic oppositions to communism. Janos Kis, for example, maintained in 1989 that "the alternative Hungary is facing now is to create a constitutional, multiparty democracy and a mixed, market economy, or to regress into economic decay and political Balkanization. The chance for the former to happen seems to be slim. Still, this is our only chance for the next generations. We cannot choose another terrain, more favorable to the realization of the values of liberty, equality and fraternity. We have to try to use this tiny bit of chance, here and now."[19]

Adam Michnik has frequently sounded a similar theme—there are but two futures for Eastern Europe, the Western future of liberal democracy and political compromise, on the one hand, and a descent into xenophobia and fractious tribalism, on the other.[20] In defense of the former, he finds that "liberal values in the era of post-communism, values codified in the writings of John Stuart Mill and Alexis de Tocqueville, and also those of Hayek, are meeting with their true renaissance. Through their resistance to communism, they rediscovered their vision of civil liberty, their dreams of parliamentarism, of cultural and political pluralism, of tolerance, and their desire for a country free of any kind of ideological dictatorship."[21] George Konrad, whose book *Antipolitics* was a veritable bible of democratic opposition to communism, has perhaps best summed up this self-understanding: "Why am I a liberal? Because I am skeptical about everything human, about our collective self; because for me there are no institutions, persons, or concepts that are sacrosanct or above criticism . . . For me, liberalism is, first of all, a style: worldly, civilized, personal, ironic."[22]

What are we to make of this apparent convergence between Western scholars and Eastern former dissidents on a liberal interpretation of 1989? There is reason, I believe, at least to discount the liberal enthusiasm among Central European intellectuals. As one commentator has noted, it is not liberalism as a philosophical or political doctrine so much as liberalism as an *attitude* that has experienced the renaissance to which Michnik refers. "Liberalism," Jerzy Szacki writes, "appears to Eastern Europe as a utopia, as a vision of the good society most glaringly opposed to the realities of the communist system."[23] The senses in which former oppositionists declare themselves to be liberals need to be unpacked; their own self-understandings, in other words, cannot be taken at face value if we wish to understand their current allegiances. In any case, there is no reason to privilege their views of the revolutions they helped to bring about. Tocqueville long ago pointed out that revolutionaries can misperceive the events in which they participate. Unintended consequences and possibilities too quickly foreclosed seem almost inevitable features of revolutionary transformations. While the words of Michnik and Konrad tell us something important, then, there is no reason to treat them as the last words on our subject.

One way to get a better handle on the supposed triumph of liberal democracy would be to disaggregate this idea into distinct claims, each of which needs to be judged on its own merit. The question, then, is not whether or not liberalism has triumphed but in which sense or senses it has triumphed. I discern at least three senses in which liberalism may be believed to have triumphed, and in none of them has the triumph been unambiguous.

First, we may speak of the practical triumph of liberal democratic institutions. It seems pretty clear that with the downfall of communism, monopolistic political regimes have given way to more "polyarchal" arrangements. The various "civic forum"–type oppositional coalitions quickly gave way to roundtable negotiations between communist leaderships and democratic political elites. Constitutions, some final, some provisional, have been established, formally organizing public offices and containing bills of rights. Liberal democratic institutions—separation of powers, regular competitive elections, party systems—have been put into place. Political parties have supplanted and co-opted democratic opposition movements, channeling and aggregating political demands in manageable, politically "normalized" ways. More or less free and fair elections have been held, and peaceful alternations of government have been accomplished. In this sense we may speak descriptively of the institutionalization of liberal democracy, a process that can be explained partly by the structural imperatives of organizing political disagreement in a large-scale modern society and partly by the financial requirements of a modern market economy operating in a global capitalist economy. It is impossible to deny the political triumph of liberalism in this sense.[24]

And yet of course political processes in Central Europe are still very much in flux. Many crucial constitutional issues—the restitution of property nationalized under communism, the so-called lustration of former Communists, and the status of the *nomenklatura* more generally—remain outstanding. The drastic and precipitous transformation of economic life and the marked decline in the standards of living of many Central Europeans have fed a widespread sense of popular resentment that has fueled chauvinistic ideologies. The problem of national minorities that is endemic to the region has exacerbated such ideologies. Authoritarian populism, in other words, is a real competitor of liberal democracy.[25] Perhaps equally ominous are the geopolitical uncertainty in the former Soviet Union and the brutal dismemberment of Yugoslavia, both of which add to the sense of popular anxiety and symbolize the insecurity of liberal democratic institutionalization in Central Europe. The tribalistic alternative against which Kis and Michnik caution still remains.

The limits of the triumph of liberalism in this first sense bring us to a second sense in which we may speak of a liberal vindication—the triumph of liberalism as an ethical-political imperative. Few liberal theorists deny the great difficulties currently besetting liberalism in Central Europe. These difficulties are viewed as obstacles to the project of constructing liberal democracy rather than as plausible alternatives in their own right. From this point of view, while the success of liberalism is not yet assured, the alternatives to it are demonstrably undesirable. Whatever its problems, liberal democracy is, we may say, following Churchill's famous quip, the least bad form of government. If we wish to live in and enjoy the advantages of a modern market economy, and if we wish to avoid civil war in societies characterized by all kinds of ineliminable differences, then liberal democracy is the order of the day. What Holmes calls "constitutional design" and Ackerman "statecraft" thus becomes a pressing need.

There is much truth to this claim as well. When we consider the Bosnian tragedy, or the rise of chauvinistic ideologies in Slovakia, Romania, and the Baltic
states, or the disturbing ascendancy of Vladimir Zhirinovsky in Russia, or the
anti-Semitic rhetoric of István Csurka in Hungary, it is impossible to question
the attractiveness of liberal constitutionalism. The wave of anticommunist
witch hunting that has plagued political debate, threatening to engulf Central
European societies in bitter recrimination about the past and offering fertile
ground for political demogoguery, makes evident the importance of typically
liberal civil liberties such as the presumption of innocence and due process of
law.[26] The insensitive and at times hostile ways in which national and religious
minorities have been treated underscores the importance of liberal toleration.[27]

As Ulrich Preuss has argued, two competing logics of citizenship continue to
jockey for position in Central Europe: a civic conception that defines as citizens
those who are subject to a common law and an ethnic conception that defines citizenship in terms of membership in a distinct ethnic or national group.[28] The
latter conception is profoundly hostile to the proceduralism of liberal representative government, and, mirroring the writings of Carl Schmitt, it relies on appeals to an ethnically homogeneous popular will against those "special interests"—national minorities, foreign capital, politicians—held to stand in the way
of authentic popular sovereignty.[29] Such a vision, not without its appeal in Central Europe today, is simply a right-wing version of the "totalitarian democracy"
long ago identified by Jacob Talmon.[30] In this light it is hard to disagree with the
judgment of Stephen Holmes: "The most difficult problem facing the countries
of Eastern Europe today is the creation of a government that can pursue effective
reforms while retaining public confidence and remaining democratically accountable . . . The main political danger, conversely, is . . . the spirit of antipar-
liamentarism . . . Hence, the challenge in Eastern Europe today is to prevent
extraparliamentary leaders from building public support on the basis of nondemocratic and nonelectoral forms of legitimacy."[31]

In this sense liberal democratization *is* an ethical-political imperative. For the
only macropolitical alternative seems to be some combination of authoritarianism, civil war, and economic decline.[32] And yet even here some caution is in order. For what is the relationship between the liberal project and the other possibilities liberals such as Holmes and Ash frighteningly project? Are these
alternatives simply obstacles to be combated? Do they answer to pressing concerns that derive from inadequacies of the liberal democratic transition itself, es-

pecially the endemic problems of economic dislocation and political alienation?[33] Can these challenges be so readily dismissed? For the purposes of my
argument I will put aside what we may call the authoritarian populist alternative, for it is clearly both antiliberal and antidemocratic, an alternative to be opposed, however politically viable it may seem. But are there no other alternatives
to liberal democracy? And might not a more radically democratic alternative in
fact play some role in combating authoritarian populism?

Here things become complicated, and we move on to the third sense in which
liberal democracy can be said to have triumphed, not simply as the practical result of structural forces or as an ethical-political imperative but as the *fulfillment*
of the democratic opposition to communism. Let us return to Gale Stokes's
claim that the transformation of Central Europe was "not a revolution of total innovation, but rather the shucking off of a failed experiment in favor of an already
existing model."[34] Many liberal commentators have offered not simply a political prognosis but a historical interpretation, to the effect that liberal democratic
institutions were the *intended outcome* of the revolutions, or at least of the most
advanced, democratic leaderships of the revolutions. Such a view recapitulates a
nice, neat nineteenth-century progressivist scheme, pitting the forces of liberation against the forces of reaction, liberal democratic reformers against Communist reactionaries in league with nationalist ideologues. Revolutionary success versus revolutionary failure. The choice seems clear.

As in the other senses in which liberal democracy can be said to have been vindicated, there is much truth to the view that liberal democracy has long been the
goal of the revolutionaries themselves. The remarks of Michnik, Kis, and Konrad
cited earlier certainly lend plausibility to it. At an even deeper level, by 1989 the
major democratic oppositions in Central Europe—the Movement for Civil Liberties and later the Civic Forum in Czechoslovakia, the Democratic Opposition
in Hungary, and the Committee for Social Self-Defense and Solidarity in Poland—had all demanded an end to Communist rule and the institution of multiparty liberal democracy, demands that accurately reflected the long-standing positions of leading activists, many of whom had begun their careers as human
rights dissidents.[35] At a deeper level still, if we examine the major writings of the
principal dissident intellectuals—Havel, Konrad, Michnik, Kuron, Kis—it is not
hard to discern that a recurrent theme is the need for limits in politics, surely a
theme with liberal resonance.

And yet here too things are more complicated. For if we examine the views of the democratic oppositionists more carefully, we discover that while they are democratic, it is not clear that they are unambiguously liberal democratic. This is not to say that they are antiliberal.[36] Liberal ideas of individual liberty and liberal institutions of constitutional government are surely valued as necessary ingredients of human freedom and dignity. But they are not viewed as sufficient for many of the democratic oppositionists. There is, if you will, a democratic "surplus value" that the liberal interpretation of 1989 quietly expropriates.

Indeed, liberals admit as much in passing. Bruce Ackerman, for example, both praises and criticizes the "antipolitical" vision shared by Konrad and Havel. Its resistance to totalitarianism was meritorious, but its calls for existential integrity, he maintains, are insufficiently practical for the task of liberal construction. Havel's "Heideggerian contempt for the Enlightenment in general and Western consumerism in particular has an authoritarian ring." Indeed, the very idea of "living in truth"—a hallmark of the democratic opposition— is "positively dangerous if the truth is understood with grim philosophical passion."[37]

Just what Ackerman means by his remark about grim philosophical passion is made clearer by a similar observation offered by Timothy Garton Ash: "Now we expect many things of politicians in a well-functioning parliamentary democracy. But 'living in truth' is not one of them. In fact the essence of democratic politics might rather be described as 'working in half-truth.' Parliamentary democracy is, at its heart, a system of limited adversarial mendacity, in which each party attempts to present part of the truth as if it were the whole."[38] Garton Ash makes explicit what Ackerman keeps implicit—that too much integrity, conscientiousness, "authenticity" is anathema to liberal democracy, which requires a certain cavalierness about truth and honesty if it is to function properly.[39] The most sophisticated argument to this effect has been presented by Elisabeth Kiss, who maintains that while the vision of "antipolitics" developed by the democratic oppositionists played a very important role in inspiring and organizing opposition to communism, this vision is insufficient as a model for ongoing, normal politics in a complex society. "The new social order that will emerge in East-Central Europe, and the extent to which it fosters democratic aspirations," she avers, "will depend in large measure on governments, parliaments, and parties." Because the "antipolitics" of the oppositionists abjured such institutions in favor of more genuine agencies, it "translates badly into the postcommunist era."[40]

Kiss puts her finger on the problem with the idea that 1989 represents a fulfillment of the opposition vision by identifying the striking tensions between the liberal democracy currently being instituted and the aspirations of many of those who struggled most vigorously against communism. With this problem in mind we can return to Holmes's observation that the principal task facing liberal democrats is "to prevent extraparliamentary leaders from building public support on the basis of nondemocratic and nonelectoral forms of legitimacy." The question is simple. Are all extraparliamentary efforts to build public support on the basis of nonelectoral forms of legitimacy antidemocratic? Or are there forms of democratic politics that are democratic precisely by virtue of going beyond parliamentary and electoral institutions? There are such forms of politics, and they were pioneered by the democratic oppositionists. Among the many meanings of 1989, one is the continuing importance of such forms of politics.

Antipolitical Politics Revisited

In many ways the Central European democratic oppositions can be seen as animated by liberal principles of state neutrality, the rule of law, the accountability of government, and the inviolability of private life. Confronting an arbitrary and repressive Communist state, these oppositions began as human rights initiatives, monitoring governmental abuses, petitioning for redress of specific grievances, and publicizing egregious violations of human rights recognized by international law and the Communist constitutions themselves.

And yet such initiatives implicated a more radically democratic kind of political praxis. The political aspect of their activity derived in part from the simple fact that in a totalitarian state all independent initiatives of any kind assumed political importance, at least implicitly challenging the party's monopoly of political legitimacy. In this sense such initiatives can be viewed as no more than tactics or at best strategies for achieving a liberal democratic opening over time. But what came to be known as "antipolitical politics," whatever its initial motivations—which surely varied from person to person—was more than a strategy. It developed into an alternative form of politics. Its very means—which were ever so scrupulously self-monitored—became its ends. Antipolitical politics was, in short, what antipolitical politics did. What it did was to organize forms of solidarity and assistance for the persecuted and marginalized under conditions of extreme duress.[41] A strong ethos of solidarity and participation was necessary to support such initiatives in the face of state repression and mass indifference or outright hostility. As one of the first appeals of KOR, the Polish Committee on Social Self-Defense, put it: "The independent social activity reemerging in the course of the past several years is based above all on the organization of authentic public opinion, on the defense against reprisals, on the formulation of genuine social demands, and on the interruption of the state monopoly over the dissemination of information. Participation in these activities is open to everyone . . . It is necessary to organize to defend one's rights."[42] In what ways did this practice of organizing "civil society against the state" in order "to defend one's rights" implicate a nonliberal but democratic form of politics? I will suggest an answer by analyzing a single initiative, the Czechoslovakian human rights group Charter 77.

As is fairly well known, Charter 77 was formed in 1976 as an ad hoc community of individuals who sought to protest the arrest of an avant-garde rock band called Plastic People of the Universe. The Charter was formed around the drafting of a declaration of protest that appealed to the principles of legality affirmed by the Helsinki Accords, to which the Czech regime had been a signatory. But it soon became the nucleus of a variety of independent initiatives aimed at the democratization of Czech society.[43]

In some ways Charter 77 *was* the declaration of protest, for from the very beginning it forswore any formal organization or explicit membership. Anyone who signed the Charter was by the very act of having done so a "Chartist."[44] The Chartists considered themselves a "civic initiative" rather than a "classic opposition" or a "movement."[45] As one Charter document put it, a civic initiative is "an ongoing common initiative by individual citizens of all ages, callings, political opinions and religious beliefs. They are linked by a sense of public responsibility for the way things are and a determination to take action to correct the present depressing state of affairs."[46] A civic initiative is an open-ended form of voluntary association, an exercise of civic responsibility for the "state of affairs." But it is not an interest group or a mass movement, for it avoids formal organization and abjures political power. It operates in the sphere of civil society, independent of official and formal political institutions, and it seeks to influence public opinion rather than directly to exercise political power.

In many ways this conception of civic initiative was adopted as a strategic necessity, out of a desire to avoid a frontal challenge to totalitarian state power.[47] But it also reflected a specific theoretical understanding of modern politics consistently elaborated in Charter documents. The 1984 "Open Letter to the British Peace Movements," for example, states:

> Charter 77 does not constitute a movement in the accepted sense. (These are not, however, "sour´grapes" on the part of some crypto-oppositional group vegetating in a totalitarian society, but a policy we have pursued consistently on the basis of our conviction that it represents a new factor in overcoming the global political and moral crisis.) Charter 77 is far more concerned to promote and extend the aforementioned sense of responsibility than to become a mass movement and win the maximum possible number of supporters; it is hardly in any position, anyway, to set itself specific political goals, leastways not in the sense that the word "politics" has been understood heretofor [sic]."[48]

This point is made even more emphatically in one of the most serious and revealing Charter documents, the "Statement on the Occasion of the Eighth Anniversary of Charter 77." The Charter rejects formal political organization or objectives, it argues, not out of opportunism or strategic necessity but because "its goal is really fundamentally different. It is deeper and more far-reaching: its goal is to rehabilitate people as the true subjects of history . . . [which] by its very nature radically transcends the framework of mere changes of the system of power, i.e., the framework of eventual exchange of one official ideology for another, one group of rulers for another. This effort represents potential criticism of every system because every system, even the best, conceals within itself a tendency to elevate itself above people. Therefore, Charter 77 has a valid purpose under any circumstances."[49] Three key ideas are expressed in these documents: that there is a "global crisis" of political and moral responsibility, that the participation of ordinary citizens is necessary to address this crisis, and that the Charter as a set of ideas and initiatives is thus relevant "under any circumstances," as a response not simply to totalitarianism but to a crisis of modern politics more generally.

These ideas have long been associated with the writings of Vaclav Havel. But the extraordinary diversity of Chartist documents makes clear that, however influential Havel undoubtedly was, these ideas had fairly wide currency among the Czech democratic oppositionists. Indeed, while the Charter included individuals of many political tendencies—radical democrats, democratic socialists, reform Communists, independent Trotskyists, liberals, religious conservatives— the very form of Charter initiatives led them to converge on a common under-

standing of the politics of their activities. They spoke of an "antipolitical politics," of a kind of ethical responsibility and initiative that went beyond politics
"in the ordinary sense" or "as commonly understood."[50] As I have argued in
Chapter 5, this was a republican politics with strong affinities with the writings
of Hannah Arendt. It was antiteleological, in the sense that what was central to
the Chartists was less the motives or the goals of action than the modes of action
themselves. And it was an effort "to reach for a new type of politics, or rather, a
revival of what was once understood by the term 'politics,' the way it was practiced, and which has, today, been almost forgotten"—an effort to revive active
citizenship.[51] These themes were elaborated in a remarkable essay by Vaclav
Benda, "The Parallel Polis," which was originally circulated in samizdat in 1978
and spawned a vigorous debate among the Czech democratic opposition.[52] Several important themes emerged from this discussion.

One is that politics is primarily a way of being and acting that affirms one's
dignity. As Ladislav Hejdanek wrote: "The beginning of all independence is
taking our lives seriously, deciding for something that is worth taking responsibility for, being prepared to devote our energy, our work, and our lives to something of value, or, more appropriately, to someone rather than something."[53]
The Arendtian resonances—creating value, resisting futility, regenerating democracy—are striking. The Chartists saw themselves as resisting the "worldlessness" and deracination characteristic of totalitarianism, and indeed of modern life more generally.

As I have shown in Chapter 5, the Chartists described their network as a
"small island in a sea of apathy."[54] The Chartists sought, through their activity,
to constitute a "parallel polis" that would at once resist the imperatives of the
communist system and protect them from being "swallowed up" by the conformity and consumerism of modern industrial society.[55] As Havel wrote: "It
seems to me that all of us, East and West, face one fundamental task from which
all else should follow. That task is one of resisting vigilantly, thoughtfully, and
attentively, but at the same time with total dedication, at every step and everywhere, the irrational momentum of anonymous, impersonal and inhuman
power—the power of ideologies, systems, apparat, bureaucracy, artificial languages, and political slogans."[56]

The islands of civic engagement and solidarity improvised by the Czech democrats represented a strategic but also an ethical experiment in political resistance. Through their efforts the Chartists transformed themselves from sub-

jects into citizens of "elementary republics" of their own making. As should be clear, the independent initiatives of Charter 77, especially the vigorous quasi-public debate about opposition that itself constituted perhaps its most significant kind of initiative, implied a theory of democratic power, the most articulate statements of which were Havel's famous essays "The Power of the Powerless" and "The Politics of Conscience."[57] On this view, totalitarianism was a most extreme, malignant, and grotesque version of the more general tendency of modern society to subject individuals to "the irrational momentum of anonymous, impersonal, and inhuman power—the power of ideologies, systems, apparat, bureaucracy, artificial languages, and political slogans." Modern politics, in other words, including liberal democratic politics, is a politics of civic disempowerment justified by the advantages—sometimes palpable, often illusory—of a mass society. As Havel put it, the individual is treated as "an obedient member of a consumer herd"; "instead of a free share in economic decision-making, free participation in political life, and free intellectual advancement, all people are actually offered is a chance freely to choose which washing machine or refrigerator they want to buy."[58] The Chartists, agreeing with radical democrats such as John Dewey and Hannah Arendt, considered this a Faustian bargain that doomed modern individuals to lives of passivity, conformity, and political irresponsibility. The acquiescence to totalitarianism was the extreme form of such irresponsibility, but it was hardly the only form. For problems of human rights, ecological disaster, economic insecurity, and the threat of war all point toward the need for the kind of civic initiative that cuts against the grain of a modern industrial society.

It was this broader sense of civic responsibility that animated the Czechoslovakian democratic opposition, and it would not be hard to demonstrate that it also played an important role in animating the other Central European democratic oppositions. This sense of responsibility led these oppositions to resist totalitarian power and to advocate liberal democratic institutions. But it also led them to consider such institutions insufficient insofar as "every system, even the best, conceals within itself a tendency to elevate itself above the people."[59] Because liberal democracy is itself a system, it is liable to this corruption. Yet in spite of their critique of liberal democratic party politics and its own "technologies of power," the Chartists recognized the value of liberal constitutionalism at the same time that they recognized its limits in an age of consumerism and bureaucratic power.

Both of these points were brought home in Charter 77's open letter to the British peace movements: "Your 'sideways' stand, as it were, in relation to the classical democratic structures and political mechanisms is very close to the sense and forms of our own efforts. (Here, again, we must stress, however, our deep conviction that these structures constitute a vital basis which has been denied or falsified always at the cost of greater evil; but at the same time we are aware that the decline of those structures has done much to create the present global crisis, and that without radical new impulses and regenerating transformations no way out of the crisis can be found.)"[60] Liberal democratic institutions, in other words, are "a vital basis" of human freedom. But they need to be supplemented and reinvigorated by "radical new impulses," civic initiatives that challenge the way these institutions typically function and the corruption to which they are perpetually liable.

Civic Initiative and Liberal Democracy

As I have suggested, in many ways the vision of civic initiative that resists intolerable power seems unambiguously liberal. It affirms the importance of setting limits to the exercise of collective authority. It values liberal democratic political institutions. Its emphasis on the importance of protest and dissent is surely consistent with liberal political theory and the practices of liberal constitutionalism.[61] In all of these respects the politics of Central European democratic opposition falls squarely within liberal parameters. On an even deeper level, the injunction to "live in truth" seems perfectly consistent with John Rawls's view that there are a multitude of ways to live "the good life," and that the great evil in politics is to make one of them mandatory.[62] For the Central European antipolitics of civil society was explicitly voluntary and self-consciously insular. While open to all who might be interested, it never intended to incorporate masses of people into a hegemonic political project, much less to coerce people to live "authentically." In this sense it saw itself as one way of being among many others, and was remarkably respectful of other ways of being, a political orientation wholly consistent with liberal theory and practice.[63]

And yet it would be a mistake to infer that it therefore fits neatly into a liberal perspective. Antipolitical politics is clearly not antiliberal, but neither is it liberal. For all its common ground with liberalism, there are also points of tension between them.

Antipolitical politics disagrees not about the importance of liberal democratic institutions but about the way they typically function in a modern industrial society. On the liberal democratic view, the principal task of politics is to provide limited, accountable institutions that are responsive to claims of justice. The great virtue of existing liberal institutions—representative parliaments, competitive parties, independent judiciaries, impartial legal systems, civil service bureaucracies—is that they fulfill this task not, to be sure, perfectly, but better than all possible alternatives. For this reason the imperative of liberal democratic politics is to strengthen these institutions and, through "institutional design," to make them work better, more fairly and responsively.

Antipolitical politics rejects the claim that existing liberal institutions do fulfill this task. What emerges clearly from the Chartist literature, and from the literature of Central European dissent more generally, is the belief that the impersonality and consumerism of modern society, the bureaucratization of political agencies, and the debasement of political communication through the cynical manipulation of language and images produce a shallow politics, a disengaged citizenry, and the domination of well-organized corporate interests.

In this sense the literature of dissent parallels the writings of pragmatist critics of American democracy such as John Dewey and C. Wright Mills. Like these writers, the Chartists believe that liberalism currently functions more as an ideology than as a utopia. In 1956 C. Wright Mills wrote:

> Perhaps nothing is of more importance . . . than the rhetorical victory and the intellectual and political collapse of American liberalism . . . liberalism has been organizationally impoverished . . . liberalism-in-power devitalized independent liberal groups, drying up the grass roots, making older leaders dependent upon the federal center and not training new leaders . . . It is much safer to celebrate civil liberties than to defend them; it is much safer to defend them as a formal right than to use them in a politically effective way . . . as a rhetoric, liberalism's key terms have become the common denominators of the political vocabulary; in this rhetorical victory . . . liberalism has been stretched beyond any usefulness as a way of defining issues and stating policies.[64]

Mills's point was not that there is anything wrong with liberal values of individual autonomy or liberal practices of constitutional government. It was that the actual institutions of liberal societies pay lip service to such values and practices but do not effectively support them.

A very similar sentiment is developed by the Chartists when they note that while liberal democratic structures are too important to be dismissed, "we are aware that the decline of those structures has done much to create the present global crisis, and that without radical new impulses and regenerating transformations no way out of the crisis can be found."[65] Because the liberal democratic structures have declined, it is necessary to foster new impulses and undertake civic initiatives simply to realize liberal values. Because the Central European democrats operated with a highly critical understanding of the actual functioning of liberal democratic politics, they saw such civic initiatives as being significant not only as a way of opposing communism but as a way of sustaining individual freedom and empowerment in a modern mass society.

The kind of civic initiatives that they practiced—petitions, protests, vigorous critical debate, civil disobedience—are not illiberal. But they are in deep tension with the "normal" institutions of liberal politics.[66] They are, as Holmes says, extraparliamentary. They impose ethical demands upon politicians contrary to the organized "adversarial mendacity" of which Garton Ash speaks. They involve a different style of politics, one more rebellious and more participatory than the normal forms of liberal democratic politics. They do not present themselves as wholesale alternatives to liberal democracy. For the Chartists, it is both inconceivable and undesirable that everybody could "live in truth" together in a modern industrial society. Most people are preoccupied with other things, and the institutions of liberal democracy, imperfect as they are, typically suit them just fine. But these institutions are chronically liable to corruption, and the advantages they confer—security, economic opportunity—are therefore precarious. A more rebellious politics is therefore necessary to reinvigorate them and keep them honest.

Just as these political practices are in tension with normal liberal politics, their guiding ideals are in tension with certain liberal ideals. Liberal political philosophy is distinguished by what Rawls has aptly called a "thin theory of the good."[67] Liberal justice is the codification of certain basic rights and liberties that allow individuals to pursue their own versions of the good life. Liberal politics is the legitimate avenue for protecting basic rights and liberties, for making sure that the exercise of political power is responsive to public opinion yet does not infringe on individual liberties. The liberal view of "the priority of right" over public goods has concisely been stated by Benjamin Constant: "Our freedom must consist of peaceful enjoyment and private independence. The share which in antiquity everyone held in national sovereignty was by no means an abstract presumption as it is in our own day . . . Lost in the multitude, the individual can almost never perceive the influence he exercises. Never does his will impress itself upon the whole; nothing confirms in his eyes his own cooperation."[68] Constant does not deny that politics is important. Liberal representative government is a device intended to regulate common affairs so that individuals can pursue their private goods. It is thus essential for individuals to monitor their government and hold it accountable through the political process. But for Constant politics is in the service of a civil society that is itself properly beyond politics. Like Rawls, he sees the creation of any public goods beyond a certain "thin" minimum as threatening to individual liberty.[69]

Havel and Konrad share the liberal belief that the effort to constitute a single homogeneous "general will" is tyrannical. They support the idea that any free society must provide spaces for autonomous individual initiative. But they question the faith that liberals place in representative institutions and implicitly they challenge the view of civil society as properly beyond politics.[70] Recall Ivan Jirous's remark that civic initiatives allow people "to resist the futility that threatens to swallow them up." For antipolitical politics, the impersonality, bureaucratization, and domination characteristic of modern society threaten to swallow people up in manifold ways. On this view, Constant's description of liberal man—that "nothing confirms in his eyes his own cooperation"—is an all too accurate description of the political disempowerment and alienation characteristic of modern industrial society. If such experiences are not to produce frustration and resentment, they need to be channeled in healthy ways and resisted by civic initiative. Wherever injustice is experienced, then, it needs to be challenged. And while the state is a principal source of much injustice in our world, it is not the only source.[71]

Freedom, then, requires a conscientious engagement in public affairs. While such engagement is not contrary to liberal individualism, it relies on a stronger sense of solidarity than that typically supported by liberal political theory or liberal political institutions. Liberal ideals tend to emphasize the importance of protecting individuals from extra-individual—typically political—forces; antipolitical politics involves a more Arendtian view of individuals as inhabiting a common world that, in complex ways, imposes on them certain ethical responsibilities. To ignore these responsibilities is to lack care for the world; it is also to be untrue to yourself, to exchange your dignity for certain advantages, to submit yourself to some kind of *dictat* for the sake of convenience or sociability. Such submission is dangerous, shortsighted, wrong—it is hard to find exactly the right moral term here—though it does not follow that submission could or should be proscribed. Civic responsibility is thus not a strictly political imperative; it would be both impossible and undesirable to mandate it. Indeed, the effort to mandate it is inconsistent with it, for civic initiative is essentially voluntary. But it is more than a moral imperative in Rawls's sense, a matter of simple and wholly capricious individual choice. It is an ethical imperative, a strong obligation to act in the name of a dignity that is jeopardized by the tendencies of modern social life.[72] It occupies a middle ground between individual liberty and state power, and its proper sphere of expression and assertion is civil society.[73]

It is understandable why such people as Kis, Konrad, and Michnik would gravitate toward liberalism, both because its rights-based philosophy offers a powerful antidote to the kind of collectivism long enforced by communism and because it is the only feasible macropolitical alternative to right-wing populism. The practice of antipolitical politics under the conditions of postcommunism has great risks, for it is an unsettling politics and the conditions of postcommunism seem to demand settlement and order, and it is an ethically exacting politics at a time when most people seem to want normality. If Holmes is correct and the building of stable parliamentary institutions is the order of the day, it would seem a strategic imperative to abjure antipolitical politics and to take the liberal side. But two important caveats are in order.

First, it is important to see that such a move would involve a taking of sides, a marked shift from a politics of civic initiative and suspicion of institutionalized power to a politics of political "normalization." In this sense we must reject the Whiggish reading of liberal democratization as a fulfillment of the democratic opposition. Second, having learned, with Popper, of the dangers of acting according to a confidence that our tasks are prescribed by History, we should proceed with caution before the suggestion that a single choice is the order of the day. Indeed, Havel and Konrad and many other democratic oppositionists sympathetic to liberalism *have* proceeded with such caution. They have managed to navigate a difficult path, combining support for liberal democracy with more radical civic initiatives. This path deserves more attention. In the spirit of Popperian skepticism, then, we must see that the antipolitics of the Central Euro-

pean democratic oppositions is not passé, that it is of continuing relevance both
to the "emerging democracies" of Central Europe and to democratic politics in
advanced industrial societies more generally.

The Legacies of Antipolitical Politics

Stephen Holmes is right when he asserts that the institutionalization of parliamentary democracy is a pressing task. But he is only partly right. For it does not
follow from this imperative that all energies must be channeled in this direction
or that those energies that are channeled elsewhere constitute extraparliamentary threats to a democratic transition. Though antipolitical politics cannot
claim to be the sole vehicle of democratic politics in the postcommunist era, it is
not therefore a candidate for liquidation in the name of democracy. Indeed, in
many ways antipolitical politics can be seen to occupy the same space that it occupied under communism, that of a marginalized minority of democrats undertaking civic initiatives in the hope—perhaps faith—that, in Havel's words, "a
purely moral act that has no hope of any immediate and visible effect can gradually and indirectly, over time, gain in political significance."[74] Such a politics remains of continuing relevance to Central European politics in at least three
ways. A brief consideration of these ways will also lead us to a broader assessment of the relevance of antipolitics to democratic politics in general.

The first is organizational. Put simply, antipolitical civic initiatives continue
to operate in the postcommunist era. Charter 77, for example, has not dissolved,
in spite of the fact that many of its founders and leaders have now become active
in partisan politics. Though in many ways it has been deprived of its principal
raison d'être—opposition to the Communist party-state—it continues to act on
behalf of human rights and in support of democratic civil liberties.[75] It also continues to have a "radiating effect" on democratic efforts in other parts of Central Europe.

In late 1991, for example, many members of the Hungarian democratic opposition formed Charter '91, a "civic initiative" in many ways like the Czech Charter 77. Reacting to the perception that the Hungarian government—led by the
conservative party called Hungarian Democratic Forum—was endangering
constitutional liberties, the Charter presented seventeen points on behalf of liberal democracy. Within two months more than 5,000 people had signed. George
Konrad, one of the cofounders, described Charter '91 as "a made in Hungary
civic initiative . . . Civil society continually searches for and experiments with ap-

propriate forms for expressing itself. It does not want to replace representative democracy, only to place the political class, and, more narrowly, the governing administration, in the environment of a democratic society . . . It is important that politics, or the polis, namely the discussion of all of our affairs, should not become some far-off chattering on high." Konrad emphasizes that the Charter is not a new discovery but "a further development of the tool-box of the democratic movement, in the genre of self-organization of civil opinion, the genre, above all, for individuals."[76]

The Charter is an explicitly pro-liberal democratic initiative. But it is also explicitly extraparliamentary and "antipolitical," seeking to raise the level of public debate about the political system and to nourish a more participatory political culture. It sees a liberal democratic political class as being necessary *and* dangerous, in need of support *and* of intense, skeptical civic monitoring and criticism. As one commentator points out, the Charter emerges out of the disaffection of many former members of the democratic opposition with "the new power-oriented and bureaucratized politics." The Charter "shows that this intelligentsia is partly returning to its pre-1989 role: as the 'mediacracy' in the forming of cultured public opinion . . . But its voice will no longer be as influential as it was; it will be lost in the din of battle between different social interests. The former Democratic Opposition's task will be to articulate the opinions of different politicizing groups, and once again to expand and explore the space between state and society. In this respect, the Democratic Charter has given the old opposition a chance to find a new role for itself."[77]

Another initiative that draws on the experience of antipolitical politics is the Helsinki Citizens' Assembly, an outgrowth of the international links formed between Central European dissidents and West European peace activists. Inspired by Charter 77's famous 1985 "Prague Appeal," the Assembly was established in 1990 to nurture an "international civil society," a network of citizens' organizations and initiatives that transcends the borders of the nation-state. Mary Kaldor, one of the Assembly's founders, has described its politics: "It is not addressed to governments except in so far as they are asked to guarantee freedom of travel and freedom of assembly so that citizens' groups can meet and communicate. It is a strategy of dialogue, an attempt to change society through the actions of citizens rather than governments . . . in short, to create a new political culture. In such a situation, the behaviour of governments either changes or becomes less and less relevant."[78] As the Assembly's 1990 Prague Appeal states: "Overcoming the division of Europe is the job above all of civil society, of citizens acting together in self-organized associations, movements, institutions, initiatives and clubs across national boundaries."[79]

The Assembly is organized into six ongoing working commissions on problems of democratization. It monitors human rights and discrimination against minorities and women, publishes a regular newsletter and special reports, and provides networking and support for civic initiatives throughout Central Europe. It sees itself not as an antagonist or rival of the formal process of liberal democratization but as a democratic adjunct to that process, offering outlets for more vigorous and direct participation in grass-roots politics and the formation of public opinion. "So what kind of organization are we?" asks Kaldor. "We are not a representative of civil society; we are a part of civil society. If we were representative of civil society we would be no different from a parliament . . . In fact, we don't represent anyone except the movements and institutions in which we are involved. In many cases, we represent no one but ourselves. And our power rests not on whom we represent but in what we do—in what we say, in our ideas, in our quest for truth, in the projects we undertake. It rests on our energy and commitment."[80]

As Andras Bozoki points out, such initiatives will necessarily be marginalized in the postcommunist period by the structural logics of liberalization and marketization and by the general banality brought on by the ascendancy of consumerism.[81] But they were marginalized under the old regime as well. A cynic could claim that when Kaldor says that the Assembly's power rests on civic initiative, she is really saying that it has no power at all, for the power of civic initiative surely pales in comparison with the power of more organized, well-connected political forces. Indeed, whether the issue is European integration, the rights of minorities, or peace in Yugoslavia, it is clear that the Assembly's efforts have borne little fruit. And yet their failure to make a clear and immediate impact on policy does not make them without moral and even political significance.[82] If the experience of democratic opposition under communism has taught anything, it is that such efforts can have a surprising and incalculable impact below the surface of appearances, helping to incubate certain values so that they may surface with effect under the right circumstances.

As for the second sense in which antipolitical politics remains relevant, the more directly political sense, any assessments are necessarily impressionistic and incomplete, but it is possible to make some judgments on this score, and the

Czech case is instructive. There is first the example of Havel, who in a matter of months went from being an imprisoned dissident writer to president of a newly liberated republic. What is most remarkable about Havel is that he seems to represent a new type of politician, someone capable of personal reflection and public articulation of the difficulties of practicing democratic politics and the need for more responsible forms of citizenship. Havel has issued a steady stream of public addresses on the challenges of the new situation. In his address to the opening session of the Helsinki Citizens' Assembly he reflected on the readjustments made necessary by the transition from dissidence to leadership. "It turns out," he observed, "that no matter how difficult it is to bring down a totalitarian system, it is even more difficult to build a newer and better system from its ruins. Since we entered the world of high politics, we have realized that in this world one has to take account of various interests, of various ambitions, of the balance of power represented by different groupings . . . Thus a person in the world of high politics is forced to behave diplomatically, to maneuver. Simply, we now find ourselves in a different arena . . . and have a totally different kind of responsibility from when we were in opposition." This sounds like a concession to Garton Ash; "living in truth," it would seem, is now passé. And yet Havel continues that the requirements of "high politics" cannot alter "the essence of our efforts and ideals, even though the forms and the ways in which these ideals are being implemented have been modified."[83]

The refusal to allow the new circumstances to change his essential ideals and efforts explains, of course, why this head of state, alone among European heads of state, considered it worthwhile to address the Assembly. In *Summer Meditations* Havel presents a telling and personal account of his efforts to advance and incarnate the ideals of "living in truth" in a way that remains consistent with the requirements of public office.[84] Is Havel simply a unique individual whose leadership style has no general importance? What good has this leadership style gotten him, anyway? It certainly failed to prevent the breakup of Czechoslovakia, nor has it been able to stem the tide of political recrimination. These are legitimate questions. But it is worth considering how much more difficult things might well have turned out were Havel not the kind of president he is. Yet the political relevance of antipolitics extends beyond the question of Havel's rhetoric or leadership style. For Havel has engaged in a highly charged and politically significant public debate with Prime Minister Vaclav Klaus over the meaning of civil society. Klaus, following Friedrich Hayek, has maintained that civil society is the sphere of individual transactions. Havel has insisted that civil society "gives people social space to assume their share of responsibility for social developments, cultivates the feeling of solidarity between people and love of one's community, and makes it possible to live a full, varied life."

At stake in this philosophical debate are some very important political issues. One is the pace and character of economic reform. Klaus sees the rapid expansion of the market as the essence of freedom; Havel sees the market as a necessary institution but one that also threatens many important forms of association, and thus needs to be regulated in certain ways.[85] The second is regional administrative reform. Klaus sees decentralization as a way of weakening the political agencies of economic shock therapy; Havel sees it as a way of providing important avenues of democratic citizenship. Perhaps the most interesting debate concerns the adoption of a law on nonprofit organizations. Havel has made it clear that he sees such organizations as crucial elements of civil society, and has strongly supported a law that would lay out the rules for nonprofit organizations and exempt them from taxation. As Radio Free Europe reported, in his 1994 New Year's Day speech "Havel made it clear that he considered the decentralization of state administration and the adoption of a law on nonprofit organizations to be the two most important steps the Czech Republic should take in creating the social and legal conditions for civil society."[86]

Havel's position in these debates suggests that antipolitical politics can inform important public policy questions, placing emphasis on the ways in which legal and political arrangements can provide support for the development of voluntary associations and civic initiatives. Indeed, strikingly similar arguments have been made by Jacek Kuron, who has decried the relentless privatization of Polish society and emphasized the need for new forms of self-organization—housing cooperatives, agrarian cooperatives, labor cooperatives—consistent with the spirit of solidarity.[87] As the arguments of Havel and Kuron suggest, while civic initiatives are always voluntary and never the creation of the state, a democratic state may be able to nourish such initiatives. Between the "democratic tool-box" of grass-roots activity and the "institutional design" of political elites, then, there may be room for some creative political learning.[88]

Antipolitical politics, then, continues to exist organizationally and to have some impact on Central European political culture and public policy. But perhaps its greatest relevance is hermeneutic or interpretive. Even if antipolitical politics currently had no palpable existence and no evident influence whatsoever, it would still remain relevant as a crucial historical moment of the recent past. In *The Book of Laughter and Forgetting*, Milan Kundera presents a striking scene:

> In February 1948, Communist leader Klement Gottwald stepped out on the balcony of a Baroque palace in Prague to address the hundreds of thousands of his fellow citizens . . . Gottwald was flanked by his comrades, with Clementis standing next to him. There were snow flurries, it was cold, and Gottwald was bareheaded. The solicitous Clementis took off his own fur cap and set it on Gottwald's head. The party propaganda section put out hundreds of thousands of copies of a photograph of that balcony with Gottwald, a fur cap on his head and comrades at his side, speaking to the nation. . . . Four years later Clementis was charged with treason and hanged. The propaganda section immediately airbrushed him out of history, and, obviously, out of all the photographs as well. Ever since, Gottwald has stood on that balcony alone. Where Clementis once stood, there is only bare palace wall. All that remains of Clementis is the cap on Gottwald's head.[89]

Kundera's target was the Communists' obliteration of history, a common target of dissident writers. He points out the absurdity of the attempt to airbrush history, and indicates that the effort can never be wholly successful, for traces of the past remain. Kundera's point has a broader relevance. "The struggle of man against power," he says, "is the struggle of memory against forgetting."[90] Hannah Arendt offers a similar point: "What saves the affairs of mortal men from their inherent futility is nothing but this incessant talk about them, which in turn remains futile unless certain concepts, certain guideposts for future remembrance, and even for sheer reference, arise out of it."[91] The political initiatives of the Central European democratic opposition testify to what conscientious and responsible citizens can do to defend their dignity and empower themselves in difficult circumstances. Such efforts may not be part of the normal repertoire of liberal democratic politics. They may represent fleeting moments of democratic action, destined to fade away or be incorporated by more bureaucratic organizations and institutions.[92] But this is all the more reason to remember them. For the traces of such initiatives remain, in the freedoms now recognized by the law, in the current initiatives that continue to be inspired by them, and in the fertile embryos of initiatives yet to be undertaken.

Timothy Garton Ash recognizes this process when he asks whether the onset of consumerism will sweep the "treasures" of the opposition period away in the rush for affluence. In such an eventuality, he says, "something would remain, at least in memory, in culture, in spirit. At the very least the Europeans from over there would have offered us, with a clarity and firmness born of bitter experience, a restatement of the value of what we already have, of old truths and tested models . . . of liberal democracy."[93] Garton Ash is right that the democratic initiatives that led to 1989 furnish a valuable symbolic legacy. But I find his view of them too reassuring. Surely they may remind us that liberal democracy is worth struggling for, and that it is indeed the outcome of hard struggle. As Frederick Douglass long ago noted with reference to the American Revolution: "To say now that America was right, and England wrong, is exceedingly easy. Everybody can say it, the dastard, not less than the noble brave, can flippantly discant on the tyranny of England . . . It is fashionable to do so; but there was a time when . . . [it] tried men's souls. They who did so were accounted in their day plotters of mischief, agitators and rebels, dangerous men. To side with the right against the wrong, with the weak against the strong, and with the oppressed against the oppressor! here lies the merit, and the one which, of all others, seems unfashionable in our day."[94] But for Douglass the point of remembering the Revolution was not to reassure Americans about the value of what they already had; it was to *disturb* their pervasive sense of assurance, to unsettle them and to defend new, abolitionist initiatives that went beyond the constitutional politics of the day. Historical recollection of the antipolitics of democratic opposition and of the glorious revolutions of 1989 that it helped to bring about can serve a similar function. It can also remind us of a kind of courage and conviction and a kind of creative political agency that cut against the grain of liberal democratic normality.

Here we return to the question with which we began. Does 1989 represent simply the triumph of old liberal values or of something new? It should now be clear that neither alternative as baldly stated is plausible. Liberal democracy has triumphed, but haltingly and with uncertain results. Antipolitical politics does resonate with liberalism, yet it is not unambiguously liberal. It is new, but it is not wholly new. The kinds of civic initiatives pioneered by the democratic oppositions did not spring up *de novo*. They had antecedents and exemplars; surely they were inspired by previous revolts against communism and by nonviolent political struggles in the twentieth century more generally. Garton Ash refers to them as a "treasure." Perhaps unwittingly, this language recalls Hannah Arendt's discussion of "the revolutionary tradition and its lost treasure." There were surely novelties in the "democratic tool-box" of the Central European dissidents—the concept of a "self-limiting revolution," the successful practice of nonviolence against a post-totalitarian dictatorship, perhaps even the very idea of a "civic initiative." But at a deeper level antipolitical politics can be seen as simply one of many instances in modern history when ordinary citizens have improvised new forms of democratic agency and new forms of opposition to oppressive power.[95] It was not new; but neither was it assimilable to the repertoire of normal liberal democratic politics.

Such a treasure is now in danger of being buried. But it has not yet receded from politics, nor has it receded from memory. It will continue to play some role in Central Europe—a marginal one, to be sure, but perhaps a significant one in sustaining a democratic political culture and in offering outlets for healthy political participation. Yet its significance is not limited to the postcommunist world. Indeed, it has great relevance for the Western world, the world of advanced capitalism and liberal democracy. For if I am correct, while antipolitical politics can remind us of the value of what we have, it can also remind us of the limits of what we have.[96]

In the East the tasks of liberal construction impose constraints on antipolitics. Political resources and energies are scarce, and though the contest between liberal democratic transition and civic initiative does not constitute a zero-sum game, there are surely many times when it must seem as though it does.[97] And however much political theorists may endorse a healthy sense of the tragic ambiguities in politics, there are times in politics when high stakes are on the table and one must act. If liberal democrats in parliament are under attack by authoritarian populists, there are times when it may be necessary for democrats to hold their tongues and allow their own mendacities to pass. At a time when anarchy threatens, it may be necessary to avoid civil disobedience even though it seems wholly justifiable in principle. In Central Europe antipolitical politics still has a role to play, but there are times when it will take a back seat to more conventional liberal democratic politics. It is wrong to overestimate the "threat" that civic initiatives may pose to constitutional order. Indeed, as Charter '91 exemplifies, there are times when civic initiative provides indispensable support for such order. But at other times the claims of "normalization" will win out.

But if postcommunist societies experience a deficit of liberalism, liberal democratic societies may well experience a surfeit of liberalism. It is becoming increasingly obvious that liberal democracy in the West is suffering from a kind of legitimacy crisis, a growing and widespread sense that its institutions are no longer adequate to support coherent public policy, a meaningful way of life, or a sense of popular empowerment. The symptoms of this crisis proliferate—a pervasive feeling of frustration with politicians, political parties, "special interests," and the mass media; the rise of new social movements that operate outside of established channels and politicize new realms of social life, whether they be gender, sexuality, race, or ecology; a conservative and often xenophobic backlash against these movements that has acquired a powerful rhetorical force.[98] If democracy involves some kind of identification between citizens and the laws that govern them, what is most striking about the current moment is the pervasive sense of alterity and alienation experienced by ordinary citizens of liberal democracies. Just as Constant described, most citizens feel "lost in the multitude"; nothing confirms in their own eyes their "own cooperation." As Constant saw, the "danger" of liberal democracy is that people will become so absorbed in private life that sources of power will evolve beyond their control. Lacking a sense of empowerment and lacking a vision of healthy civic initiative, such a citizenry is fertile ground for anxiety, resentment, and authoritarianism.[99] It is this virtually total eclipse of democratic public life in Western liberal democracy that makes the experience of antipolitical politics supremely relevant, as a source of both inspiration and concrete examples.[100] While the Central Europeans have much to learn from the West about the workings of liberal democracy, we have much to learn from them about the practice of democratic citizenship.

What, then, are the meanings of 1989? One is that liberal democracy is the most attractive way to organize politics at the level of the nation-state, and that the transition to liberal democracy in Central Europe, and in other parts of the world, is an ethical and political imperative. Another is that civic initiative still has remarkable power to resist the "anonymous, impersonal, inhuman power" whose "irrational momentum" Havel decried, and that it is imperative for civic initiatives to resist the corruption endemic to liberal democracy. How to reconcile these conclusions? Need they be reconciled? Perhaps the strategic requirements of political maneuvering or constitutional design require that a choice sometimes be made. But perhaps we should heed the words of Albert Camus: "In the difficult times we face, what more can I hope for than the power to exclude nothing and to learn to weave from strands of black and white one rope tautened to the breaking point?"[101] If 1989 has a single meaning, it is that any kind of monism, even liberal monism, is hostile to life, and that the effort to exclude certain perspectives in the name of expediency or History is doomed to failure.

8

I have not given you, oh Adam, a definite seat or a special
appearance, or any function of your own. The seat or the
appearance or the function which you want, you may have
and keep by your own desire and your own counsel. The other
creatures have a defined nature which is fixed within limits
prescribed by me. You, unhampered, may determine your
own limits according to your own will, into whose power I have
placed you. I have set you in the center of the world; from there
you can better see whatever is in the world. I have made you,
neither heavenly nor terrestrial, neither mortal nor immortal, in
order that, like a free and sovereign artificer, you can fashion your
own form out of your own substance. You can degenerate to the
lower order of the brutes; you can, according to your own will,
recreate yourself in those higher creatures which are divine.

GOD SPEAKING TO ADAM
IN PICO DELLA MIRANDOLA,
Oration on the Dignity of Man (1486)

Nothing can prepare you for the stink of refugees. When you
enter a sports hall filled with women and children who have
not washed for a month, or when you enter a cowshed filled with
male prisoners who have not washed for two or three months, you
smell something new, and it is terrible. You think that somebody
has wrapped a discarded dishrag around your face, and that you
must inhale air through it. Of course the smell is disgusting. It
is the smell of filth, of animals. We have an easy time thinking
of animals as animals in part because they smell like animals.
That's a difference between us and them. But what are you
supposed to think when you find a group of humans who smell
no better than cows, even worse? It reminds you that humans are
animals, with the ability to stink like pigs, and kill like wolves.

PETER MAAS, *Love Thy Neighbor: A Story of War* (1996)

Political theory at its best takes its bearings from political experience, and seeks to offer an interpretation of the challenges and possibilities of what C. Wright Mills called "the present as history and the future as responsibility." This book has offered a set of extended reflections on the prospects for democracy in our time. Much of it can be seen as an effort to come to terms with what I have called "the meanings of 1989," with the kind of political praxis that was enacted by the democratic activists struggling against communism, and with the relevance of that praxis for politics east and west. These activists struggled against great odds, and if their eventual success in overcoming communist oppression was not due entirely to their own efforts, their commitment, and the way in which they acted on this commitment, it is nonetheless a legitimate source of hope and inspiration. I stand by the conviction that any meaningful democratic theory for the twenty-first century must come to terms with this political experience of courageous, rebellious, and self-limiting civic initiative, and that this experience contains indispensible resources for rethinking democratic politics.

But if silence about or ignorance of this experience is folly, it would be no less mistaken to privilege this form of politics or to ignore its limitations or the challenges it confronts. One way to think about this would be to consider the extraordinary outpouring of literature that testifies to the growing irrelevance and demoralization of the former democratic oppositionists in their own countries. What was being celebrated only a few short years ago as an exemplary political idealism is now widely viewed as passé. Russians are no longer interested in Brodsky and Solzhenitsyn when they have access to *Playboy* and *People*.[1] Alexander Kwasniewski, one of many former Communists to be democratically returned to power, explains his victory over Lech Walesa in the Polish presidential elections by noting that "the divisions between those who are former Communists and those who were with Solidarity are not so important outside intellectual circles of Warsaw. People think more of the future than they dwell on the past."[2] So much for historical memory. The littérateurs of revolt in East Central Europe have been relegated to a marginality that perhaps even exceeds their marginality under communism. As Adam Michnik has observed: "The time for people like myself to engage in politics has come to an end . . . today politics is becoming normal, and for those who did not treat politics as a game but as a way to defend basic values it is becoming difficult to find a space. It will become even harder in the future."[3]

Another way to think about this would be to consider the contemporary marginality of democracy in any form. Why ground a political theory of democracy on the experience of democratic transition in South Africa rather than on the genocide in Rwanda? Why present an argument about the promise of civic initiative based on the experience of conscientious opposition to communism in Czechoslovakia rather than on the experience of "ethnic cleansing" in Bosnia? A political theory based on "the meanings of Bosnia" would, I daresay, present a rather different picture than one based on "the meanings of 1989."

This concluding chapter can be viewed as an essay on the meanings of Bosnia. For without such a corrective, any arguments based on the meanings of 1989 would be both irresponsible and irrelevant. I have been concerned in this book with developing a certain perspective about democracy in the dark times in which we live, times that remain in too many ways inhospitable to human decency and to responsible forms of political empowerment. I do think that there are certain possibilities for democracy in our time, for the successful institutionalization and reform of liberal democratic practices in some places, and for the continued practice of more robust, rebellious forms of democratic politics beyond the confines of normal citizenship within the nation-state. But such forms of politics, when successfully practiced, will be forms of democracy practiced in dark times. And I think from the vantage point of the present it is important to emphasize how dark these times are and will continue to be, and to consider how such darkness ought to temper our sense of what is politically possible.

The Meanings of Bosnia

Bosnia is a place in the heart of Europe. What can it mean to speak of the "meanings" of a place? It all depends. In some contexts, to speak of the meaning of a place is clearly to succumb to a kind of political romanticism, to appeal to collective passions and invoke associations in a hyperbolic way. Thus "Remember the Alamo" can be seen as an incitement to action against the Mexicans, and "the meaning of Eretz Israel" as a patriotic call to arms on behalf of an expansionist agenda in pursuit of "Greater Israel." There are good reasons to be suspicious of the idea that profound meaning can be derived from an evocation of place. But in some situations a place name can come to symbolize more than mere sentimentality, something historical and profound. Auschwitz is such a place name for the generation that survived World War II. In many ways, I think, Bosnia is such a place name for those of us who inhabit advanced industrial societies and who believe ourselves to enjoy the fruits of civil and political freedom.

When the history of twentieth-century political thought is written, the decade of the 1990s will claim credit for, among other things, a unique and distinctive contribution to the lexicon of politics—the concept of "ethnic cleansing." Bosnia is the site of this philosophic innovation. It is not as if the activities to which this concept is linked are novel. To the contrary, they have become chronic features of our political landscape. And yet, as linguistic philosophers tell us, the invention of a concept is the enactment of a world. What is this world that has been enacted in Bosnia, and what is its significance for thinking about democracy in our time?

If in other parts of East Central Europe the demise of communism liberated democratic oppositions and helped to set in motion a process—for good and ill—of political and economic liberalization, in Yugoslavia it set in motion a process of rapid and precipitous political implosion. The republics of Slovenia, Croatia, and Bosnia quickly declared their independence and moved toward secession; anxious Serbian ethnic minorities within these areas recoiled in fear; and into this political caesura stepped Slobodan Milosevic, the Serbian ex-Communist dictator of Yugoslavia, who used the crisis as an opportunity to enforce the political project of a "Greater Serbia." A thorough and detailed account of events or an intensive analysis of historical causality is beyond the scope of my argument here. The unfolding of events was no doubt complicated; political corruption, vice, and violence were practiced in many forms by many parties to what is a complex conflict. But I think it is possible nonetheless to offer a thumbnail sketch of the inhumanity in question, and no one has offered a better one than David Rieff:

This is what happened. Two hundred thousand Bosnian Muslims died, in full view of the world's television cameras, and more than two million other people were forcibly displaced. A state formally recognized by the European Community and the United States . . . and by the United Nations . . . was allowed to be destroyed. While it was being destroyed, United Nations mili-

tary forces and officials looked on, offering "humanitarian" assistance and
protesting . . . that there was no will in the international community to do
anything more. Two successive American Presidents, one Republican, the
second Democratic, declared over and over that they represented the last remaining superpower and yet simultaneously insisted that they were help-
less . . . And this was not, as so many pretended, the result of some grim,
ineluctable law of history, but rather a testimony of specific choices made
by those who governed the rich world and by civil servants who adminis-
tered the international system that they had created.[4]

The Bosnian "civil war" began in the summer of 1991; it was brought to an
official end only in the summer of 1995, when the Dayton Accords brokered by
the United States ratified the independence of Slovenia and Croatia and the de
facto partition of Bosnia. In the intervening years a brutal war of "ethnic cleansing" was waged by Bosnian-Serb forces against the Muslim population of Bosnia. Towns and villages were depopulated and destroyed; mosques and cultural
institutions were systematically pillaged and razed; a policy of mass rape was
practiced against Muslim women; a network of concentration camps was set up
throughout those parts of Bosnia captured by Bosnian-Serb forces; and a campaign of terror and mass murder—of genocide—was undertaken against the
Muslim population. It complicates the picture, but in no way mitigates the horror or minimizes the enormous responsibility of Milosevic and his Bosnian-
Serb allies, to point out that the Croat dictator, Franjo Tudjman, organized a similar reign of terror on a smaller scale. Many people of all ethnic identifications
suffered, as did many more who lacked a clear ethnic identification altogether.
But none suffered more than the Bosnian Muslims, who were "cleansed" by
Serbs, harrassed by Croats, and helped by no one.[5] While the Dayton Accords
brought an official end to these atrocities, the "peace" that has been established
is an uncertain one. Fear and resentment persist. Injustice goes unpunished.
Paramilitary militias remain armed. The Bosnian Serbs remain in control of
most of the territory and the property that they conquered and forcibly expropri-
ated. These facts are beyond question.[6]

The question regards their meaning. What do they signify, what lessons can
we draw from them? What are their implications for democratic politics, or for
politics in general? These questions, of course, have no single or easy answer. Indeed, they are matters about which commentators are sure to argue for years to

come, as events continue to unfold. Yet I think some tentative answers are possible.

The most important thing to say about events in Bosnia is that there is no reason to consider them aberrational. Francis Fukuyama has contended that such events are entirely "marginal," and in no way signify that liberal democracy has "plausible ideological competitors." He writes: "More extreme nationalist states like Serbia that violate fundamental liberal principles of tolerance have not fared well. Because populations are not homogeneous, their emphasis on ethnic purity leads them to conflict, war, and destruction of the economic basis of modern power. It is thus not surprising that Serbia has failed to become a model society for anyone in Europe, East or West ... Although ethnic conflict is a severe threat to democracy in the short run, there are a number of reasons for thinking that it will be a transitional phenomenon."[7] This is a strange remark. The description of Serbia as "intolerant"—rather than, say, brutally repressive or genocidal—is a striking understatement. And what does it mean to say that ethnonationalist ideology does not represent a "plausible" ideological competitor of liberalism? A great deal hinges on the meaning of the term "plausible." For Serbian nationalist ideology surely has fared quite well in achieving its objectives. And if Serbia has hardly become a spiritual model for the West, the West has nonetheless demonstrated little difficulty accepting its violation of "fundamental liberal principles."

Many meanings can be attributed to the destructive and violent scenario still being enacted in Bosnia. Among them four stand out. And contrary to Fukuyama, they implicate some general and disturbing realities that no one who is serious about democracy can afford to gloss over.

First, the Bosnian debacle can be seen as a symptom of a broader crisis in international relations in a postcolonial and postcommunist age, a "foreign policy" crisis of tremendous proportions that tests the resources of liberal democratic states and their strategies of promoting a more organized and "liberal" world order.[8] The downfall of communism in Europe has let loose what Daniel Patrick Moynihan has called a "Pandaemonium" of destructive forces, of which the Bosnian civil war is only one example.[9] Similar ethnonationalist conflicts have broken out or threaten to break out throughout the formerly communist world—in Nagorno-Karabakh, Kosovo, Georgia, the Crimea, and, most notably, Chechnya, among many other places.[10] But such hostilities are not limited to the former Soviet sphere. Similar conflicts are unfolding in Turkey and Iraq (and, though better repressed, in Syria and Iran), where Kurds are struggling for independence; in Afghanistan; in Palestine; and throughout Africa. Indeed, in 1996 a mass of mostly Hutu refugees were making their way from Zaire into Rwanda at a rate of 15,000 people *every hour*, men, women, and children walking thirty miles a day, victims (and victimizers) of a brutal civil war that has taken well over half a million lives and seen the displacement of millions more, a vivid symbol of the prevalence of ethnonationalist conflict in our time.[11]

What has any of this to do with democracy? Aren't these events taking place in the *nondemocratic* parts of the world? Don't they testify to the value of and the need for democracy? Perhaps they do, but they also testify, contra Fukuyama, to how marginal democracy is in our world today. Since the end of the eighteenth century Western humanists have envisioned a world of ever-increasing cosmopolitanism, humanitarianism, legality, and self-government. And yet, at the dawn of the twenty-first century, we confront a world that gives the lie to these expectations. More than thirty years have passed since Jean-Paul Sartre, in his famous preface to Frantz Fanon's *Wretched of the Earth*, wrote of the "inhumanity" of this European humanism "stained with blood."[12] But Sartre credulously wrote in the name of a more "authentic" humanism, a humanism of oppressed peoples—Third World peoples and national minorities—who would rise up against European neocolonialism and free themselves from oppression, who would make real the humanist impulses only given lip service by Western imperialism. We now know that this "humanism" was no more plausible than the one it so sneeringly disparaged.

The postcolonial and postcommunist world is a world of tremendous violence and chaos, destruction and despair. As the journalist Robert D. Kaplan reports, the vast majority of the world's population today lives amidst relentless disease, environmental devastation, soil degradation, population explosion, and grinding poverty, subject to ever-present violence and political predation.[13] It is of course important not to overgeneralize. Each situation is unique. Each political crisis presents its own possibilities. Bosnia is not Burundi, Burundi is not Burma. Yet all of these places, each in its own way, are beset by intractable problems thrown up by a postcolonial world. They testify to the disorder of this world, and to its recalcitrance toward democratic values and democratic political forms. The point is not that Western liberal democracies are complicit in these problems, though they are, by virtue of their economic and diplomatic ties and their not insignificant role as arms suppliers, a factor that deserves much more attention than it receives. It is that, at the very least, the Bosnias of the world defy democratic expectations and stand as severe reproaches to them. In the long run, these reproaches may pass from the scene, though it is surely more likely that they will not; but in the long run, as John Maynard Keynes famously quipped, we are in any case all dead.

Bosnia symbolizes more than a kind of moral or spiritual reproach to democracy, a barrier beyond which democracy seems unable to pass. For if one feature of the world in which we live is the everpresence of suffering, displacement, and violence, another is the utter porousness of the borders, literal and figurative, that keep these problems "there" rather than "here." In this deeper sense Bosnia can be viewed as the future of democracy in those very places where it seems to flourish. For the dynamic of persecution and dispossession is not, and cannot be, safely quarantined "over there." It is *here*, within our societies and within ourselves. What do I mean?

First, that Bosnia is here, within liberal democracy, because the Bosnians themselves are here. The world is currently experiencing a refugee crisis of truly global proportions. According to the Office of the United Nations High Commissioner on Refugees, in 1993 alone 18.2 million people—10,000 people every day—were forced to leave their countries for fear of persecution and violence. This is a conservative estimate. It does not include those millions who were forced to leave their countries under exigencies that do not officially qualify as politically violent. And it does not include the 24 million others displaced within the borders of their own countries. According to the U.N., "roughly one in every 130 people on earth has been forced into flight."[14] This is an incredible statistic.

Where do these people go when they are forced to leave their homes, those places in which, however tenuously, they have long resided and labored? They go elsewhere, abroad. They leave "there," wherever "there" is, and come "here." The Bosnian "ethnic cleansing" alone displaced two million people. Many wound up in concentration camps. Some found refuge in Slovenia, or Croatia, or even Belgrade. Hundreds of thousands made their way to Western Europe, to Germany or Austria or Switzerland. They became refugees in the heart of "civilized" Europe, resident aliens of liberal democratic nation-states. In this regard they share the fate of millions of others—Turks, Arabs, Africans, Asians, Mexicans and Central Americans—ethnic minorities who have changed the demographics of Western liberal democracies and introduced a series of challenges vaguely registered by the concept of "multiculturalism." The challenges are immense. To what extent should these peoples be allowed, and to what extent refused, entry into our countries? To what extent should their cultures be assimilated, to what extent granted legal recognition? To what extent are they entitled to the welfare benefits available to citizens? To what extent are they, many of them residents and productive contributors to the economy for generations, entitled to the rights of citizenship itself?[15] There are no easy answers to these questions, nor is there any reason to think that such questions can be answered in a single way at all times and in all places; but if liberal democracy is to remain a viable form of government anywhere, it will increasingly be compelled to answer them, and to do so in ways that remain true to core liberal democratic values of equal respect and political fairness. Liberal democratic regimes have not, till now, proved themselves up to this task, and their failure is likely to become magnified with the passage of time and the further straining of civic resources. Bosnia is here, then, in the sense that the problems of the rest of the world present themselves to liberal democracies not simply as problems of foreign but of domestic policy, problems of managing conflict and constituting political identity in an increasingly pluralistic and increasingly fractious world.

Bosnia is present in a more insidious sense as well—as a spirit of ethnonationalist exclusionism and political resentment that is becoming increasingly prevalent in liberal democratic societies. We do not have to go all the way with Hans Magnus Enzensberger's *Civil Wars* to recognize that public life in what used to be called "the West" has become increasingly acrimonious, and that the kind of arrogance, meanness, and cruelty characteristic of the Bosnian genocide has become, in much smaller doses to be sure, a staple of the civic culture of liberal democracy.[16] The impressive gains made by Jean-Marie Le Pen's National Front in France are just one example; the significant growth of neo-fascist movements and parties in Italy, Austria, and Germany is another.[17] The anti-immigrant sentiment that has spread throughout Western Europe and the United States is a sign of pervasive insecurity and fear on the part of "native" populations, who are experiencing the effects of economic dislocation and fiscal austerity, and who jealously guard the national patrimony through which they can vicariously derive a sense of security and belonging.[18] The emergence of right-wing populist movements that play upon ethnic and racial divisions to constitute and enforce an antiliberal vision of homogeneous community represents a significant challenge to liberal democracy.[19] Equally significant are the uprisings of aggrieved minorities that dot the political landscape, from African-Americans in Los Angeles and St. Petersburg to Algerians in Paris and Turks in Berlin. Responding to economic inequality and cultural marginality, these groups often project their own forms of fundamentalism which are no less hostile to the normal workings of liberal democracy.[20]

Here we can think of Bosnia as being present among us in an ethical and perhaps metaphysical sense, as the challenge of otherness that has exploded into the political arena. Multiculturalism, after all, is not simply about toleration or public recognition of ethnic, racial, or national groups. It is about a complex set of ways in which political identities are currently being contested, about the veritable explosion of a cultural politics centered on identity that has erupted since the 1960s. The problem of Bosnians among us is a problem of dealing with (literal) strangers and with the hostility that they bring out in the society; it is also a problem of how to deal with strangeness itself, how to envision and to regulate the contestation of gender identity, sexual identity, racial identity, the human relationship with the nonhuman world ("ecology"), and indeed how to deal with the complex identities and conflicts that reside in the soul of each individual human being.[21] As Julia Kristeva puts it: "Strangely, the foreigner lives within us: he is the hidden face of our identity, the space that wrecks our abode, the time in which understanding and affinity founder. By recognizing him within ourselves, we are spared detesting him in himself. A symptom that precisely turns 'we' into a problem, perhaps makes it impossible. The foreigner comes in when the consciousness of my difference arises, and he disappears when we all acknowledge ourselves as foreigners, unamenable to bonds and communities."[22] Bosnia, then, is also a sign of the complexity of the social and political world in general and of the need for liberal democratic citizens to generate the ethical and political resources to grapple with this world in all of its complexity. Here, too, their performance leaves little cause for optimism.

Bosnia thus also stands for a moral crisis of humanism itself. By insisting that Bosnia is a sign of moral crisis, I mean that the very fact that the genocide could be carried out constitutes an instance of egregious ethical irresponsibility, and that the abdication, if not complicity, of the rest of the world—especially the so-called advanced and civilized world—in the face of so glaring an atrocity symbolizes an equally egregious failure of ethical responsibility in our time. For four years the Bosnian debacle went on in our midst. It went on before our very eyes, as the bloodshed and displacement were broadcast virtually nightly on CNN to every corner of the globe.[23] We citizens of advanced liberal democracies knew

that it was happening. And yet we—and the agencies of intellectual enlightenment and political empowerment that supposedly represent us—did virtually
nothing to prevent it from happening or to stop it once it began. This is what David Rieff means when he writes about the "failure of the West"—failure to name
the genocide as genocide, and failure to act on the refrain of "Never again" that
has so frequently been invoked in the wake of the Holocaust perpetrated by the
Nazis.

Like the events in Bosnia, this failure is an accomplished fact. What does it
mean to call it a crisis of ethical responsibility? Ethical responsiblity is a complicated thing, something that philosophers, novelists, and poets have wrestled
with for centuries. Suffice it to say that is has long been a presumption of our
modern, "enlightened" societies that a certain conception of ethical responsibility is enabled by the institutions of liberal democratic self-government: that to be
responsible is to be able to perceive what is going on around you, to make certain
judgments about the rights and wrongs in which you are implicated, and to be
capable of taking some kind of action within the limits of your power to limit
wrong and to abet right.[24] It has long been believed that liberal democracy is
uniquely hospitable to such ethical responsibility because of its freedom of expression, its freedom of the press, its forms of universal public education, its independent judiciary, and its system of responsible and deliberative self-
government. Bosnia puts the lie to such beliefs. Of course this is not the first
time the lie has been put to them. Indeed, in many ways the history of twentieth-
century politics can be viewed as an extended narrative about the failure of these
benign expectations in the face of violence and injustice. Hannah Arendt was
not alone in viewing the Holocaust as an "unprecedented" crime that was nonetheless anticipated by other barbarities, such as the Turkish genocide of Armenians, and a precedent for future barbarities.[25] We should not be surprised by the
possibility of Bosnia. And yet it is nonetheless striking precisely because it has
taken place in the heart of Europe, fifty years after our supposed moral luminaries asserted "Never again," and in the midst of a veritable euphoria over the defeat of communism and the triumph of a liberal "New World Order" in which
democracy was ordained to flourish.[26]

The fact that this crime could occur is due partly to the failure of nerve of political leaders reluctant to offend diplomatic protagonists or to inflame popular
passions by calling genocide by its name. It is due partly to the failure of the mass

media to educate and to outrage; indeed, the freedom of expression long ago hailed by Jefferson and his peers as a guarantee of civic virtue proved itself in practice to promote mass confusion and cynicism.[27] Bosnia signals a failure of organized political response and of civic responsibility, but at an even deeper level it can be argued that it signals a striking evacuation of responsibility altogether, of the increasing prevalence of a callow indifference among citizens of the "free world" that simply masks itself as an exercise of freedom. As a victim of Soviet persecution, the Nobel Prize–winning poet Joseph Brodsky penned a poem called "The Berlin Wall Tune" to call attention to the oppressions and hypocrisies of communism.[28] How ironic, then, that, but three years after the demise of communism, he would be moved to write a sequel, "Bosnia Tune," to call attention to the ethical debility of "freedom" itself. His words are apposite:

> As you sip your brand of scotch,
> crush a roach, or scratch your crotch,
> as your hand adjusts your tie,
> people die.
>
> In the towns with funny names,
> hit by bullets, caught in flames,
> by and large not knowing why,
> people die.
>
> In small places you don't know
> of, yet big for having no
> chance to scream or say good-bye,
> people die.
>
> People die as you elect
> brand-new dudes who preach neglect,
> self-restraint, etc.—whereby
> people die.
>
> Too far off to practice love
> for thy neighbor/brother Slav,
> where your cherubs dread to fly,
> people die.

> While the statutes disagree,
> Cain's version, history
> for its fuel tends to buy
> those who die.
>
> As you watch the athletes score,
> check your latest statement, or
> sing your child a lullaby,
> people die.
>
> Time, whose sharp blood-thirsty quill
> parts the killed from those who kill,
> will pronounce the latter band
> as your brand.[29]

Brodsky's poem brilliantly captures the incredible, shocking juxtaposition of political murder "there" and absorption in the commerce of daily life "here"; it also sharpens the sense that there are no "here" and "there," that we inhabit a single ethical universe, that the suffering "they" (and their killers) are here too, on our television screens, at our borders, and on our streets, within reach, and yet we choose to ignore them.[30] It is widely reported that accident victims who lose a limb will long after the event experience the limb as if it existed. Brodsky's poem seeks to induce in us a similar effect, of becoming palpably aware of something—ethical responsibility—by heightening the experience of its utter absence. It is impossible to read the poem and not be moved to think about an ethical responsibility that has been abdicated.

This ethical failure, as I have insisted, is an accomplished fact. And so, even more important, are the injustices that have been committed in part as a result of such failure. This reflection leads me to the final significance of Bosnia, what I will call, speaking loosely, the irremediability of injustice that it instantiates. Political theory is not only about justice. It is also about injustice, about identifying injustice and remedying it, about righting the wrongs that have been done.[31] Just as liberal democracy has long been imagined to be a form of government uniquely suited to regulating problems of conflict and to fostering an ethos of respect and responsibility, it has also been imagined to be a way of enacting and enforcing legality, of being responsive to the claims of those who have been wronged. That Bosnia is the site of horrifying wrong is beyond doubt. And

yet in what ways are the victims of this wrong being compensated? Who is responsible for such remediation? Who is empowered to enforce it? Is such remediation even possible?

Bosnia is a symbol of mass persecution and violence and widespread destruction. It is also a symbol of the extreme difficulty—indeed, I fear, the impos-
siblity—of compensation. There is no remedy for the losses. There is obviously
no chance of bringing back the dead. And it seems equally impossible to restore
the property of the dispossessed, or to restore the dignity and confidence of
those who have been terrorized, raped, and incarcerated. And it appears that
there is little political will to enforce any kind of justice for those most politically
responsible for organizing and perpetrating such violence.[32] To the extent that
this is true, it is not simply the past that is poisoned, but the future as well, for
those who have suffered, but also, I submit, for those who stood by, and continue
to stand by, doing nothing to assist them, incapable of offering rescue or remedy.[33] In his famous "Theses on the Philosophy of History," Walter Benjamin
described "the angel of history" thus:

> His eyes are staring, his mouth open, his wings are spread. This is how one
> pictures the angel of history. His face is turned toward the past. Where we
> perceive a chain of events, he sees one single catastrophe which keeps pil-
> ing up wreckage upon wreckage and hurls it in front of his feet. The angel
> would like to stay, awaken the dead, and make whole what has been
> smashed. But a storm is blowing from Paradise; it has got hold of his wings
> with such violence that the angel can no longer close them. This storm irre-
> sistibly propels him into the future to which his back is turned, while the
> pile of debris before him grows skyward. This storm is what we call
> progress.[34]

Such a grim picture is, of course, one-sided; wreckage is surely not all that our
recent history has wrought. But wreckage is an absolutely critical part of the
story of our contemporary history, a part that most political scientists and political theorists who write about democracy attend to all too little. The most powerful image in Benjamin's parable is that of a world irremediably torn, one that
cannot be made whole or restored to some balance and some semblance of justice. Bosnia symbolizes this problem. It symbolizes it juridically, as an instance
of the incapacity of legal authorities to bring the perpetrators of violence to justice, an inability that only continues to fuel a cycle of fear, resentment, and ha-

tred toward all possible violators. It symbolizes the problem politically, by virtue of the incessant waves of refugees it produces, continually uprooting peoples and taxing the fiscal and civic resources of liberal democratic states. And it symbolizes it ethically, as an expression of profound civic cynicism that helps to reinforce the growing sense that meaningful public action on behalf of justice or solidarity is impossible.

The Pathos of Modern Freedom

The epigraphs with which this chapter began are intended to juxtapose two powerful images—the image of freedom and creative possiblity that inaugurated the modern world, and the image of degradation and bestiality that in so many ways marks the world in which we live. Our world is the product of that earlier world, of its dreams of creative possibility and of the unanticipated and disturbing ways in which some of these dreams have been fulfilled.

Liberal democracy, I believe, represents in many respects the greatest political fulfillment of such dreams. It represents a way of organizing public offices and distributing political power that, at its best, promotes peaceful conflict resolution, legality, and the accountable exercise of public authority. Liberal democracy is a creation of the modern world, which is to say it is a way of organizing human energies and a way of limiting the scope of their expression, and of doing so on a mass scale, at the level of the nation-state. In *Peasants into Frenchmen*, Eugen Weber details the complex and contingent processes whereby civic identity in a nation-state is constituted through human artifice. The very processes of ongoing social life in liberal democracies—peaceful and law-abiding conduct, extensive commercial activity, the flourishing of private life—and the ongoing operations of government testify to the power of this construction. The extraordinary physical and cultural infrastructure of advanced industrial societies further testify to the power of liberal democratic politics. Liberal democracy has been productive of much that is good.

And yet these achievements are inextricably linked to those forms of darkness that it has been the purposes of this chapter to identify—the injustices and forms of violence beyond borders in which liberal democracy is complicit; the cultural and political exclusions enforced by the juridical form of the nation-state; the forms of political resentment engendered by economic inequality and political alienation; and the mass indifference of liberal democratic citizens to the demands of solidarity whether at home or abroad. Many people will of course argue that these problems may plague the world in which we live, but they have little to do with the juridical and political institutions of liberal democracy and in no way impeach these institutions. How, they may ask, can the pervasiveness of illiberalism and barbarity be taken as a sign of the debilities of liberal democracy, a form of government that seems to stand as the antithesis of illiberalism and barbarity? In one respect this rejoinder is correct. Liberal democracy is in no self-evident way the *cause* of the problems symbolized by Bosnia, and there is no good reason to hold it responsible for these phenomena in any simpleminded sense. Indeed, nothing in the normative or juridical organization of liberal democracy would prevent it from addressing at least some of these problems in a meaningful and effective way. Further, whatever its limitations in this regard, it is hard to imagine any wholesale alternative to liberal democracy that might do any better. So in a way the disturbing meanings I have sought to draw from the story of Bosnia could be taken together as an endorsement of liberal democracy rather than as a reproach to it. If only the rest of the world had it, one might argue, then we would have a lot less to be troubled about. In a way, this is true; but only in a way.

For of course things are not that simple. As I have tried to show, Bosnia symbolizes not simply the Other of liberal democracy but the legal, political, and ethical challenges that are endemic to liberal democracy and that it has yet to address successfully. There are many ways of thinking about these challenges. As I have indicated repeatedly, my own way of thinking about them is influenced by the writings of Hannah Arendt, especially her notion of the "worldlessness" or "world alienation" of modern society. Drawing from Martin Heidegger and from Max Weber before him, Arendt argued that the social processes of the modern world relentlessly engender "the instrumentalization of the whole world and the earth, this limitless devaluation of everything given, this process of growing meaninglessness where every end is transformed into a means and which can be stopped only by making man himself the lord and master of all things"[35] Arendt criticizes this worldlessness both as a metaphysic of human power without limit and as a social formation that renders individuals "superfluous," subject to forces beyond their control and often beyond even their comprehension. Better than any other modern social critic, she saw that the elaborate web of interrelationships that we modern humans have woven has only made us more vulnerable, that our power has produced a sense of powerlessness and our wealth an experience of privation and dislocation.

Democratic sovereignty as modern political theory conceives it represents the ultimate form of empowerment and productivity, the mobilization—as the social contract theorists saw—of prodigious political will behind the authority of the nation-state. And yet the democratic nation-state today is marked by a profound immobility in the face of the social forces thrown up by the modern world. New forms of globalization produce massive economic disruption and the devaluation of labor.[36] New forms of communication and mass media promote the banalization of public discourse and a growing sense that nothing is truly real and nothing truly matters.[37] The relentless technological imperatives of "creative destruction" produce ecological devastation and ever-increasing risk.[38] Economic dislocation and political persecution engender pervasive ethnonational conflict and the dispossession and global movement of vast numbers—millions upon millions—of refugees.[39] Each of these processes is severe; in combination they constitute a single explosive mixture that presents a serious challenge to democratic governance.[40]

It is again worth noting that these challenges are not all that characterizes the current moment. If there is much darkness, there is also light. As theorists such as Jürgen Habermas have insisted, the resources for a revitalized liberal democratic politics have not been thoroughly extinguished. They survive in the form of liberal constitutionalism, and also in the form of a multiplicity of new social movements and political associations that promote inclusivity, mutual respect, and democratic deliberation.[41] Though civil society in many liberal democratic societies is impoverished, it continues to serve as an important source of secondary association and normative vitality.[42] And yet it is important to draw the balance between these resources and the challenges that they will increasingly be called upon to meet. Here I think it is hard to avoid the conclusion that democracy is an important force but also an increasingly marginalized and demoralized one, marginalized and demoralized less by an exultant ideological competitor than by the exhaustion of its own resources. The formal processes of liberal democratic government are increasingly constrained by the forms of "worldlessness" beyond their control, and as a result are increasingly in disrepair and disrepute. The liberal democratic nation-state is an important achievement, and it is difficult to imagine its disappearance. But it is increasingly eclipsed by the darkness surrounding it, and is decreasingly viewed as the repository of genuinely democratic ideals of self government. Secondary associations and social movements continue to emerge and to operate in the public sphere, but they are perpetually in danger of being eclipsed by the forces of privatism, cynicism, and trivialization. Indeed, in many ways the most vital social movements at present seem to be those—whether religious fundamentalist or right-wing populist— whose authoritarianism and antiliberalism can hardly furnish comfort to those committed to democratic values.

For this reason I find Arendt's idea of "oases in the desert" appealing, for it captures, as I argued earlier, two indispensable insights: the marginality and precariousness—indeed, the preciousness—of democratic values and those civic initiatives necessary to advance and embody them; and the ineliminable plurality and partiality of such initiatives. Arendt saw, I believe correctly, that the liberal democratic nation-state could serve only in the most imperfect and inadequate way as a vehicle for democratic values in the current age. And she saw that this politics needed to be supplemented by a robust and fractious politics "from below" that would energize and more fully embody a democratic ethos. Such a politics from below—sometimes called a "grass-roots" politics—is distinguished not by its geographical localism but by its partiality, by its persistent operation outside the boundaries of and at cross-purposes with the liberal democratic nation-state, seeking to forge new associational forms and new political identities capable of securing a sense of human dignity and political empowerment. Such efforts are up against such great and inescapable obstacles that Sheldon Wolin can aptly describe democracy today as a "fugitive," a pariah with no secure home and no rest.[43] For many liberal political theorists democracy signifies a constructive political vision, an ordering of political authority in a way that is intended to solve the basic problems of social living. There is much to be said for this vision; and the effort to act on it to craft liberal democratic constitutional arrangements is a valuable one. But if I am correct, this effort comes up against obstacles that it does not seem able to surpass. Furthermore, even in its successes such an effort is limited; for all of the constitutional engineering, electoral and campaign finance reform, and subsidizing of secondary associations and quasi-official deliberative forums that political scientists may imagine will in the end come up against the unpleasant truth that the dominant economic, technological, communicative, and political forces in our world conspire against them. In a worldless world political reform is both exceedingly difficult and increasingly inadequate. To this extent a more skeptical, Arendtian view of democracy recommends itself as a corrective, one that envisions democracy as largely a defensive reaction, a practice of rebellion—or more properly rebellions— against the injustices and imperatives of a worldless world.

On the eve of the revolutions of 1848, which raised the banner of the democratic nation-state throughout Europe, two relatively obscure social theorists issued their now-famous critique of capitalism: "Modern . . . society with its relations of production, of exchange and of property, a society that has conjured up such gigantic means of production and of exchange, is like the sorcerer who is no longer able to control the powers of the nether world whom he has called up by his spells."[44] As most readers will recognize, this passage comes from *The Communist Manifesto*. In many ways it hardly constitutes an emblematic statement of political philosophy; few political theorists writing about democracy today, liberal or otherwise, would seek their lineage there. And yet in an important way this text *is* emblematic. It articulates, perhaps more strongly than any other statement in modern political thought, the belief—indeed, the faith—that the modern world is a world of tremendous human capacity, a capacity that threatens to confuse and overwhelm us, but that can, in the end, be brought under control, reorganized under the self-conscious guidance of a legitimate collective purpose. And in the contemporary world such a purpose has gone by the name of democracy. Whether socialist or, more fashionably today, liberal, democracy has been seen as a way of ordering political authority within territorially based communities—nation-states—so as to exercise political power in a constructive, problem-solving way, to institutionalize the sovereignty of ordinary people over the conditions of their lives, to bring the world of their making under their collective control.

Yet the record of the twentieth century suggests that this vision of the democratic nation-state as a vehicle of collective purpose and remedial agency is, however noble, in important ways mistaken. Perhaps the defining feature of the late modern world is not that humankind creates problems that it can solve but that humankind has created a host of problems that it cannot solve, that it lacks both the vision and the will to solve them, and that this incapacity has engendered cynicism and weariness. Perhaps the most significant fact of the human condition today is not our power but a self-produced and self-perpetuating liability, an irremediable vulnerability in the face of powers called up by our own magic.

The pathos of modern freedom is the fact that we are subject to the forces of our own creation, expressions of our freedom, and yet the resources available to mitigate these forces are literally pathetic—limited, fragile, destined to be incomplete, frustrating, and unsatisfying. The political world is increasingly like a wasteland, subject to processes of encroaching and intensifying desertification. The effort to irrigate the desert is not without merit, and in those places where the resources for it exist, the task is worth undertaking. But in many places the resources for this task do not exist or are in short supply; and in any case, the task, even when successfully accomplished, is incomplete and scarcely adequate to the challenges it confronts. Even in the most flourishing of the gardens we create the desert encroaches. For this reason it is equally important, perhaps even more so, to cultivate and to preserve those oases in the desert where freedom still thrives, those small and marginal spaces that strive to keep the desert at bay.

What kinds of democratic responses do I have in mind when I invoke such flowery metaphors about oases and deserts? How is this talk of oases anything more than a retreat before the problems confronting us, perhaps even a justification for the kind of gated communities that increasingly dot our landscape?

The kind of politics I have in mind is not invidiously utopian; it very much takes its bearing from the initiatives and activities seen in such associations as Charter 77 and the Industrial Areas Foundation, the Algebra Project and Médecins sans Frontières. These are imperfect forms of political response, yet they are exemplary precisely by virtue of their imperfection. Such efforts perform a variety of tasks: they provide mutual aid, develop networks of information and empowerment, express—sometimes adamantly—public protest and indignation, and alter public opinion, sometimes in small ways. They are not grand schemes of political transformation or even institutional reform, but rather more modest and self-limiting efforts to generate forms of solidarity and participation to attack specific injustices and to present limited remedies to specific problems. These efforts do not, cannot, and should not replace the forms of mass politics and parliamentary governance in liberal democratic societies. But in an era in which these more "normal" forms of politics are in disrepair and disrepute, political theory ought to take the full measure of such oases, and to consider, in the words of the Hungarian George Konrad, what they add to the "tool-box" of democratic politics.[45]

Perhaps it would be more useful to speak literally rather than metaphorically. What might the citizens of liberal democratic societies have done, what may they still do to address the actual problems thrown up by the brutal civil war that continues to smolder in Bosnia? How can this Arendtian conception of politics respond to these difficulties? The answer is that there is no single answer. The idea that political theory can discern the grand strategy or institutional reform that might have prevented this war or might prevent such wars in the future is precisely what I call into question. The idea that some vision of geopolitics or international law or Kantian republicanism might secure us from these disasters seems naive. Given the way the world is, the Bosnian debacle in all of its ramifications was hard to avoid. "Hard" does not mean "impossible." But avoidance runs counter to the dominant forces in our world. Extraordinary political foresight is required, and, even more important, extraordinary political will. Yet it is precisely this will that is in such short supply, and none of the schemes of well-meaning political scientists, theorists, and constitutional engineers are likely to counterbalance this fact. I do not say that nothing can be done; but what can be done—what is being done—comes up against strong, probably insurmountable obstacles. Yet such efforts are important. Trying—in the face of the black hole that is the mass media—to meaningfully publicize information about atrocities and suffering, and to promote a public debate about the politics of rescue.[46] Raising money for relief aid. Agitating for a sensitive and humane immigration policy to provide sanctuary for refugees, and using existing resources—community, religious—to offer such sanctuaries. Undertaking seemingly small but symbolically and materially meaningful acts such as seeking the help of Western university libraries in the effort to preserve the books of the Sarajevo library. Supporting "peace caravans" such as those organized by the Helsinki Citizens' Assembly. Trying to promote forms of mutual respect and dialogue, at the grassroots level, sometimes far removed from the battle-scarred territory of the conflict, among the antagonists. These are not things that might be done—though they might be done by more people; they are things that have been done and that are being done.

But what about military intervention? What about new forms of security? What about international law and the enforcement of justice against war criminals? These are all important things. They are also things that are highly unlikely to address such problems as Bosnia effectively, at least not until after the Bosnias have already been destroyed. Such measures can be contemplated seriously only in a civil society in which other forms of solidarity exist. If they do exist, and if they combine in certain ways, then it is of course possible, under rare but propitious circumstances, that they might in fact support meaningful state action or meaningful institutional reform, such as new forms of federalism, or the reform of immigration law, or foreign policies that extend aid to the Bosnians of our world and perhaps even undertake to rescue them. But it is more likely that they will not. This is why they are best conceived not as supports for a bigger, more important form of politics but as a kind of politics sui generis, probably the best, most meaningful forms of democratic politics that we can aspire to experience. These activities, to be sure, cannot fully or satisfactorily remedy the problems to which they address themselves. But they can have significance, however limited. Think about the specific children aided by Médecins sans Frontières. Or the refugees given another chance by the activities of sanctuary groups. Or the specific volumes—and the cultural value they bear—saved by the effort to rescue books. These activities matter, however infrequently they occupy the attention of political theorists and public policy analysts. And just as important, a sense of dignity, solidarity, and empowerment is engendered among those who practice these activities and who thus through their very efforts constitute the oases in the desert. They are ways of doing good and doing politics, having a say and making a difference.

In his powerful book *A Miracle, a Universe*, Lawrence Weschler quotes a passage from the Hebrew Mishnah: "Therefore was one single man created first, Adam, to teach you that if anyone destroys a single soul from the children of Man, Scripture charges him as though he had destroyed a whole Universe—and whoever rescues a single soul from the children of Man, Scripture credits him as if he had saved a whole Universe."[47] The passage makes a nice contrast to Pico della Mirandola's "Oration." Adam here—the human being—stands not for a "free and sovereign artificer" but for a fragile creature in an equally fragile world, a world that is broken and in need of repair, and in which small, modest acts—and failures to act—can assume great significance.

It will of course be said, and with some reason, that the kind of politics I am describing and endorsing is nothing but an "ethic of the Red Cross," a pessimistic and despairing effort to place bandages on the wounded without seeking truly to secure justice and to make the world whole.[48] Or it may be said that it represents not a serious view of politics at all but simply a plea for "attitude adjustment," for a scaling back of political vision, a retreat from serious struggle against injustice and for democracy.[49] I can only reply that on this score I agree with Camus: "My conviction is that we can no longer hope to save everything, but that we can at least try to save lives, so that some kind of future, if not the ideal one, will remain possible." Rather than advancing an ambitious vision of reforming or remaking political structures, I am suggesting a "modest thought-fulness which, without pretending to solve everything, will always be ready to give human meaning to everyday life."[50] I am proposing not political quiescence but political realism. In an emergency room a Red Cross ethic is required. And the world today is an emergency room, with one caveat—there is no outside, we are all inside together, vulnerable and anxiously seeking some way to stanch the bleeding. This image is a kind of attitude adjustment. It is a more chastened view of collective action and democratic citizenship. But it is not a retreat from the struggle against injustice, just an abandonment of the idea that there *is* a grand struggle that subsumes all the rest.

I have asserted that political theory takes its bearings from political experience. We are experiencing in our time an impressive resurgence of liberal democratic constitutionalism, and it is important that political theory attend to this revival and, so far as is possible, abet it. But we are also experiencing an equally impressive demonstration of the limits of this constitutionalism and of the liberal democratic nation-state that is its principal vehicle. In confronting these limits, we need to take the full measure of a different kind of politics, one less official and less institutional, more chastened and yet more idealistic, a politics that cannot and does not seek to dispel the darkness but seeks only to create some protective spaces of light and warmth where the damage may be contained. As Hannah Arendt wrote, "even in the darkest of times we have the right to expect some illumination . . . from the uncertain, flickering, and often weak light that some men and women, in their lives and in their words, will kindle under almost all circumstances and shed over the time span that was given them on earth."[51] The light may be flickering, uncertain, and weak, the light of a candle rather than a blazing sun. But it is perhaps the only illumination we can expect in the dark times settling upon us. And in any case it is a beacon of hope, and a sign that if we are not "unhampered," like "free and sovereign artificers," there is still a spark of "divinity" within us and among us, an ability to make the world we inhabit together, through our own precarious and unaided efforts, a more just and hospitable place.

Introduction

1. See Samuel Huntington, *The Third Wave: Democratization in the Late Twentieth Century* (Norman: University of Oklahoma Press, 1991).

2. See Larry Diamond, "Is the Third Wave Over?" *Journal of Democracy* 7 (July 1996), 20–37.

3. See Charles Maier, "Democracy and Its Discontents," *Foreign Affairs* 73 (July/August 1994), 48–67.

4. For an interesting statement of this idea, see Göran Therborn, "The Life and Times of Socialism," *New Left Review*, no. 194 (July/August 1992), 17–32. See also the range of interesting contributions in Robin Blackburn, ed., *After the Fall: The Failure of Communism* (London: Verso, 1991).

5. The strongest statement of this theme is Jean Cohen and Andrew Arato, *Civil Society and Political Theory* (Cambridge: MIT Press, 1992).

6. In 1990 Michael Walzer hopefully suggested that the demise of communism might enhance the prospects for a more authentic social democratic politics. See "A Credo for This Moment," *Dissent* 37 (Spring 1990), 160. I obviously strongly disagree with this judgment, which has not been borne out by subsequent events; but I suspect that Walzer too now takes a more chastened view.

7. A primary outlet for these discussions is the *Journal of Democracy*, a publication of the National Endowment for Democracy's International Forum for Democratic Studies. See also Adam Przeworski et al., *Sustainable Democracy* (New York: Cambridge University Press, 1995). I discuss this literature in Chapter 7.

8. I criticize much of this literature in "Situating Hannah Arendt on Action and Politics," *Political Theory* 21 (August 1993), 534–40.

9. Hannah Arendt, *Men in Dark Times* (New York: Harcourt, Brace & World, 1968), p. viii.

10. See, for example, Jean Baudrillard, "Simulations and Simulacra," in Mark Poster, ed., *Jean Baudrillard: Selected Writings* (Cambridge: Polity Press, 1988).

11. The most recent reiteration of this old and mistaken charge is to be found in Richard Wolin, "Hannah and the Magician," *New Republic*, October 9, 1995, pp. 27–37.

12. One of the few theorists to absorb this fact is Sheldon Wolin, who notes that "de-

mocracy has no continuous history following the absorption of Athens into the Macedonian empire," in "Fugitive Democracy," *Constellations* 1 (April 1994), 22.

13. See Karl Mannheim, *Ideology and Utopia* (New York: Harcourt, Brace, 1936), p. 205.

14. See Stephen Holmes, "Liberalism for a World of Ethnic Passions and Decaying States," *Social Research* 61 (Fall 1994), 599–610.

15. See Jürgen Habermas, *Legitimation Crisis* (Boston: Beacon Press, 1975); *The Theory of Communicative Action*, vol. 2: *Lifeworld and System: A Critique of Functionalist Reason* (Boston: Beacon Press, 1987); and "The New Obscurity: The Crisis of the Welfare State and the Exhaustion of Utopian Energies," in *The New Conservatism* (Cambridge: MIT Press, 1989); Cohen and Arato, *Civil Society and Political Theory*; and Seyla Benhabib, *Critique, Norm, and Utopia: A Study of the Foundations of Critical Theory* (New York: Columbia University Press, 1986) and "Deliberative Rationality and Models of Democratic Legitimacy," *Constellations* 1 (April 1994), 26–52.

16. Habermas, "The New Obscurity," p. 67.

17. Here I concur with Seyla Benhabib's critique of the "obsolescence of social theory" today, in her "Response" to "The Strange Silence of Political Theory," *Political Theory* 23 (November 1995), 679–80.

18. See especially William E. Connolly, *Identity\Difference: Democratic Negotiations of Political Paradox* (Ithaca: Cornell University Press, 1991), and "The Ethical Sensibility of Michel Foucault," *Political Theory* 21 (August 1993), 365–89; Bonnie Honig, "Toward an Agonistic Feminism," in Bonnie Honig, ed., *Feminist Interpretations of Hannah Arendt* (University Park: Penn State University Press, 1995), and "Differences, Dilemmas, and the Politics of Home," *Social Research* 61 (Fall 1994), 563–98; and Wendy Brown, "Wounded Attachments," *Political Theory* 21 (August 1993), 390–410.

19. I have explored these ethical concerns in *Arendt, Camus, and Modern Rebellion* (New Haven: Yale University Press, 1992), pp. 105–76.

20. Connolly, *Identity\Difference*, pp. 94, 121.

21. Ibid., p. 85.

22. Honig, "Differences, Dilemmas, and the Politics of Home," p. 589.

23. As the mere mention of Arendt makes clear, the contrast I want to denote here, which marks only a difference and not a source of privilege, is itself complicated and problematic, for Arendt herself (and Camus as well) was inspired in part by Nietzsche, and Bonnie Honig has invoked Arendt in support of her own agonistic view. See especially Bonnie Honig, *Political Theory and the Displacement of Politics* (Ithaca: Cornell University Press, 1993), pp. 76–125.

24. Connolly, *Identity\Difference*, pp. 84–85.

25. Such efforts, I would add, are perhaps best conceived as existing in a healthy tension with the forms of cultural politics that concern agonistic writers, though, in fairness, writers such as Honig also write about the importance of "coalition politics," and to this extent what we are dealing with here is a matter of emphasis. See Honig, "Difference, Dilemmas, and the Politics of Home," p. 587.

26. Albert Camus, "Neither Victims nor Executioners," in *Between Hell and Reason:*

Essays from the Resistance Newspaper "Combat," 1944–1947, ed. and trans. Alexandre de Gramont (Hanover, N.H.: Wesleyan University Press, 1991), p. 139.

Chapter 1. The Return of the Repressed; or, The Limits of Democratic Theory

1. Francis Fukuyama, "The End of History?" *National Interest*, no. 16 (Summer 1989), 4.

2. Marc F. Plattner, "The Democratic Moment," in Larry Diamond and Marc F. Plattner, eds., *The Global Resurgence of Democracy* (Baltimore: Johns Hopkins University Press, 1992), p. 28.

3. National Endowment for Democracy, *Strategy Document* (Washington, D.C., 1992), pp. 1, 5.

4. George Bush, "Inaugural Address: A New Breeze Is Blowing," *Vital Speeches of the Day* 55 (February 15, 1989), 258.

5. "U.S. Foreign Policy in a Changing World," *Vital Speeches of the Day* 56 (May 1990), 418.

6. "The Battle for Democracy," *U.S. News & World Report*, May 22, 1989, p. 38.

7. Ibid., p. 35.

8. Ibid.

9. Joshua Muravchik, *Exporting Democracy: Fulfilling America's Destiny* (Washington, D.C.: American Enterprise Institute, 1992), p. xiv.

10. Jean-François Revel, *Democracy against Itself: The Future of the Democratic Impulse* (New York: Free Press, 1993), pp. 14–15.

11. Samuel P. Huntington, "No Exit: The Errors of Endism," *National Interest* 17 (Fall 1989), 3–11. For a similar argument see also Jean-François Revel's essay "But We Follow the Worse . . ." *National Interest* 17 (Winter 1989/90), 99–103, which calls for "a deliberate, *democratic policy*, an activist policy, world-wide."

12. For a journalistic statement of this theme, see Morton Kondrake, "Freedom Bummer: Democratization's Hangover," *New Republic*, September 26, 1990, pp. 21–24. See also David Aikman, "Interview: A Doctor for Young Democracies," *Time*, June 10, 1991, pp. 12–13; "Replacing Communism: So Little Time, So Much to Do," *Economist*, January 20, 1990, pp. 49–51; and, more skeptically, Walter Shapiro, "America's Dubious Export," *Time*, September 4, 1989, p. 72.

13. Revel, *Democracy against Itself*, pp. 17, 19.

14. See "Is Russian Democracy Doomed?" a special section of *Journal of Democracy* (April 1994), 3–41.

15. Craig R. Whitney, "Little Big Men: They're All Speaking Perot's Lines," *New York Times*, April 3, 1994, Section 4, p. 1.

16. Philippe C. Schmitter, "Democracy's Future: More Liberal, Preliberal, or Postliberal?" *Journal of Democracy* 6 (January 1995), 16. See also his "Dangers and Dilemmas of Democracy," *Journal of Democracy* 5 (April 1994), 57–74.

17. See Judith Shklar, *After Utopia: The Decline of Political Faith* (Princeton: Princeton University Press, 1969).

18. Hannah Arendt, *The Origins of Totalitarianism* (New York: Harcourt Brace Jovanovich, 1973), pp. v–vi.

19. See Jeffrey C. Isaac, *Arendt, Camus, and Modern Rebellion* (New Haven: Yale University Press, 1992), pp. 37–67.

20. See David Ricci, *The Tragedy of Political Science: Politics, Scholarship, and Democracy* (New Haven: Yale University Press, 1984), especially pp. 115–32, where he discusses the influence of Karl Popper and his notion of the "open society." See Karl Popper, *The Open Society and Its Enemies*, 2 vols. (Princeton: Princeton University Press, 1966). See also Karl Popper, "The Open Society and Its Enemies Revisited," *Economist*, April 23, 1988, 18–22.

21. For a clever and compelling recitation of some of these debates, see C. Douglas Lummis, *Radical Democracy* (Ithaca: Cornell University Press, 1996), pp. 1–8, 14–44.

22. Robert A. Dahl, *A Preface to Democratic Theory* (Chicago: University of Chicago Press, 1956); Giovanni Sartori, *Democratic Theory* (New York: Praeger, 1965); and Henry Mayo, *An Introduction to Democratic Theory* (Ann Arbor: University of Michigan Press, 1960). Also influential was Seymour Martin Lipset, "Some Social Requisites of Democracy: Economic Development and Political Legitimacy," *American Political Science Review* 53 (March 1959), 69–105, later incorporated in his *Political Man* (New York: Doubleday, 1963).

23. This point is also made by Sheldon Wolin, "Fugitive Democracy," *Constellations* 1 (April 1994), 16–25.

24. An exception can be found in early essays on socialist political theory written by Robert A. Dahl, reprinted in his *Democracy, Liberty, and Equality* (Oslo: Norwegian University Press, 1985). Yet in his most influential works of democratic theory this concern is not evident. On this problem, see my "Dilemmas of Democratic Theory," in Ian Shapiro and Grant Reeher, eds., *Power, Inequality, and Democratic Politics: Essays in Honor of Robert A. Dahl* (Boulder, Colo.: Westview Press, 1988).

25. See, for example, Sartori, "The Machiavellians: Mosca, Pareto, Michels," in his *Democratic Theory*, pp. 40–42, where he applauds the "realism" of these thinkers but dismisses their "anti-democratic" sentiments as being of little consequence, unrelated to their empirical concerns. My point is not that democratic theorists such as Sartori and Lipset were unfamiliar with such theorists. Indeed, it is clear that postwar behavioralists were well schooled in the history of political thought. My point is that they did not treat such ideas with a great deal of intellectual seriousness.

26. See John L. Stanley, ed., *From Georges Sorel: Essays in Socialism and Philosophy* (New York: Oxford University Press, 1976); Robert Michels, *Political Parties*, trans. Eden and Cedar Paul (New York: Dover, 1959); and David Beetham, "From Socialism to Fascism: The Relation between Theory and Practice in the Work of Robert Michels," *Political Studies* 25, nos. 1–2 (1980). See also the many writings of Lenin, especially "The State and Revolution," in Robert C. Tucker, ed., *The Lenin Anthology* (New York: Norton, 1975). On the currency of "democracy" among Marxists seeking to advance the "democratic dictatorship

of the proletariat," see especially Roy Medvedev, *Leninism and Western Socialism* (London: Verso, 1981).

27. See Bernhard Schlink, "Why Carl Schmitt?" *Constellations* 2 (January 1996), 429–41.

28. Carl Schmitt, *The Crisis of Parliamentary Democracy* (Cambridge: MIT Press, 1988), pp. 6–8. For a brilliant critique of Schmitt, see Richard Wolin, "Carl Schmitt: The Conservative Revolutionary Habitus and the Aesthetics of Horror," *Political Theory* 20 (August 1992), 424–47.

29. See J. L. Talmon, *The Origins of Totalitarian Democracy* (Boulder, Colo.: Westview Press, 1985).

30. Schmitt, *Crisis of Parliamentary Democracy*, pp. 14–17.

31. See especially chap. 2 of Dahl's *Preface to Democratic Theory*, which draws in part on the classic analysis provided in Kenneth Arrow, *Social Choice and Individual Values*, 2d ed. (New Haven: Yale University Press, 1963).

32. The most famous statement of the idea that nonparticipation might be a good thing for a democracy can be found in Bernard R. Berelson, Paul Lazarsfeld, and William N. McPhee, *Voting: A Study of Opinion Formation in a Presidential Campaign* (Chicago: University of Chicago Press, 1954). See also Robert A. Dahl's discussion of "homo civicus" in *Who Governs?* (New Haven: Yale University Press, 1961). The classic liberal statement of this theme is Benjamin Constant, "The Liberty of the Ancients Compared with That of the Moderns," in *The Political Writings of Benjamin Constant*, trans. and ed. Biancamaria Fontana (New York: Cambridge University Press, 1988).

33. For a useful overview, see Philippe Schmitter and Terry Karl, "What Democracy Is . . . and Is Not," in Diamond and Plattner, *Global Resurgence of Democracy*.

34. A classic statement of this theme is Nelson Polsby, *Community Power and Political Theory*, 2d ed. (New Haven: Yale University Press, 1980). For criticism, see my *Power and Marxist Theory: A Realist View* (Ithaca: Cornell University Press, 1987).

35. See Joseph Schumpeter, *Capitalism, Socialism, and Democracy* (New York: Harper, 1942), and Anthony Downs, *An Economic Theory of Democracy* (New York: Harper, 1957).

36. Dahl, *Preface to Democratic Theory*, p. 130. In *Who Governs?* Dahl describes the processes whereby political elites present themselves and their programs as "democratic rituals" in which the appearance of responsiveness and accountability is more significant than their reality.

37. Schumpeter, *Capitalism, Socialism, and Democracy*, p. 269.

38. See, for example, David Held, *Models of Democracy* (Stanford: Stanford University Press, 1987), pp. 164–85.

39. Sartori, *Democratic Theory*, pp. 228–50. Sartori's political agenda is clear. As he writes, with the challenge presented by the Italian Communist Party perhaps in the back of his mind: "Where democracy is challenged, provisional answers will not do. . . . The fundamental values and beliefs of our civilization are at stake, and it is through definitions and the corresponding images of democracy that we are playing the game and that we are

going to win or lose it, because it is through definitions, and the ideas that they convey, that we make our choices" (p. 11).

40. Gabriel Almond and Sidney Verba, *The Civic Culture: Political Attitudes and Democracy in Five Nations* (Princeton: Princeton University Press, 1963).

41. Sartori, *Democratic Theory*, p. 246.

42. See Stephen Holmes, *The Anatomy of Antiliberalism* (Cambridge: Harvard University Press, 1993).

43. For a similar argument, see Terence Ball, "American Political Science in its Postwar Context," in James Farr and Raymond Seidelman, eds., *Discipline and History: Political Science in the United States* (Ann Arbor: University of Michigan Press, 1993), pp. 207–22.

44. On the logic of this process, see Downs, *Economic Theory of Democracy*.

45. On the American version of this theme, see Alan Wolfe, *America's Impasse* (New York: Pantheon, 1986); Godfrey Hodgson, *America in Our Time* (New York: Vintage, 1985).

46. See Francis Fukuyama, "Democracy's Future: The Primacy of Culture," *Journal of Democracy* 6 (January 1995), 7–14.

47. Charles S. Maier, "Democracy and Its Discontents," *Foreign Affairs* 73 (July/August 1994), 48–64.

48. See Schmitter, "Democracy's Future: Liberal, Preliberal, or Postliberal?" and François Furet, "Europe after Utopianism," in *Journal of Democracy* 6 (January 1995).

49. See Jürgen Habermas, "Citizenship and National Identity: Some Reflections on the Future of Europe," *Praxis International* 12 (April 1992), 1–19.

50. An American contribution to this discourse is Peter Brimelow, *Alien Nation* (New York: Free Press, 1994), a best-seller about the danger foreign immigrants pose to the American way of life.

51. See Chantal Mouffe, "The End of Politics and the Rise of the Radical Right," *Dissent* 42 (Fall 1995), 498–502.

52. See, for example, Anna Elisabetta Galeotti, "Citizenship and National Identity: A Place for Toleration," *Political Theory* 21 (April 1993), 585–605; and Norma Claire Moruzzi, "A Problem with Headscarves: Contemporary Complexities of Political and Social Identity," *Political Theory* 22 (November 1994), 653–720. See also William Kymlicka, *Multicultural Citizenship* (New York: Oxford University Press, 1995).

53. See Lester Thurow, *The Future of Capitalism* (New York: Morrow, 1996); Benjamin Barber, *Jihad vs. McWorld* (New York: Times Books, 1995); and Bennett Harrison, *Lean and Mean: The Changing Landscape of Corporate Power in the Age of Flexibility* (New York: Basic Books, 1994). See also David Gordon, *Fat and Mean: The Corporate Squeeze of Working Americans and the Myth of Managerial Downsizing* (New York: Free Press, 1996).

54. See Ulrich Beck, "The Reinvention of Politics: Towards a Theory of Reflexive Modernization," in Ulrich Beck, Anthony Giddens, and Scott Lash, *Reflexive Modernization:*

Politics, Tradition, and Aesthetics in the Modern Social Order (Stanford: Stanford University Press, 1994), p. 8. See also Beck, *Risk Society: Towards a New Modernity* (London: Sage, 1992) and *Ecological Politics in the Age of Risk* (Cambridge: Polity Press, 1994).

55. On the causes of this decline of the welfare state, see Jürgen Habermas, *Legitimation Crisis* (Boston: Beacon Press, 1975); Claus Offe, *Contradictions of the Welfare State* (Cambridge: MIT Press, 1984); Nancy Fraser, *Unruly Practices: Power, Discourse, and Gender in Contemporary Social Theory* (Minneapolis: University of Minnesota Press, 1989); and, in another vein, Christopher Lasch, *The True and Only Heaven: Progress and Its Critics* (New York: Norton, 1991), especially pp. 476–532.

56. Jürgen Habermas, "The New Obscurity: The Crisis of the Welfare State and the Exhaustion of Utopian Energies," in *The New Conservatism: Cultural Criticism and the Historians' Debate* (Cambridge: MIT Press, 1989), pp. 50–51.

57. See Samuel P. Huntington, "The Democratic Distemper," *Public Interest*, July 1976, pp. 9–38.

58. In a fascinating retrospective, David Easton has also mentioned the role of McCarthyism in promoting an "end of ideology" conformism, "driving underground an interest in social reform and critical theory." See David Easton, "Political Science in the United States: Past and Present," in David Easton, John G. Gunnell, and Luigi Graziano, *The Development of Political Science: A Comparative Survey* (New York: Routledge, 1991), pp. 280–81.

59. See Claus Offe, "New Social Movements: Challenging the Boundaries of Institutional Politics," *Social Research* 52 (Winter 1985), 817–68.

60. Robert A. Dahl, *Democracy and Its Critics* (New Haven: Yale University Press, 1991). See also Charles Lindblom, *Politics and Markets* (New York: Harper Torchbooks, 1977), and John Manley, "Neopluralism: A Class Analysis of Pluralism I and II," *American Political Science Review* 77 (June 1983), 268–83.

61. See Amy Gutmann and Dennis Thompson, *Deliberative Democracy* (Cambridge: Harvard University Press, 1996); James Fishkin, *Democracy and Deliberation: New Directions for Democratic Reform* (New Haven: Yale University Press, 1991) and *The Voice of the People: Public Opinion and Democracy* (New Haven: Yale University Press, 1995); and Jean Elshtain, *Democracy on Trial* (New York: Basic Books, 1995).

62. See Robert D. Putnam, *Making Democracy Work: Civic Traditions in Modern Italy* (Princeton: Princeton University Press, 1993), "Bowling Alone: America's Declining Social Capital," *Journal of Democracy* 6 (January 1995), 65–78, and "The Strange Disappearance of Civic America," *American Prospect*, no. 24 (Winter 1996), 34–38. And see the symposia about this work featured in *Politics and Society* 24 (March 1996) and *American Prospect*, no. 25 (March/April 1996).

63. The literature on civil society that has developed since 1989 is immense. See especially Jean Cohen and Andrew Arato, *Civil Society and Political Theory* (Cambridge: MIT University Press, 1992); and the special section, "Rethinking Civil Society," *Journal of Democracy* 5 (July 1994).

Chapter 2. The Strange Silence of Political Theory

1. See Timothy Garton Ash, *The Magic Lantern* (New York: Random House, 1991).

2. See Francis Fukuyama, "The End of History," *National Interest* 16 (Summer 1989); Jean-François Revel, *Democracy against Itself: The Future of the Democratic Impulse* (New York: Free Press, 1993); and Larry Diamond and Marc Plattner, eds., *The Global Resurgence of Democracy* (Baltimore: Johns Hopkins University Press, 1993).

3. Jean-Luc Nancy's *"La Comparution/*The Compearance: From the Existence of 'Communism' to the Community of 'Existence,' "* Political Theory* 20 (August 1992), 371–98, is an extraordinarily dense essay that makes no explicit reference to political events or movements but seems occasioned by the so-called end of history.

4. Robert H. Dix, "Eastern Europe's Implications for Revolutionary Theory," *Polity* 24 (Winter 1991), 227–42, presents a critial review of the explanatory approach of Theda Skocpol.

5. Many of these articles are collected in Diamond and Plattner, *Global Resurgence of Democracy.*

6. Immanuel Kant, *On History*, ed. Lewis White Beck (Indianapolis: Bobbs-Merrill, 1963), p. 148.

7. R. R. Palmer, *The Age of the Democratic Revolution* (Princeton: Princeton University Press, 1959).

8. Milan Kundera, "The Tragedy of Central Europe," *New York Review of Books*, April 26, 1984. See also Timothy Garton Ash, "Does Central Europe Exist?" in *The Uses of Adversity: Essays on the Fate of Central Europe* (New York: Random House, 1989), and Tony Judt, "The Rediscovery of Central Europe," *Daedalus* 119 (Winter 1990), 23–54.

9. See, for example, Richard Rorty, "Philosophy as a Kind of Writing: An Essay on Derrida," in *Consequences of Pragmatism* (Minneapolis: University of Minnesota Press, 1982), pp. 90–109.

10. See my "Civil Society and the Spirit of Revolt," *Dissent* (Summer 1993), 356–61; Jean Elshtain, "Politics without Cliche," *Social Research* 60 (Fall 1993), 433–44; Jeffrey C. Goldfarb, *Beyond Glasnost: The Post-Totalitarian Mind* (Chicago: University of Chicago Press, 1989) and *After the Fall: The Pursuit of Democracy in Central Europe* (New York: Basic Books, 1992); and especially Jean Cohen and Andrew Arato, *Civil Society and Political Theory* (Cambridge: MIT Press, 1992).

11. Ralf Dahrendorf offers such an interpretation in *Reflections on the Revolution in Europe* (New York: Random House, 1990). A similar though more nuanced interpretation is presented in Jürgen Habermas, "What Does Socialism Mean Today? The Revolutions of Recuperation and the Need for New Thinking," in Robin Blackburn, ed., *After the Fall: The Failure of Communism and the Future of Socialism* (London: Verso, 1991), pp. 25–46.

12. I briefly address this theme in "Adam Michnik: Politics and the Church," *Salmagundi*, no. 103 (Summer 1994), 198–212, an essay on Michnik's pathbreaking *The Church and the Left*, ed. and trans. David Ost (Chicago: University of Chicago Press, 1992).

13. See David Truman, "Disillusion and Regeneration: The Quest for a Discipline," *American Political Science Review* 59 (December 1965), 867–74.

14. See J. Peter Euben, "Political Science and Political Silence," in Sanford Levinson, ed., *Power and Community* (New York: Vintage, 1970), and William E. Connolly, *Political Science and Ideology* (New York: Atherton, 1967).

15. Thomas Kuhn, *The Structure of Scientific Revolutions*, 2d ed. (Chicago: University of Chicago Press, 1972), p. 35.

16. Quentin Skinner, "Meaning and Understanding in the History of Ideas," *History and Theory* 8 (1969), 3–53.

17. For an overview, see John Gunnell, *Political Theory: Tradition and Interpretation* (Boston: Winthrop, 1979).

18. See, for example, Michael Shapiro, "Eighteenth-Century Intimations of Modernity: Adam Smith and the Marquis de Sade," *Political Theory* 21 (May 1993), 273–93; Stephen K. White, "Burke on Politics, Aesthetics, and the Dangers of Modernity," *Political Theory* 21 (August 1993), 507–27; and William E. Connolly, *The Augustinian Imperative: A Reflection on the Politics of Morality* (Newbury Park, Calif.: Sage, 1993).

19. On this aversion see Ian Shapiro, "Gross Concepts in Political Argument," *Political Theory* 17 (1989), 51–76, and *Political Criticism* (Berkeley: University of California Press, 1990), pp. 265–98.

20. Fred Dallmayr, "Postmetaphysics and Democracy," *Political Theory* 21 (February 1993), 101.

21. For Lefort's work, which came out of his very practical reflections as a Trotskyist associated with the French journal *Socialisme ou Barbarie?* see John B. Thompson, ed., *The Political Forms of Modern Society* (Cambridge: MIT Press, 1986). For Ackerman's explorations of this dialectic, see *We the People: Foundations* (Cambridge: Harvard University Press, 1991) and *The Future of Liberal Revolution* (New Haven: Yale University Press, 1992).

22. William E. Connolly, "The Politics of Territorial Democracy," in *Identity\ Difference: Democratic Negotiations of Political Paradox* (Ithaca: Cornell University Press, 1991), p. 219. My criticism of the way this passage avoids first-order inquiry is also registered by Iris Marion Young in her review of the book in *Political Theory* 20 (August 1992), 513.

23. Michel Foucault, "Nietzsche, Genealogy, History," in *The Foucault Reader*, ed. Paul Rabinow (New York: Pantheon, 1984), p. 76.

24. See, for example, Bonnie Honig, "Toward an Agonistic Feminism," in Bonnie Honig, ed., *Feminist Interpretations of Hannah Arendt* (University Park: Penn State University Press, 1995), and Wendy Brown, "Wounded Attachments," *Political Theory* 21 (August 1993), 390–410. Some of Connolly's earlier work on American politics, originally published in the short-lived journal *democracy*, also bears mention in this connection. See especially the essays collected in his *Politics and Ambiguity* (Madison: University of Wisconsin Press, 1987).

25. For an interesting criticism of the tendency to confuse the difference between aca-

demic discourse and political reality beyond the ivory tower, see Henry Louis Gates Jr., "The Master's Pieces: On Canon Formation and the Afro-American Tradition," in Dominick LaCapra, ed., *The Bounds of Race: Perspectives on Hegemony and Resistance* (Ithaca: Cornell University Press, 1991).

26. To call attention to this fact is not to invoke some kind of nativist preference for "plain English," nor is it to deny the insight that has been derived from these French and German idioms. Far be it from me, someone whose last book was on Hannah Arendt and Albert Camus, to deny that. It is, though, to call attention to the intellectual and literary styles often associated with specific Continental idioms, such as Derridaean deconstruction and Habermassian critical theory, and to note some of the drawbacks of these styles.

27. George Orwell, "Politics and the English Language," in *A Collection of Essays* (New York: Harcourt, Brace, 1953), p. 166.

28. Daniel J. Boorstin, *The Genius of American Politics* (Chicago: University of Chicago Press, 1953).

29. The writing of George Kateb seeks to capture this spirit. See *The Inner Ocean: Individualism and Democratic Culture* (Ithaca: Cornell University Press, 1992).

30. See Peter T. Manicas, *A History and Philosophy of Science* (London: Blackwell, 1989), and C. Wright Mills, *Sociology and Pragmatism* (London: Oxford University Press, 1948).

31. I am not claiming that either the critique of Marxism or the history of ideas has been rendered pointless, but only that it is astonishing how much more powerfully they seem to concern political theorists than recent events that certainly place a different coloration on these pursuits.

32. C. Wright Mills, *The Sociological Imagination* (London: Oxford University Press, 1959).

33. On this score see John G. Gunnell, *The Descent of Political Theory* (Chicago: University of Chicago Press, 1993).

34. While Wolin's book has helped to license an excessive preoccupation with "the tradition of political philosophy" among many political theorists, his own work has always been marked by an engagement with current political concerns, from his interventions during the Berkeley Free Speech Movement (see Seymour Martin Lipset and Sheldon S. Wolin, eds., *The Berkeley Student Revolt* [New York: Anchor, 1965]), to his editorship of the journal *democracy*, to some of the essays published in *The Presence of the Past* (Baltimore: Johns Hopkins University Press, 1989).

35. For some indications of this concern with subdisciplinary identity, see William E. Connolly, "From the Editor," *Political Theory* 17 (February 1989), 3–7; and Tracy Strong, "From the Editor," *Political Theory* 18 (February 1990), 3–5, and "From the Editor," *Political Theory* 20 (February 1992), 4–7.

36. For an interesting reflection, see George Steiner, "The Ephemeral Genre and the End of Literature," *New Perspectives Quarterly* 13 (Fall 1996), 46–49.

37. Vaclav Havel, "The Power of the Powerless," in *Living in Truth* (London: Faber & Faber, 1989), p. 54.

38. Ralph Waldo Emerson, "The American Scholar," in Robert E. Spiller, ed., *Selected Essays, Lectures, and Poems of Ralph Waldo Emerson* (New York: Pocket Books, 1977), p. 68.

Chapter 3. Hannah Arendt as Dissenting Intellectual

1. The classical reading of Arendt is nicely stated in John Gunnell, *The Descent of Political Theory* (Chicago: University of Chicago Press, 1994). This view is still quite prominent, especially among non-political theorists unfamiliar with the nuances of Arendt's texts. But it has recently come under fire. See, for example, Dana Villa, "Beyond Good and Evil: Arendt, Nietzsche, and the Aestheticization of Political Action," *Political Theory* 20 (1992), 274–308, and the criticisms offered in Bonnie Honig, "The Politics of Agonism," and my own "Situating Hannah Arendt on Action and Politics," in *Political Theory* 21 (August 1993), 528–40. A number of recent books situate Arendt in the twentieth-century context. See Elisabeth Young-Bruehl's authoritative biography, *Hannah Arendt: For Love of the World* (New Haven: Yale University Press, 1982); Dagmar Barnouw, *Visible Spaces: Hannah Arendt and the German-Jewish Experience* (Baltimore: Johns Hopkins University Press, 1990); Margaret Canovan, *Hannah Arendt: A Reinterpretation of Her Political Thought* (Cambridge: Cambridge University Press, 1992); Jeffrey C. Isaac, *Arendt, Camus, and Modern Rebellion* (New Haven: Yale University Press, 1992); and Richard Bernstein, *Hannah Arendt and the Jewish Question* (Cambridge: MIT Press, 1996).

2. Joanna Vechiarelli Scott, "The Methodology of Reaction: Hannah Arendt and the Uses of History," paper presented at the 1988 Meeting of the American Political Science Association, Washington, D.C., p. 12; Alexander Bloom, *Prodigal Sons: The New York Intellectuals and Their World* (New York: Oxford University Press, 1986), p. 220.

3. Alan Wald, *The New York Intellectuals: The Rise and Decline of the Anti-Stalinist Left from the 1930s to the 1980s* (Chapel Hill: University of North Carolina Press, 1987), p. 269.

4. Hannah Arendt, "On Hannah Arendt," in Melvyn A. Hill, ed., *Hannah Arendt: The Recovery of the Public World* (New York: St. Martin's Press, 1979), p. 334.

5. Albert Camus, "Return to Tipasa," in *Lyrical and Critical Essays* (New York: Knopf, 1968), p. 165.

6. Irving Howe, "This Age of Conformity," *Partisan Review* 21 (January/February 1954), 8.

7. On Macdonald, a close friend of Arendt, who was at the center of the intellectual circles in which she moved, see Gregory Sumner, *Dwight Macdonald and the "politics" Circle* (Ithaca: Cornell University Press, 1996).

8. On this matter see Peter Clecak, *Radical Paradoxes: Dilemmas of the American Left, 1945–1970* (New York: Harper & Row, 1973).

9. See Maurice Isserman, *If I Had a Hammer: The Death of the Old Left and the Birth of the New Left* (New York: Basic Books, 1987), pp. 77–124.

10. Young-Bruehl recounts this incident in *Hannah Arendt*, pp. 308–18. For interesting discussions of this particular matter, see Hannah Pitkin, "The Return of 'The Blob,'"

in Bonnie Honig, ed., *Feminist Reinterpretations of Hannah Arendt* (University Park: Penn State University Press, 1995).

11. See James Bohman, "The Moral Costs of Political Pluralism: The Dilemmas of Difference and Equality in Arendt's 'Reflections on Little Rock,'" in Larry May and Jerome Kohn, eds., *Hannah Arendt: Twenty Years Later* (Cambridge: MIT Press, 1996).

12. See Herbert J. Spiro and Benjamin R. Barber, "Counter-Ideological Uses of 'Totalitarianism,'" *Politics and Society* 1 (November 1970), 3–22, and Les K. Adler and Thomas G. Patterson, "Red Fascism: The Merger of Nazi Germany and Soviet Russia in the American Image of Totalitarianism, 1930s–1950s," *American Historical Review* 75 (April 1970), 1046–64.

13. The following arguments draw from chap. 2 of *Arendt, Camus, and Modern Rebellion*.

14. On this theme see James D. Wilkinson, *The Intellectual Resistance in Europe* (Cambridge: Harvard University Press, 1981).

15. This essay is discussed in Dwight Macdonald, "The Root Is Man," *politics* 3 (April and July 1946), 97–115, 194–214.

16. Many of its themes can be discerned in Arendt's essay "Organized Guilt and Universal Responsibility," *Jewish Frontier*, January 1945, pp. 19–23, which strongly influenced Dwight Macdonald's famous essay "The Responsibility of Peoples."

17. Hannah Arendt, *The Origins of Totalitarianism* (New York: Harcourt Brace Jovanovich, 1973), p. vii.

18. See Robert Booth Fowler, *Believing Skeptics: American Political Intellectuals, 1945–1964* (Westport, Conn.: Greenwood Press, 1978).

19. See her paraphrase of Constant's remark about Rousseau in *The Human Condition* (Chicago: University of Chicago Press), published in 1958, hardly a moment hospitable to Marxist ideas in the American academy: "Certainly, I shall avoid the company of detractors of a great man. If I happen to agree with them on a single point I grow suspicious of myself; and in order to console myself for having seemed to be of their opinion . . . I feel that I must disavow and keep these false friends away from me as much as I can" (p. 79).

20. Young-Bruehl, *Hannah Arendt*, pp. 274–92.

21. Hannah Arendt, "The Ex-Communists," *Commonweal*, March 20, 1953, p. 596.

22. Ibid., p. 599. For a parallel, see Henry Steele Commager, *Freedom, Loyalty, Dissent* (New York: Oxford University Press, 1954), especially p. 58.

23. Young-Bruehl, *Hannah Arendt*, p. 287.

24. See Peter Coleman's useful if uncritical *The Liberal Conspiracy: The Congress for Cultural Freedom and the Struggle for the Mind of Postwar Europe* (New York: Free Press, 1989), pp. 15–32.

25. Hannah Arendt, "The Aftermath of Nazi Rule: Report from Germany," *Commentary* 19 (October 1950), 342–53.

26. Hannah Arendt, "Dream and Nightmare," *Commonweal*, September 10, 1954, p. 553.

27. For an interesting reconstruction of the ideological temper of this moment, see Tony Judt, *Past Imperfect: French Intellectuals, 1944–1956* (Berkeley: University of California Press, 1992).

28. Arendt, "Dream and Nightmare," pp. 578–80. See also Karl Jaspers, *The Future of Mankind* (Chicago: University of Chicago Press, 1961). Jonathan Schell, *The Fate of the Earth* (New York: Knopf, 1982), sounds Arendtian themes, especially on pp. 118–78.

29. Hannah Arendt, "The Cold War and the West: An Exchange," *Partisan Review* 29 (Winter 1962), 11–13.

30. Ibid., p. 19.

31. Quoted in Young-Bruehl, *Hannah Arendt*, p. 208.

32. Daniel Boorstin, *The Genius of American Politics* (Chicago: University of Chicago Press, 1953).

33. Hannah Arendt, *On Revolution* (New York: Penguin, 1977), pp. 215–82. These issues are discussed in more detail in Chapter 5 below.

34. Hannah Arendt, *Crises of the Republic* (New York: Harcourt Brace Jovanovich, 1972), pp. 39–40.

35. Ibid., p. 173.

36. For incisive elaborations on this theme on the part of postcolonial writers, see Kwame Anthony Appiah, *In My Father's House: Africa in the Philosophy of Culture* (New York: Oxford University Press, 1992); Kanan Makiya, *Cruelty and Silence: War, Tyranny, Uprising and the Arab World* (New York: Norton, 1993); and Wole Soyinka, *The Open Sore of a Continent: A Personal Narrative of the Nigerian Crisis* (New York: Oxford University Press, 1996).

37. Arendt, "On Violence," in *Crises of the Republic*, 105–11, 116, 118, 89.

38. Arendt, *On Revolution*, p. 278.

39. See Chapter 5 below.

40. Arendt, "Thoughts on Politics and Revolution," in *Crises of the Republic*, p. 232.

41. Hannah Arendt, "Truth and Politics," in *Between Past and Future* (New York: Penguin, 1977), pp. 241–42.

Chapter 4. A New Guarantee on Earth: Human Dignity and the Politics of Human Rights

1. Many of these themes are taken up in Judith Shklar, "Obligation, Loyalty, Exile," *Political Theory* 21 (May 1993), 181–97.

2. See Elisabeth Young-Bruehl, *Hannah Arendt: For Love of the World* (New Haven: Yale University Press, 1982).

3. Hannah Arendt, *The Origins of Totalitarianism* (New York: Harcourt Brace Jovanovich, 1973), p. ix.

4. See Eric Voegelin, "The Origins of Totalitarianism," and Arendt, "A Reply," *Review of Politics* 15 (1953), 68–85, and Jeffrey C. Isaac, *Arendt, Camus, and Modern Rebellion* (New Haven: Yale University Press, 1992), pp. 68–73, 102–4.

5. Arendt, writing about work, comments on "the instrumentalization of the whole

world and the earth, this limitless devaluation of everything given, this process of growing meaninglessness where every end is transformed into a means," in *The Human Condition* (Chicago: University of Chicago Press, 1958), p. 157.

6. On this theme, see Richard Falk, *Human Rights and State Sovereignty* (New York:
Holmes & Meir, 1981), and Stanley Hoffman, *Duties beyond Borders: On the Limits and Possibilities of Ethical International Politics* (Syracuse: Syracuse University Press, 1981).

7. See "We Refugees," in Hannah Arendt, *The Jew as Pariah*, ed. Ron Feldman (New
York: Grove Press, 1978).

8. *Origins of Totalitarianism*, pp. 284–86. Reflecting sardonically on her own experience in a French internment camp, Arendt wrote: "Apparently nobody wants to know that
contemporary history has created a new kind of human beings—the kind that are put into
concentration camps by their foes and internment camps by their friends," in "We Refugees," p. 56.

9. See Immanuel Kant's classic essay "Perpetual Peace: A Philosophical Sketch," in
Political Writings, ed. Hans Reiss, trans. H. B. Nisbet (New York: Cambridge University
Press, 1991).

10. Dwight Macdonald wrote of World War II: "One of the many things I cannot get accustomed to in this war is the fact that the most ancient, beautiful buildings of Europe
may be blasted to bits in a few hours. Rome, Paris, Assisi . . . who knows before they will
join Warsaw, Bath, Coventry, Nuremberg, Frankfort, Kiev, Cologne, Palermo, Naples,
Rotterdam, Cracow, London, and Berlin? It is like living in a house with a maniac who
may rip up the pictures, burn the books, slash up the rugs and furniture at any moment"
(quoted in Gregory Sumner, *Dwight Macdonald and the "politics" Circle* [Ithaca: Cornell
University Press, 1996], pp. 52–53).

11. On this indifference, see Zygmunt Bauman, *Modernity and the Holocaust* (Ithaca:
Cornell University Press, 1989).

12. Hannah Arendt, "Organized Guilt and Universal Responsibility," in *Jew as Pariah*,
pp. 234–45.

13. See Edmund Burke, *Reflections on the Revolution in France* (Harmondsworth: Penguin, 1970), p. 150.

14. A similar point, drawn explicitly from Arendt, is made by Julia Kristeva in *Strangers
to Ourselves*, trans. Leon S. Roudiez (New York: Columbia University Press, 1991), pp.
151–54.

15. Ibid., p. 153.

16. George Kateb, "Death and Politics: Hannah Arendt's Reflections on the American
Constitution," *Social Research* 54 (1987), 612–13. For a similar view, see Martin Jay, "Hannah Arendt," *Partisan Review* 45 (1978), 348–68. For both Kateb and Jay, Arendtian action
is disconnected from moral principles and thus inhospitable to the rights that are the
achievement of liberal democracy. Jay explicitly links Arendt to the discourse of "political
existentialism" also developed by Carl Schmitt and other proto-fascist writers.

17. Kateb cites this assertion from *On Revolution* in "Death and Politics," p. 613.

18. See Isaac, *Arendt, Camus*, pp. 110–18.

19. This Arendtian point is developed beautifully in Vaclav Havel's essay "A Word about Words," in *Open Letters: Selected Writings, 1965–1990* (New York: Vintage, 1992).

20. Hannah Arendt, "What Is Existenz Philosophie?" *Partisan Review* 13 (1946), 37.

21. See Burke's lament that "all the pleasing illusions . . . are to be dissolved by this new conquering empire of light and reason. All the decent drapery of life is to be rudely torn off. All the super-added ideas, furnished from the wardrobe of a moral imagination . . . as necessary to cover the defects of our naked shivering nature, and to raise it to dignity in our own estimation, are to be exploded as a ridiculous, absurd, antiquated fashion" (*Reflections*, p. 171).

22. Note the importance of promising, consent, and dissent in Arendt's work. See Arendt, *Human Condition*, pp. 243–47, and "Civil Disobedience," in *Crises of the Republic* (New York: Harcourt Brace Jovanovich, 1972), pp. 83–102.

23. A similar point is developed in Wayne Booth, "Individualism and the Mystery of the Social Self; or, Does Amnesty International Have a Leg to Stand On?" in Barbara Johnson, ed., *Freedom and Interpretation: The Oxford Amnesty Lectures 1992* (New York: Basic Books, 1993).

24. Vaclav Havel, "Letter to Gustav Husak," in *Living in Truth* (London: Faber & Faber, 1986), p. 12.

25. A quite similar point is made in connection with the problem of Third World poverty in Amartya Sen, "Freedom and Needs," *New Republic*, January 10–17, 1994, pp. 31–38.

26. She writes that "one is tempted to recommend the story as required reading in political science for all students who wish to learn something about the enormous power potential inherent in non-violent action and in resistance to an opponent possessing vastly superior means of violence" (*Eichmann in Jerusalem* [New York: Penguin, 1977], p. 171). For a discussion of the importance of resistance to totalitarianism as a model of praxis for Arendt, see Isaac, *Arendt, Camus*, chap. 2.

27. Many commentators have failed to see the importance of these themes in Arendt's writing because of an unfortunate tendency to dehistoricize Arendt. See Isaac, "Situating Hannah Arendt on Action and Politics," *Political Theory* 21 (August 1993), 534–40.

28. Arendt, "What Is Existenz Philosophie?" pp. 55–56.

29. Arendt, *Human Condition*, pp. 26–27.

30. Arendt, *Origins of Totalitarianism*, p. 296.

31. Ibid., pp. 297–98.

32. On this score there are, I believe, similarities between Arendt and Claude Lefort, particularly regarding Lefort's notion of a "right to have rights," that is, the power to articulate rights claims. See "Politics and Human Rights," in *The Political Forms of Modern Society* (Cambridge: MIT Press, 1986). It is ironic that Lefort misses this similarity in his essay "Hannah Arendt and the Political," in *Democracy and Political Theory* (Minneapolis: University of Minnesota Press, 1988), p. 55.

33. Hannah Arendt, *On Revolution* (New York: Penguin, 1977), p. 108.

34. Hannah Arendt, "The Ex-Communists," *Commonweal* 57 (1953), 599.

35. Arendt experienced both of these limits in a very personal way during the 1950s, when she feared that her husband, Heinrich Blucher, might be deported for his radicalism under the terms of the McCarran-Walters Security Act, which allowed for the expulsion of foreign-born and thus tainted "subversives." See Young-Bruehl, *Hannah Arendt*, p. 288. As Blucher wrote to Arendt: "it seems that one can now deprive someone of citizenship with a simple denunciation . . . And how soon these 'Born American' people could become a Master Race" (p. 275).

36. Arendt, *Eichmann in Jerusalem*, pp. 270–73. See also Karl Jaspers, *The Future of Mankind* (Chicago: University of Chicago Press, 1961).

37. For an endorsement of this idea based explicitly on the writings of Arendt, see Alain Finkelkraut, *Remembering in Vain: The Klaus Barbie Trial and Crimes against Humanity* (New York: Columbia University Press, 1992).

38. Hannah Arendt, "Karl Jaspers: Citizen of the World," in *Men in Dark Times* (New York: Harcourt, Brace & World, 1968), pp. 83–84. This sentiment was influentially developed during the early 1980s by Jonathan Schell in *The Fate of the Earth* (New York: Knopf, 1979), which explicitly credits the influence of Arendt.

39. Arendt, "Karl Jaspers," p. 93.

40. See Jürgen Habermas, "Historical Consciousness and Post-Traditional Identity," in *The New Conservatism* (Cambridge: MIT Press, 1990), and "Citizenship and National Identity: Some Reflections on the Future of Europe," *Praxis International* 12 (1992), 1–19. See also Yael Tamir, *Liberal Nationalism* (Princeton: Princeton University Press, 1993), and Julia Kristeva, *Nations without Nationalism* (New York: Columbia University Press, 1994).

41. Hannah Arendt, "Peace or Armistice in the Near East," in *Jew as Pariah*, p. 201.

42. On this subject see Dagmar Barnouw, *Visible Spaces: Hannah Arendt and the German-Jewish Experience* (Baltimore: Johns Hopkins University Press, 1990), and Richard J. Bernstein, *Hannah Arendt and the Jewish Question* (Cambridge: MIT Press, 1996). For argument along Arendtian lines, see Mark Heller and Sari Nusseibeh, *No Trumpets, No Drums: A Two-State Settlement of the Israeli-Palestinian Conflict* (New York: Hill & Wang, 1991).

43. As she writes: "Politics deals with men, nationals of many countries and heirs to many pasts" (*Men in Dark Times*, p. 81).

44. See Arendt, *On Revolution*, pp. 88–89, for an interesting discussion of the difference between the sentiments of compassion and pity and solidarity, the latter "a principle that can guide action."

45. Albert Camus, "Neither Victims nor Executioners," in *Between Hell and Reason*, trans. Alexandre de Gramont (Hanover, N.H.: Wesleyan University Press, 1991), pp. 135–36.

46. Hannah Arendt, "Thoughts on Politics and Revolution," in *Crises of the Republic* (New York: Harcourt Brace Jovanovich, 1972), pp. 231–33. I have elaborated at length on the affinities and connections between Arendt and Camus in my *Arendt, Camus*, especially on pp. 105–76.

47. See James Miller, "The Pathos of Novelty: Hannah Arendt's Image of Freedom in the Modern World," in Melvyn A. Hill, ed., *Hannah Arendt: The Recovery of the Public World* (New York: St. Martin's Press, 1979).

48. My point here bears some similarity to the argument made in Ernesto Laclau and Chantal Mouffe, *Hegemony and Socialist Strategy* (London: Verso, 1985). On the theme of complex identity formation, see Bonnie Honig, "Difference, Dilemmas, and the Politics of Home," *Social Research* (Fall 1994), 563–98.

49. On these links see H. Gordon Skilling, *Samizdat and an Independent Society in Central and Eastern Europe* (London: Macmillan, 1989), and Hilary Wainwright, *Arguments for a New Left* (London: Routledge, 1994).

50. Mary Kaldor, Introduction to *The New Détente*, ed. Mary Kaldor et al. (London: Verso, 1989), p. 15.

51. Mary Kaldor, "Speech to the Closing Session of the Helsinki Citizens' Assembly," in *Europe from Below: An East–West Dialogue*, ed. Mary Kaldor (London: Verso, 1991), p. 215.

52. See United Nations High Commissioner for Refugees, *The State of the World's Refugees, 1993: The Challenge of Protection* (New York: Penguin, 1993), and Aristide Zolberg et al., *Escape from Violence: Conflict and the Refugee Crisis in the Developing World* (New York: Oxford University Press, 1989).

53. Human Rights Watch, *Human Rights Watch World Report, 1992* (New York, 1992), p. 1.

54. Arendt, *Origins of Totalitarianism*, p. vii.

Chapter 5. Oases in the Desert: Hannah Arendt on Democratic Politics

1. Sheldon Wolin, "Hannah Arendt: Democracy and the Political," *Salmagundi* 60 (Spring/Summer 1983), 3.

2. Hannah Arendt, *On Revolution* (New York: Penguin, 1977), pp. 275–76.

3. See Margaret Canovan, "The Contradictions of Hannah Arendt's Political Thought," *Political Theory* 6 (February 1978), 5–6. Canovan's article, because of its sophisticated treatment of ambiguities in Arendt, is particularly notable because even she assumes that Arendt's talk of elites must be antidemocratic. See also George Kateb, "Arendt and Representative Democracy," *Salmagundi*, no. 60 (Spring/Summer 1983), 20–59. A more nuanced account, one more consistent with my argument, can be found in Canovan, *Hannah Arendt: A Reinterpretation of Her Political Thought* (New York: Cambridge University Press, 1992), pp. 233–43.

4. See Ian Hampsher-Monk, "The Historical Study of Democracy," in Graeme Duncan, ed., *Democratic Theory and Practice* (New York: Cambridge University Press, 1983), and Russell Hanson, "Democracy," in Terence Ball, James Farr, and Russell Hanson, eds., *Political Innovation and Conceptual Change* (New York: Cambridge University Press, 1989).

5. On the elusive, almost mythical character of Arendt's construction of a revolution-

ary tradition, see James Miller, "The Pathos of Novelty: Hannah Arendt's Image of Freedom in the Modern World," in Melvyn Hill, ed., *Hannah Arendt: The Recovery of the Public World* (New York: St. Martin's Press, 1979).

6. The classic statement of this theme is Robert Michels, *Political Parties: A Sociological Study of the Oligarchical Tendencies of Modern Democracy*, trans. Eden and Cedar Paul (New York: Crowell-Collier, 1962), especially pp. 43–51.

7. Canovan, "Contradictions," p. 15.

8. See Arendt, *On Revolution*, pp. 255–75. Arendt also commented, "From the revolutions of 1848 to the Hungarian revolution of 1956, the European working class, by virtue of being the only organized and hence the leading section of the people, has written one of the most glorious and probably the most promising chapter of recent history" (*The Human Condition* [Chicago: University of Chicago Press, 1958], p. 215).

9. This is why she so strenuously objected to Rousseau's conception of the "general will" (*On Revolution*, pp. 74–89). Arendt rejects the idea that there is a single authoritative source of power, and that "the people" can be seen as a homogeneous entity in which this power resides. The clearest statements of the theme of plurality are to be found in Arendt, *The Human Condition*, and *Lectures on Kant's Political Philosophy*, ed. Ronald Beiner (Chicago: University of Chicago Press, 1982).

10. See Robert A. Dahl, *Who Governs?* (New Haven: Yale University Press, 1961).

11. See Wolin, "Hannah Arendt," pp. 5–6.

12. See Richard Wolin, *The Politics of Being: The Political Thought of Martin Heidegger* (New York: Columbia University Press, 1990), and Stephen K. White, *Political Theory and Postmodernism* (New York: Cambridge University Press, 1991), pp. 31–54.

13. See Alan Megill, *Prophets of Extremity* (Berkeley: University of California Press, 1985), and Jürgen Habermas, *The Philosophical Discourse of Modernity* (Cambridge: MIT Press, 1987).

14. John Dewey, *The Public and Its Problems* (Chicago: Swallow Press, 1927), pp. 134–35.

15. C. Wright Mills, *The Sociological Imagination* (New York: Oxford University Press, 1959), pp. 170–73.

16. George Kateb acknowledges this stance in *Hannah Arendt: Politics, Conscience, Evil* (Totowa, N.J.: Rowman & Allanheld, 1983), pp. 70–74.

17. Arendt, *Human Condition*, p. 159.

18. The metaphorical character of the connection between mass politics and democratic participation has long been acknowledged by democratic theorists. Dahl, for example, strenuously distinguishes between democracy and polyarchy, claiming that the latter only approximates the values of the former. Under polyarchy elections are the central means of citizen participation, and elections reflect the preferences of the citizens in only the roughest of senses, "insuring that political leaders will be *somewhat* responsive to the preferences of *some* ordinary citizens." See Robert A. Dahl, *A Preface to Democratic Theory* (Chicago: University of Chicago Press, 1956), pp. 130–32.

19. The same point can be made about her argument for excluding "the social" from politics—that "the social" is for her a functional rather than a structural category, de-

noting an unreflective *way of being* rather than any particular kinds of concerns. See Bonnie Honig, *Political Theory and the Displacement of Politics* (Ithaca: Cornell University Press, 1993), pp. 76–125, and "Toward an Agonistic Feminism," in Bonnie Honig, ed., *Feminist Reinterpretations of Hannah Arendt* (University Park: Penn State University Press, 1995); and Nancy Fraser, *Unruly Practices: Power, Discourse, and Gender in Contemporary Social Theory* (Minneapolis: University of Minnesota Press, 1989). I examine inconsistencies in Arendt's treatment of the social in *Arendt, Camus, and Modern Rebellion* (New Haven: Yale University Press, 1992), pp. 158–66. Arendt's view of the social question does not sit easily with any conception of democracy, though it is not, I believe, inconsistent with democracy. But for the purposes of this chapter, which is concerned principally with Arendt's conception of elementary republics and elites, I will bracket her treatment of the social question.

20. Her method is indicated in an essay on Walter Benjamin, in which she writes about a kind of thinking that "delves into the depths of the past . . . not in order to resuscitate it the way it was and to contribute to the renewal of extinct ages [but to help it] survive in new crystallized forms and shapes." See "Walter Benjamin, 1892–1940," in *Men in Dark Times* (New York: Harcourt, Brace & World, 1968), pp. 205–6.

21. Arendt, *On Revolution*, p. 256.

22. See John F. Sitton, "Hannah Arendt's Argument for Council Democracy," *Polity* 20 (Fall 1987), 80–100, and Canovan, *Hannah Arendt*, pp. 232–38.

23. Canovan, "Contradictions," p. 18.

24. Ibid., p. 19.

25. Kateb, "Representative Democracy," pp. 56–58; see also George Kateb, *The Inner Ocean: Individualism and Democratic Culture* (Ithaca: Cornell University Press, 1992), pp. 1–76.

26. See Michels, *Political Parties*; Otto Kirchheimer, "Germany: The Vanishing Opposition," in Robert A. Dahl, ed., *Politial Opposition in Western Democracies* (New Haven: Yale University Press, 1966); Franz Neumann, *The Democratic and the Authoritarian State* (New York: Free Press, 1957); and Carl Schmitt, *The Crisis of Parliamentary Democracy* (Cambridge: MIT Press, 1988). The same problems were identified even earlier by Max Weber in "Parliament and Government in a Reconstructed Germany (A Contribution to the Critique of Officialdom and Party Politics)," in his *Economy and Society: An Outline of Interpretive Sociology*, ed. Guenther Roth and Claus Wittich, trans. Ephraim Fischoff et al., 2 vols. (Berkeley: University of California Press, 1978), 2:1381–469. For a more recent account, see Jürgen Habermas, *The Structural Transformation of the Public Sphere* (Cambridge: MIT Press, 1989).

27. See the excellent discussion in Robert R. Westbrook, *John Dewey and American Democracy* (Ithaca: Cornell University Press, 1991).

28. C. Wright Mills, *The Power Elite* (New York: Oxford University Press, 1956).

29. Hannah Arendt, "The Ex-Communists," *Commonweal* 57 (March 1953), 599.

30. See *On Revolution*, pp. 32–33, 268–69, for acknowledgments of the virtues of representative government, and p. 108 on "the protecting mask of a legal personality."

31. See especially her discussion of legality and favorable references to Montesquieu in *The Origins of Totalitarianism* (New York: Harcourt Brace Jovanovich, 1973), pp. 465–67. It is worth noting that Arendt was a consistent supporter of civil liberties. See also Elisabeth Young-Bruehl, *Hannah Arendt: For Love of the World* (New Haven: Yale University Press, 1982), pp. 273–75, 288–89.

32. These themes are explicitly developed in Arendt, *Crises of the Republic* (New York: Harcourt Brace Jovanovich, 1972).

33. See Martin Jay, "The Political Existentialism of Hannah Arendt," in *Permanent Exiles: Essays on the Intellectual Migration from Germany to America* (New York: Columbia University Press, 1986), pp. 237–56; George McKenna, "Bannisterless Politics: Hannah Arendt and Her Children," *History of Political Thought* 5 (1984), 333–60; and Richard Wolin, "Hannah and the Magician," *New Republic*, October 9, 1995, pp. 27–36.

34. See Arendt, "Civil Disobedience," in *Crises of the Republic*, pp. 82–102.

35. See especially Arendt's essay on judgment, "Truth and Politics," in *Between Past and Future* (New York: Penguin, 1977), and her *Lectures on Kant's Political Philosophy*. See also my *Arendt, Camus*, pp. 166–76.

36. Schmitt, *Crisis of Parliamentary Democracy*, pp. 15–17, 9.

37. It is true that Arendt often failed to couch her aguments in these democratic terms, thus lending credence to those who criticized her for counterposing civic virtue and democratic rights. The most egregious instance of this counterposition was her notorious essay "Reflections on Little Rock," *Dissent* 6 (Winter 1959), 45–56, in which she criticized federal efforts to desegregate southern schools in the name of republican values. The subject of this subtle and complex essay is beyond the scope of this chapter, but it is clear that at least in this instance Arendt's conception of extraparliamentary elementary republics put her in close proximity to the "state's rights" arguments of southern segregationists, however different her reasoning was. See the discussion of the antidemocratic potential of grass-roots politics with specific reference to the Ku Klux Klan and the southern White Citizens' Councils in Sara M. Evans and Harry C. Boyte, *Free Spaces: The Sources of Democratic Change in America* (New York: Harper & Row, 1986), pp. 52–60. I am indebted to Michael Wreszin and Frank Warren for calling attention to this problem in Arendt's writing. For an interesting commentary, see James Bohman, "The Moral Costs of Political Pluralism: The Dilemmas of Difference and Equality in Arendt's 'Reflections on Little Rock,'" in Larry May and Jerome Kohn, eds., *Hannah Arendt: Twenty Years Later* (Cambridge: MIT Press, 1996), pp. 53–80.

38. See James Wilkinson, *The Intellectual Resistance in Europe* (Cambridge: Harvard University Press, 1981), and Gregory D. Sumner, *Dwight Macdonald and the "politics" Circle* (Ithaca: Cornell University Press, 1996).

39. Dwight Macdonald, "The Root Is Man, Part II," *politics* 3 (April 1946), 194–214.

40. Sumner, *Dwight Macdonald*, pp. 172–76.

41. See Mills, *Sociological Imagination*, pp. 177–94.

42. Albert Camus, *The Plague*, trans. Stuart Gilbert (New York: Modern Library, 1948), p. 177.

43. Arendt, *On Revolution*, p. 280.

44. Arendt, *Between Past and Future*, pp. 3–4. See Jeffrey C. Isaac, "Civil Society and the Spirit of Revolt," *Dissent* 40 (Summer 1993), 356–61.

45. This kind of criticism is presented in different ways in Canovan, "Contradictions," and Wolin, "Hannah Arendt." Miller, "Pathos of Novelty," offers a more appreciative account, as does Canovan, *Hannah Arendt*.

46. See H. Gordon Skilling, *Charter 77 and Human Rights in Czechoslovakia* (London: Allen & Unwin, 1981), and *Samizdat and an Independent Society in Central and Eastern Europe* (Columbus: Ohio State University Press, 1989). For a more sustained discussion of Charter 77 and its relevance, see Chapter 7 below.

47. Quoted in Vaclav Benda et al., "Parallel Polis, or an Independent Society in Central and Eastern Europe: An Inquiry," *Social Research* 55 (Spring/Summer 1988), 227–29.

48. Quoted ibid., pp. 242–43.

49. Vaclav Havel, "Politics and Conscience," in *Open Letters: Selected Writings, 1965–1990* (New York: Vintage, 1992), p. 267. As I discuss in Chapter 7, Havel consistently relates the tyranny of communism to broader tendencies of modern industrial life and mass society.

50. See Havel, "The Power of the Powerless" in *Open Letters*, pp. 167–71, on "dissident" as a label that is attached to "ordinary people with ordinary cares, different from the rest only in that they say aloud what the rest cannot say or are afraid to say."

51. Quoted in Benda et al., "Parallel Polis," p. 237.

52. Kateb, "Arendt and Representative Democracy," pp. 43–59.

53. See E. E. Schattschneider, *The Semisovereign People* (New York: Holt, Rinehart & Winston, 1960); Theodore Lowi, *The End of Liberalism* (New York: Norton, 1969); and Robert A. Dahl, *Democracy and Its Critics* (New Haven: Yale University Press, 1989).

54. See Quentin Skinner, "The Empirical Theorists of Democracy and Their Critics: A Plague on Both Their Houses," *Political Theory* 4 (1973), 287–306.

55. See Carole Pateman, *Participation and Democratic Theory* (Cambridge: Cambridge University Press, 1970).

56. This criticism has been leveled against writers such as Benjamin Barber, whose *Strong Democracy: Participatory Democracy for a New Age* (Berkeley: University of California Press, 1984) is one of the most influential "participatory" critiques of liberal democracy.

57. See Harry C. Boyte, *The Backyard Revolution: Understanding the New Citizen Movement* (Philadelphia: Temple University Press, 1980), and *Commonwealth* (New York: Free Press, 1989). Andrew Szasz presents a superb account of the environmental justice movement that is consistent with my argument in *Ecopopulism: Toxic Waste and the Movement for Environmental Justice* (Minneapolis: University of Minnesota Press, 1994). One anonymous reviewer asks whether Operation Rescue would also qualify as a grass-roots democratic movement. This is a difficult question to answer within the terms of Arendt's theory. On the one hand, she does not offer any explicit principles of right or justice that would allow one to distinguish Operation Rescue from Planned Parenthood. In some re-

spects both groups represent examples of independent civic initiative and association. On the other hand, Arendt does insist on certain values—equality, participation, plurality, reflexivity—that would exclude certain kinds of political formations—such as neo-fascist organizations or revolutionary sects that are authoritarian in both their methods and their goals—from being considered democratic. These values would also clearly exclude the most extreme anti-abortion protest groups. The question is whether Operation Rescue is such an extreme group. Arendt would probably hold that Operation Rescue is an example of democratic civic initiative as long as it operates in a respectful, peaceful, self-limiting way. She clearly does not offer a theory of prepolitical rights—such as the right to privacy central to liberal democratic theory—on which grounds one could criticize Operation Rescue. This may be a serious limitation of her thought. On the other hand, debates about whether abortion rights are natural or conventional, and about whether they are appropriately secured through the courts or through political contestation, suggest that Arendt's view has certain merits in underscoring the political—contestable—character of such matters.

58. Literature on the importance of civil society develops similar themes, and occasionally acknowledges Arendt's influence. See Jean Cohen and Andrew Arato, *Civil Society and Political Theory* (Cambridge: MIT Press, 1992); John Keane, *Democracy and Civil Society* (London: Verso, 1988); Claude Lefort, *The Political Forms of Modern Society* (Cambridge: MIT Press, 1986); and Alain Touraine, "Social Movements, Revolution, and Democracy," in Reiner Schürmann, ed., *The Public Realm: Essays on Discursive Types in Political Philosophy* (Albany: State University of New York Press, 1989).

59. This point is aptly made in Michael Walzer, "Constitutional Rights and the Shape of Civil Society," in Robert E. Calvert, ed., *The Constitution of the People: Reflections on Citizens and Civil Society* (Lawrence: University of Kansas Press, 1991).

60. See Elisabeth Kiss, "Democracy without Parties?" *Dissent* 39 (Spring 1992), 26–31.

61. See Michael Harrington, *Socialism: Past and Future* (New York: Arcade, 1989), and Gösta Esping-Anderson, *Politics against Markets: The Social Democratic Road to Power* (Princeton: Princeton University Press, 1985).

Chapter 6. The Poverty of Progressivism

1. E. J. Dionne Jr., *Why Americans Hate Politics* (New York: Simon & Schuster, 1991). See also William Greider, *Who Will Tell the People: The Betrayal of American Democracy* (New York: Simon & Schuster, 1992).

2. Dionne's book nicely charts this ascent of the New Right. The best full-length study is Alan Crawford, *Thunder on the Right: The "New Right" and the Politics of Resentment* (New York: Pantheon, 1980). For firsthand accounts, see Richard A. Viguerie, *The New Right: We're Ready to Lead* (Falls Church, Va.: Viguerie, 1981), and Robert W. Whitaker, ed., *The New Right Papers* (New York: St. Martin's Press, 1982).

3. Greider, *Who Will Tell the People*, documents this process. See also Robert D. Put-

nam's "The Strange Disappearance of Civic America," *American Prospect*, no. 24 (Winter 1996).

4. On "culture wars" generally, see Arthur M. Schlesinger Jr., *The Disuniting of America* (New York: Norton, 1992), and David A. Hollinger, *Postethnic America* (New York: Basic Books, 1995). On right-wing extremism, see James Coates, *Armed and Dangerous: The Rise of the Survivalist Right* (New York: Hill & Wang, 1995). After the Oklahoma City bombing the *New York Times* and the *Washington Post* ran innumerable stories about the connections between the rise of the militia movements and the anti-Washington, antiliberal rhetoric of the conservative Republicans.

5. See Chris Tilly, "The Politics of the 'New Inequality,'" *Socialist Review* 20 (January–March 1990), 103–20; Kevin Phillips, *Boiling Point: Democrats, Republicans, and the Decline of Middle-Class Prosperity* (New York: HarperCollins, 1993); Bennett Harrison, *Lean and Mean: The Changing Landscape of Corporate Power in the Age of Flexibility* (New York: Basic Books, 1994); Edward N. Wolff, "How the Pie Is Sliced: America's Growing Concentration of Wealth," *American Prospect*, no. 22 (Summer 1995), 58–65; and Simon Head, "The New, Ruthless Economy," *New York Review of Books*, February 29, 1996.

6. This imbalance is pronounced in John Rawls, *Political Liberalism* (New York: Columbia University Press, 1993), especially pp. xxiv–xxx, 58–62, 133–50. A glance at Rawls's index reveals that there are only nine references to the difference principle in this book, many of them passing. See also Stephen Holmes, "Liberalism for a World of Ethnic Passions and Decaying States," *Social Research* 61 (Fall 1994), 599–610, and "Gag Rules or The Politics of Omission," in Jon Elster and Rune Slagstad, eds., *Constitutionalism and Democracy* (New York: Cambridge University Press, 1988). In a different vein, see Jean Elshtain, *Democracy on Trial* (New York: Basic Books, 1994).

7. See especially James S. Fishkin, *Democracy and Deliberation: New Directions for Democratic Reform* (New Haven: Yale University Press, 1991), and Amy Gutmann, "The Disharmony of Democracy," in John W. Chapman and Ian Shapiro, eds., *NOMOS XXXV: Democratic Community* (New York: New York University Press, 1993).

8. See Robert Putnam, "Bowling Alone," *Journal of Democracy* 6 (January 1995), 65–78; Michael Walzer, "Multiculturalism and Individualism," *Dissent* 41 (Spring 1994), 185–91; Benjamin R. Barber, "An American Civic Forum: Civil Society between Market Individuals and the Political Community," *Social Philosophy and Policy* 13 (Winter, 1996), 269–83; John Keane, *Democracy and Civil Society* (London: Verso, 1991), and Jean Cohen and Andrew Arato, *Civil Society and Political Theory* (Cambridge: MIT Press, 1992).

9. The most explicit attempt to link the communitarian critique of "rights-based liberalism" with the Progressives is Eldon J. Eisenach, *The Lost Promise of Progressivism* (Lawrence: University of Kansas Press, 1994). It is worth noting that this linkage was anticipated some time ago by Michael Sandel in "The Procedural Republic and the Unencumbered Self," *Political Theory* 12 (February 1984), especially pp. 91–95.

10. See Robert Bellah et al., *The Good Society* (New York: Pantheon, 1992), which draws

explicitly on the turn-of-the-century Progressive writers Graham Wallas, Walter Lippmann, and John Dewey.

11. See Cass Sunstein, *After the Rights Revolution* (Cambridge: Harvard University Press, 1991), which echoes the legal realism of Oliver Wendell Holmes.

12. Michael Piore, *Beyond Individualism* (Cambridge: Harvard University Press, 1995), pp. 173, 183.

13. Stanley Greenberg, "After the Republican Surge," *American Prospect*, no. 23 (Fall 1995), 72.

14. Stanley Greenberg, *Middle-Class Dreams: The Politics and Power of the New American Majority* (New York: Times Books, 1995), p. 278.

15. John B. Judis, "From Hell," *New Republic*, December 19, 1994, p. 18.

16. Wellstone and Fingerhut quoted in Joel Bliefus, "Working in Opposition," *In These Times*, January 23, 1995, pp. 12–13.

17. Ruy A. Teixera and Joel Rogers, "Who Deserted the Democrats in 1994?" *American Prospect*, no. 23 (Fall 1995), 76.

18. Jeff Faux, "A New Conversation: How to Rebuild the Democratic Party," *American Prospect*, no. 21 (Spring 1995), 36–39.

19. John B. Judis and Michael Lind, "For a New American Nationalism," *New Republic*, March 27, 1995, p. 27.

20. E. J. Dionne Jr., *They Only Look Dead: Why Progressives Will Dominate the Next Political Era* (New York: Simon & Schuster, 1996), p. 16.

21. Jacob Weisberg, *In Defense of Government: The Fall and Rise of Public Trust* (New York: Scribner's, 1996).

22. Alan Brinkley's prognosis mirrors Dionne's almost verbatim: "Liberals now need to make the case, in an inhospitable climate, that government is not intrinsically bad. They must show that it can and must play an ameliorative role in social and economic life . . . They must be able to demonstrate that institutions of government are capable of performing their functions effectively and, equally important, that they are capable of continually 'reinventing' themselves in response to the changing world around them." "Liberalism's Third Crisis," *American Prospect*, no. 21 (Spring 1995), 32–33.

23. Lind's argument here spins off of the path-breaking assessments of the decline of American liberalism presented in Dionne, *Why Americans Hate Politics*, and Thomas Byrne Edsall and Mary D. Edsall, *Chain Reaction: The Impact of Race, Rights, and Taxes on American Politics* (New York: Norton, 1991).

24. Michael Lind, *The Next American Nation: The New Nationalism and the Fourth American Revolution* (New York: Free Press, 1995), pp. 301–2.

25. Michael Kazin, "The Workers' Party?" *New York Times*, October 19, 1995, op ed page. See also Kazin's less sanguine prognosis in "Alternative Politics: Is a Third Party the Way Out?" *Dissent* 43 (Winter 1996), 22–26. Kazin elaborates on these issues in *The Populist Persuasion* (New York: Basic Books, 1994).

26. Sidney Plotkin and William E. Scheuerman, *Private Interests, Public Spending:*

Balanced-Budget Conservatism and the Fiscal Crisis (Boston: South End Press, 1994), pp. 227–31.

27. See Joel Rogers, "Why America Needs the New Party," *Boston Review* 18 (January/February 1993), 1–4, and "How Divided Progressives Might Unite," *New Left Review*, no. 210 (March/April 1995), 3–32.

28. Rogers, "How Divided Progressives Might Unite," pp. 4, 5.

29. Ibid., pp. 28–30.

30. A similar argument is developed by Stanley Aronowitz in "The Situation of the Left in the United States," *Socialist Review* 23 (1994), 5–79. Aronowitz makes the Gramscian allusion explicit: "To our understandable 'pessimism of the intellect,' we urgently need a good dose of 'optimism of the will.' Composed while in a fascist prison, Gramsci's celebrated aphorism has never had more relevance than now" (p. 75).

31. The corporatist aspirations of Rogers's argument are made explicit in Joshua Cohen and Joel Rogers, "Secondary Associations and Democratic Governance," *Politics and Society* 20 (December 1992), 393–472.

32. While this chapter focuses principally on the question of political feasibility, it must be noted that the New Progressive agenda, in its emphasis on class inequality and class mobilization, gives short shrift to other forms of inequality and contestation, and is thus ethically as well as politically problematic.

33. Piore, *Beyond Individualism*, p. 183.

34. Faux, "New Conversation," p. 39.

35. Quoted in Joel Bliefus, "Working in Opposition," *In These Times*, January 23, 1995, pp. 12–13.

36. For a powerful account, see Robert Hughes, *Culture of Complaint: The Fraying of America* (New York: Oxford University Press, 1993).

37. Todd Gitlin, *The Twilight of Common Dreams: Why America Is Wracked by Culture Wars* (New York: Metropolitan Books, 1995), p. 237.

38. This point is emphasized, albeit hyperbolically, by Amarpal Dhaliwal in her "Response" to Aronowitz in *Socialist Review* 23, no. 3 (1994), 81–98.

39. Dionne, *Why Americans Hate Politics*, pp. 17, 343–55.

40. See Russell Jacoby, *The Last Intellectuals* (New York: Basic Books, 1987); and C. Wright Mills, *The Sociological Imagination* (New York: Oxford University Press, 1959).

41. Piore, *Beyond Individualism*, p. 172.

42. See Jean Baudrillard, *Jean Baudrillard: Selected Writings*, ed. Mark Poster (Stanford: Stanford University Press, 1988).

43. Sherry Turkle, *Life on the Screen: Identity in the Age of Internet* (New York: Simon & Schuster, 1995).

44. Benjamin Barber, *Jihad vs. McWorld* (New York: Times Books, 1995), pp. 64–65, 85.

45. Todd Gitlin offers a penetrating critique of television in "Glib, Tawdry, Savvy & Standardized: Television and American Culture," *Dissent* 40 (Summer 1993), 351–55, and

"Television's Anti-Politics: Surveying the Wasteland," *Dissent* 43 (Winter 1996), 76–85. The classic account is probably Neil Postman, *Amusing Ourselves to Death: Public Discourse in the Age of Show Business* (New York: Viking, 1985).

46. See Zygmunt Bauman, *Intimations of Postmodernity* (New York: Routledge, 1992).

47. See, for example, Joel Rogers's excellent discussion of the "cultural revolution" in telecommunications and consumer electronics, in "How Progressives Might Unite," p. 12.

48. Piore, *Beyond Individualism*, p. 182.

49. Greenberg, "After the Republican Surge," p. 72.

50. For a compelling critique, see Christopher Lasch, *The True and Only Heaven: Progress and Its Critics* (New York: Norton, 1991).

51. Michael Walzer, "What's Going On? Notes on the Right Turn," *Dissent* 43 (Winter 1996), 10–11.

52. As I have indicated, the Progressive era is not the only historical exemplar invoked by current progressives, but for a variety of reasons it is the most prominent and powerful. It is also paradigmatic: (*a*) for writers, who like Brinkley, urge a return to the early New Deal, because in many ways the New Deal represented a continuation of Progressivism, and (*b*) for New Party advocates such as Rogers, insofar as the Gramscian vision on which they draw was equally a product of the era of Progressivism, or what Gramsci called "Fordism."

53. See Morton Keller, *Regulating a New Society: Public Policy and Social Change in America, 1900–1933* (Cambridge: Harvard University Press, 1994).

54. See Allen F. Davis, *Spearheads for Reform: The Social Settlements and the Progressive Movement, 1890–1914* (New York: Oxford University Press, 1967), and David B. Danbom, *"The World of Hope": Progressives and the Struggle for an Ethical Public Life* (Philadelphia: Temple University Press, 1987), on turn-of-the-century Protestant reformism. On the New Christian Right, see Michael Leinisch, *Redeeming America: Piety and Politics in the New Christian Right* (Chapel Hill: University of North Carolina Press, 1993), and Clyde Wilcox, *Onward Christian Soldiers* (Boulder, Colo.: Westview Press, 1996).

55. See Robert M. Crunden, *Ministers of Reform: The Progressives' Achievement in American Civilization, 1889–1920* (New York: Basic Books, 1982).

56. See David Ricci, *The Tragedy of Politial Science: Politics, Scholarship, and Democracy* (New Haven: Yale University Press, 1984); and John Gunnell, *The Descent of Political Theory* (Chicago: University of Chicago Press, 1993).

57. See Nick Salvatore, "The Decline of Labor: A Grim Picture, a Few Proposals," *Dissent* 39 (Winter 1992), 86–92.

58. On the link between corporate liberalism and Progressivism, see Gabriel Kolko, *The Triumph of Conservatism* (New York: Free Press, 1963); James Weinstein, *The Corporate Ideal in the Liberal States, 1900–1918* (Boston: Beacon Press, 1968); and especially Martin J. Sklar, *The Corporate Reconstruction of American Capitalism, 1890–1916* (New York: Cambridge University Press, 1988). On the demise of a "Fordist" form of capital accumula-

tion, see Barry Bluestone and Bennett Harrison, *The Deindustrialization of America* (New York: Basic Books, 1982); Bennett Harrison, *Lean and Mean: The Changing Landscape of Corporate Power in the Age of Flexibility* (New York: Basic Books, 1994); and Stuart Hall, "Brave New World," David Harvey, "Flexibility: Threat or Opportunity," and Scott Lash, "Disintegrating Firms," all in *Socialist Review* 21 (January–March 1991).

59. See Herbert Croly, *The Promise of American Life* (1909; Cambridge: Harvard University Press, 1965), pp. 139, 153, 405.

60. Jeffrey C. Isaac, "Going Local," *Dissent* 42 (Spring 1995), 184–88.

61. See the profile in Robert Lavelle, ed., *America's New War on Poverty* (San Francisco: KQED Books, 1995), p. 74. The book offers profiles of similar efforts across the United States, including such groups as YouthBuild, Teach for America, Service for Shelter, and the Dudley Street Neighborhood Initiative.

62. Meta Mendel-Reyes, *Reclaiming Democracy: The Sixties in Politics and Memory* (New York: Routledge, 1995).

63. See Robert Moses et al., "The Algebra Project: Organizing in the Spirit of Ella," in Frank Fischer and Carmen Sirianni, eds., *Critical Studies in Organization and Bureaucracy* (Philadelphia: Temple University Press, 1994), pp. 497–519.

64. See especially Harry C. Boyte, *The Backyard Revolution: Understanding the New Citizen Movement* (Philadelphia: Temple University Press, 1980); *Commonwealth: A Return to Citizen Politics* (New York: Free Press, 1989); and "Community Action: Politics as Education," *Social Policy* 20 (Spring 1990), 35–42. See also the profiles of the Industrial Areas Foundation and its director, Ernie Cortes, in Lavelle, *America's New War on Poverty*, pp. 163–74, and Greider, *Who Will Tell the People?* pp. 222–41.

65. See Alice Sunshine, "Organizing Organizers: A NOA Gathering," and Robert Fisher, "Community Organizing in the Conservative '80's and Beyond," in *Social Policy* 25 (Fall 1994). For a critical perspective, see Joseph M. King and Prudence S. Posner, eds., *Dilemmas of Activism: Class, Community, and the Politics of Local Mobilization* (Philadelphia: Temple University Press, 1990).

66. Quoted in Greider, *Who Will Tell the People?* p. 223.

67. See especially Andrew Szasz, *Ecopopulism: Toxic Waste and the Movement for Environmental Justice* (Minneapolis: University of Minnesota Press, 1994). See also the special section "From the Front Lines of the Movement for Environmental Justice" in *Social Policy* 22 (Spring 1992); Giovanna Di Chior, "Defining Environmental Justice: Women's Voices and Grassroots Politics," and Robert Gottlieb, "A Question of Class: The Workplace Experience," both in *Socialist Review* 22 (October–December 1992), 93–166; and Larry Wilson, "Environmental Destruction Is Hazardous to Your Health," *Social Policy* 24 (Summer 1994), 16–24. Finally, see Lois Gibbs, *Dying from Dioxin: A Citizen's Guide to Reclaiming Our Health and Rebuilding Democracy* (Boston: South End Press, 1995).

68. See Steve Early and Larry Cohen, "Jobs with Justice: Building a Broad-Based Movement for Workers' Rights," *Social Policy* 25 (Winter 1994), 7–18; and Janice Fine and

Richard Locke, "Unions Get Smart: New Tactics for a New Labor Movement," *Dollars and Sense*, no. 207 (September/October 1996), 16–19. See also *Labor Notes*, published by the Labor Education and Research Project, which regularly covers activities such as these.

69. Hilary Wainwright, *Arguments for a New Left: Answering the Free Market Right* (Oxford: Blackwell, 1994), p. 153.

70. Hannah Arendt, *On Revolution* (New York: Penguin, 1977), p. 275. See Chapter 5.

71. In this regard there is a significant overlap between the local efforts and regional strategies of the New Party and my own view of "localist" democracy. It is the global strategy of the New Party that I question, not the feasibility of fusion candidacies or third-party local campaigns but the idea that these efforts might add up to something "hegemonic."

72. See Richard Flax, "The Revolution of Citizenship," *Social Policy* 21 (Fall 1990), 37–50; "The Party's Over—So What Is to Be Done?" *Social Research* 60 (Fall 1993), 37–90; and "Radical Democracy," *Socialist Review* 23 (1994), 445–70. There are strong affinities between my argument and Flax's strategizing, especially in his essay "Reflections on Strategy in a Dark Time," *Boston Review* 20 (December/January 1995–96), 24–29.

73. Albert Camus, *The Plague* (New York: Modern Library, 1948), pp. 117–18.

Chapter 7. The Meanings of 1989

1. See R. R. Palmer, *The Age of Democratic Revolution: The Challenge* (Princeton: Princeton University Press, 1959), and James Miller, "Modern Democracy from France to America," *Salmagundi*, no. 84 (Fall 1989), 177–202.

2. Immanuel Kant, *On History*, ed. Lewis White Beck (Indianapolis: Bobbs-Merrill, 1963), p. 148.

3. See Gale Stokes, *The Walls Came Tumbling Down: The Collapse of Communism in Eastern Europe* (New York: Oxford University Press, 1993).

4. Francis Fukuyama, "The End of History?" *National Interest*, no. 16 (Summer 1989), 4. See also *The End of History and the Last Man* (New York: Free Press, 1992), especially pp. 39–51.

5. Marc Plattner, "The Democratic Moment," in Larry Diamond and Marc Plattner, eds., *The Global Resurgence of Democracy* (Baltimore: Johns Hopkins University Press, 1992).

6. Jean-François Revel, *Democracy against Itself: The Future of the Democratic Impulse* (New York: Free Press, 1991), pp. 14–15.

7. Samuel P. Huntington, "No Exit: The Errors of Endism," *National Interest*, no. 17 (Fall 1989), 3–11.

8. See Samuel P. Huntington, *The Third Wave: Democratization in the Late Twentieth Century* (Norman: University of Oklahoma Press, 1991). See also Giuseppe di Palma, *To Craft Democracies: An Essay on Democratic Transitions* (Berkeley: University of California Press, 1990), and the essays collected in Diamond and Plattner, *Global Resurgence of Democracy*.

9. See Charles S. Maier, "Democracy and Its Discontents," *Foreign Affairs* 73 (July/August 1994), 48–64.

10. "A new breeze is blowing and a world refreshed by freedom seems reborn," declared President George Bush in his inaugural address, "for in man's heart, if not in fact, the day of the dictator is over": *Vital Speeches of the Day* 55 (February 15, 1989), 258. "The quest for democracy is the most vibrant fact of these times," proclaimed Secretary of State James Baker. See "The Battle for Democracy," *U.S. News & World Report*, May 22, 1989, p. 38.

11. Stephen Holmes, "The Scowl of Minerva," *New Republic*, March 23, 1992, pp. 27, 33.

12. Stokes, *Walls Came Tumbling Down*, p. 260.

13. Bruce Ackerman, *The Future of Liberal Revolution* (New Haven: Yale University Press, 1992), p. 1.

14. Ralf Dahrendorf, *Reflections on the Revolution in Europe* (New York: Random House, 1990), pp. 27, 75–76.

15. Timothy Garton Ash, *The Magic Lantern* (New York: Random House, 1990), p. 154. See also his "Ten Thoughts on the New Europe," *New York Review of Books*, June 14, 1990.

16. Valerie Bunce, "The Struggle for Liberal Democracy in Eastern Europe," *World Policy Journal* 7 (1990), 395–430. Similar expressions of concern can be found in "Rediscovery of Liberalism in Eastern Europe," *East European Politics and Societies* 5 (Winter 1991), special issue, especially George Schopflin, "Obstacles to Liberalism in Post-Communist Politics"; Valerie Bunce and Maria Csanadi, "Uncertainty in the Transition: Post-Communism in Hungary," *East European Politics and Society* 7 (Spring 1993); David Ost, "The Politics of Interest in Post-Communist East Europe," *Theory and Society* 22 (1993), 453–85; and Nancy Bermeo, "Democracy in Europe," *Daedalus* 123 (Spring 1994), 159–78. See also Brad Roberts, *Securing Democratic Transitions* (Washington, D.C.: Center for Strategic and International Studies, 1990).

17. Stephen Holmes, "Introducing the Center: A Project to Promote Clear Thinking about the Design of Liberal-Democratic Institutions," *East European Constitutional Review* 1 (Spring 1992).

18. Ackerman, *Future of Liberal Revolution*, p. 27.

19. Janos Kis, "Turning Point in Hungary: A Voice from the Democratic Opposition," *Dissent* 36 (Spring 1989), 241. A very similar prognosis is offered in Mihaly Vajda, "Past, Present, Future: The Collapse of Socialism," *East European Reporter* 4 (Autumn/Winter 1990), 51–53.

20. Adam Michnik, "After the Revolution," *New Republic*, July 2, 1990, and "The Two Faces of Eastern Europe," *New Republic*, November 12, 1990.

21. Adam Michnik, "The Presence of Liberal Values," *East European Reporter* 4 (Spring/Summer 1991), 70–72. Michnik also echoes Dahrendorf's assertion that the crucial issue now is simply between those who prefer "what Popper calls the 'open society,'" and those who prefer a closed society." See Janina Paradowska, "The Three Cards Game: An Interview with Adam Michnik," *Telos*, Summer 1991, p. 101.

22. George Konrad, "Chance Wanderings: Reflections of a Hungarian Writer," *Dissent* 37 (Spring 1990), 189.

23. Jerzy Szacki, "A Revival of Liberalism in Poland?" *Social Research* 57 (Summer 1990), 472.

24. This claim is different from Fukuyama's, for it does not rely on any historical metaphysic and can be causally explained in historically specific ways.

25. See Andras Bozoki and Miklos Sukosd, "Civil Society and Populism in the Eastern European Democratic Transitions," *Praxis International* 13 (October 1993), 224–41.

26. See Jon Elster, "On Doing What One Can," and the special section "Dilemmas of Justice," *East European Constitutional Review* 1 (Summer 1992), 15–22. See also Ackerman, *Future of Liberal Revolution*, pp. 69–98.

27. See, for example, Piotr Ogrodzinski and Henryk Szlajfer, "Is the Catholic Church a Threat to Democracy?" *East European Reporter* 5 (May/June 1992), 17–20, and Michnik, "Two Faces of Eastern Europe." See also Konstanty Gebert, "Anti-Semitism in the 1990 Polish Presidential Election," *Social Research* 58 (Winter 1991), 723–56. For deeper explorations of the social psychological roots of exclusivism, see Adam Michnik, "Nationalism," and Jirina Siklova, "The Solidarity of the Culpable," *Social Research* 58 (Winter 1991), 757–74, and Erazim Kohak, "Ashes, Ashes . . . Central Europe after Forty Years," *Daedalus* 121 (Spring 1992), 197–216.

28. Ulrich K. Preuss, "Constitutional Powermaking for the New Polity: Some Deliberations on the Relations between Constituent Power and the Constitution," *Cardozo Law Review* 14 (January 1993), 646–51. Jürgen Habermas has developed a similar distinction in "Historical Consciousness and Post-Traditional Identity: The Federal Republic's Orientation toward the West," in *The New Conservatism* (Cambridge: MIT Press, 1989), pp. 248–68, and in "Citizenship and National Identity: Some Reflections on the Future of Europe," *Praxis International* 12 (April 1992), 1–19.

29. See Carl Schmitt, *The Crisis of Parliamentary Democracy* (Cambridge: MIT Press, 1988), especially pp. 11–17, 68–76. For criticisms see Stephen Holmes, *The Anatomy of Antiliberalism* (Cambridge: Harvard University Press, 1993), pp. 37–60, and John Keane, *Democracy and Civil Society* (London: Verso, 1988), pp. 153–90.

30. J. L. Talmon, *The Origins of Totalitarian Democracy* (New York: Norton, 1970).

31. Stephen Holmes, "Back to the Drawing Board: An Argument for Constitutional Postponement in Eastern Europe," *East European Constitutional Review* 2 (Winter 1993), 23–24. Timothy Garton Ash has issued a remarkably similar assessment: "The immediate question, therefore, is: What variant of democratic politics can, on the one hand, provide sufficiently strong, stable, consistent government to sustain the necessary rigors of fiscal, monetary, and economic policy over a period of several years, while, on the other hand, being sufficiently flexible and responsive to absorb the larger part of the inevitable popular discontents through parliamentary or, at least, legal channels, thus preventing the resort to extraparliamentary, illegal, and ultimately antidemocratic means?"; "Eastern Europe: Après le Déluge, Nous," *New York Review of Books*, August 16, 1990, p. 54.

32. For a pessimistic assessment of the prospects for liberal democracy combined with

an interesting defense of a third possibility—an *authoritarian* liberalism—see Ken Jowitt, *New World Disorder: The Leninist Extinction* (Berkeley: University of California Press, 1992), especially pp. 299–331.

33. The literature on the economic difficulties of liberal democratic transition is immense. See especially Adam Przeworski, *Democracy and the Market: Political and Economic Reforms in Eastern Europe and Latin America* (New York: Cambridge University Press, 1991); Claus Offe, "Capitalism by Democratic Design? Democratic Theory Facing the Triple Transition in East Central Europe," *Social Research* 58 (Winter 1991); and Ellen Comisso, "Property Rights, Liberalism, and the Transition from 'Actually Existing Socialism,'" *East European Politics and Society* 5 (Winter 1991). On the problem of political demobilization and alienation, see Bozoki and Sukosd, "Civil Society and Populism," and Andrew Arato, "Constitution and Continuity in the East European Transitions, Part I: Continuity and Its Crisis," *Constellations* 1 (April 1994), 92–112.

34. Stokes, *Walls Came Tumbling Down*, p. 260.

35. See Vladimir Tismaneanu, *Reinventing Politics: Eastern Europe from Stalin to Havel* (New York: Free Press, 1992); Stokes, *Walls Came Tumbling Down*; and, for the clearest account of the final days of communism, Garton Ash, *Magic Lantern*.

36. The great weakness of Stephen Holmes's passionately argued and insightful *Anatomy of Antiliberalism* is its refusal to take seriously the difference between the antiliberalism of Schmitt and the nonliberalism of Arendt and Lasch. In an ironic way, Holmes reiterates a classic Cold War rhetorical figure—one is either with liberalism or against it.

37. Ackerman, *Future of Liberal Revolution*, pp. 32–33.

38. Garton Ash, "Ten Thoughts on the New Europe," p. 52.

39. The most penetrating philosophical account of this position offered by a contemporary liberal is Judith Shklar, *Ordinary Vices* (Cambridge: Harvard University Press, 1984).

40. Elisabeth Kiss, "Democracy without Parties? 'Civil Society' in East-Central Europe," *Dissent* 39 (Spring 1992), 230, 226.

41. For important general accounts of antipolitics, see Timothy Garton Ash, *The Uses of Adversity: Essays on the Fate of Central Europe* (New York: Vintage, 1990), and Jeffrey C. Goldfarb, *Beyond Glasnost: The Post-Totalitarian Mind* (Chicago: University of Chicago Press, 1989).

42. "Appeal to Society," reproduced in Jan Jozef Lipski, *KOR: A History of the Workers' Defense Committee in Poland, 1976–1981* (Berkeley: University of California Press, 1985), pp. 481–82.

43. On the formation of Charter 77, see H. Gordon Skilling, *Charter 77 and Human Rights in Czechoslovakia* (London: Allen & Unwin, 1981). On the many initiatives that sprang up in conjunction with it, see Skilling's very informative *Samizdat and an Independent Society in Central and Eastern Europe* (Oxford: Macmillan, 1989), especially pp. 26–32 and 43–156.

44. The Charter originally had 241 signatories, of whom 40% were workers; by 1987 130,000 people had signed. Its influence extended far wider. As Ladislav Hedjanek, one

of its principal founders, noted: "To act and live in the spirit of Charter 77 was quite possible, even without signing. The purpose of the Charter was not to gain as many signatures as possible but to persuade as many people as possible that they could and should act towards the state as free and courageous citizens and that—this was the main thing—they could and ought to act towards their fellow citizens as friends, companions and comrades" (quoted in Skilling, *Charter 77 and Human Rights*, pp. 41–43).

45. See, for example, the interview with Marta Kubisova, Vaclav Havel, Peter Uhl, and other Charter leaders, "Polish KOR Interviews Charter 77 Representatives," *Labour Focus on Eastern Europe* (January/February 1979), 5–7.

46. Charter 77, Document no. 9/1984, "Open Letter to the British Peace Movements CND and END," *Bulletin no. 25* (London: Palach Press, 1984), p. 16.

47. The classic exploration of this strategy was Adam Michnik, "The New Evolutionism," in his *Letters from Prison* (Berkeley: University of California Press, 1985). Written in 1976 during the formation of KOR, the Polish Workers' Defense Committee (later reorganized as the Social Self-Defense Committee), this essay had a strong impact on democratic oppositionists in Czechoslovakia and Hungary as well.

48. Charter 77, "Open Letter to the British Peace Movements," p. 16.

49. Charter 77, Document no. 2/1985, reprinted in U.S. Congress, Commission on Security and Cooperation in Europe, *Human Rights in Czechoslovakia: The Documents of Charter 77, 1982–1987* (Washington, D.C.: U.S. Government Printing Office, 1988), p. 150 (hereafter *Human Rights*).

50. See, for example, Vaclav Havel, "Politics and Conscience," in *Living in Truth* (London: Faber & Faber, 1987). See also George Konrad, *Antipolitics* (New York: Harcourt Brace Jovanovich, 1984).

51. Charter 77, Document no. 2/1985, p. 161. See also Charter 77, Document no. 1/1987, "A Word to Our Fellow Citizens," in *Human Rights*, pp. 276–85.

52. Benda's essay and many responses to it were published as a book, *Civic Freedom in Central Europe: Voices from Czechoslovakia*, ed. H. Gordon Skilling and Paul Wilson (New York: St. Martin's Press, 1991). For an abbreviated version of the debate, see Vaclav Benda et al., "Parallel Polis, or, An Independent Society in Central and Eastern Europe: An Inquiry," *Social Research* 55 (1988).

53. Benda et al., "Parallel Polis," pp. 242–43.

54. Ibid., p. 232.

55. As the Hungarian dissident Gyorgy Bence noted, "what the dissidents wanted to do was to erect their own ramparts and to live, behind them, a communal life worthy of free individuals" (quoted in Stokes, *Walls Came Tumbling Down*, p. 22).

56. Havel, "Politics and Conscience," p. 153.

57. See, for example, Anonymous, "Beyond the Dissident Ghetto," *Uncaptive Minds*, June–August 1988, pp. 35–39; and "Discussion within the Charter: The Ethics of Opposition," special section, *Labour Focus on Eastern Europe* 3 (May/June 1979), 16–21.

58. Vaclav Havel, "Dear Dr. Husak," in *Open Letters: Selected Writings, 1965–1990* (New York: Vintage, 1992), p. 60.

59. Charter 77, Document no. 2 / 1985, p. 150.

60. Charter 77, "Open Letter to the British Peace Movements," p. 17.

61. On civil disobedience, see John Rawls, *A Theory of Justice* (Cambridge: Belknap/ Harvard University Press, 1971), and Burton Zwiebach, *Civility and Disobedience* (New York: Cambridge University Press, 1975). On political nonconformity and contestation more generally, see George Kateb, *The Inner Ocean: Individualism and Democratic Culture* (Ithaca: Cornell University Press, 1992), pp. 1–107, 240–66.

62. John Rawls, *Political Liberalism* (New York: Columbia University Press, 1993).

63. Perhaps the most powerful articulations of this respectfulness are Adam Michnik's essays "Why You Are Not Signing . . ." and "Maggots and Angels," both in *Letters from Prison*. A fascinating debate broke out among the Chartists on this theme, provoked by Ludvik Vaculik's "Notes on Courage," reproduced in *Labour Focus on Eastern Europe* 3 (May/June 1979), 16–21.

64. C. Wright Mills, *The Power Elite* (New York: Oxford University Press, 1956), pp. 333–35. John Dewey offers a similar assessment in *The Public and Its Problems* (Chicago: Swallow Press, 1927).

65. Charter 77, Document no. 9/1984, p. 17.

66. See April Carter, *Direct Action and Liberal Democracy* (New York: Harper & Row, 1973). See also the discussion of the "repertoires" of social movement activity in Sidney Tarrow, *Power in Movement: Social Movements, Collective Action, and Politics* (New York: Cambridge University Press, 1994).

67. Rawls, *Theory of Justice*.

68. Benjamin Constant, "The Liberty of the Ancients Compared with That of the Moderns," in *The Political Writings of Benjamin Constant*, trans. and ed. Biancamaria Fontana (New York: Cambridge University Press, 1988), p. 316.

69. Some liberal democrats, of course, would go much further than Rawls in allowing the importance of participation in politics and the public sphere more generally. See Robert A. Dahl, *Democracy and Its Critics* (New Haven: Yale University Press, 1989), and Amy Gutmann, "The Disharmony of Democracy," and Alan Ryan, "The Liberal Community," in John W. Chapman and Ian Shapiro, eds., *Democratic Community: NOMOS XXXV* (New York: New York University Press, 1993). These liberal democrats still tend to place more emphasis on "constitutional design" than on civic initiative and insurgency. But there are important points of contact between such participatory liberal democrats and Chartist views. For the clearest point of contact, see Michael Walzer, "Liberalism and the Art of Separation," *Political Theory* 12 (August 1984), 315–30. Just as one can speak of the triumph of liberal democracy only in specific senses, so one needs to distinguish between different senses of liberalism and different kinds of liberalism, and cannot speak about liberalism in general. For a clever suggestion to this effect, see Leszek Kolakowski, "How To Be a Conservative-Liberal-Socialist: A Credo," in *Modernity on Endless Trial* (Chicago: University of Chicago Press, 1990), pp. 225–28.

70. See Jean Cohen and Andrew Arato, *Civil Society and Political Theory* (Cambridge: MIT Press, 1992), pp. 29–82, 345–420.

71. See Claude Lefort, "Politics and Human Rights," in *The Political Forms of Modern Society* (Cambridge: MIT Press, 1985).

72. The moral credo of antipolitics would go something like this: It is wrong to coerce, inconsistent with the demands of conscience and the requirements of civility; liberalism is the best system of politics insofar as it refuses to license legal coercion. But liberalism is insufficient in a world of injustice and evil. It is morally imperative to resist the sources of disempowerment, including those linked to liberal institutions themselves. But we cannot hope to achieve perfect justice. A self-limiting, modest search for justice is all that can be hoped for. We will practice civic initiatives, and hope that they will have some effect, without condemning those who do not or seeking to force them to do so. We accept liberal democratic values and institutions, but it is necessary and good that civic initiatives challenge them and contest their injustice.

73. For an interesting discussion of some of the implications of such a view, see Michael Walzer, "The Idea of Civil Society: A Path to Social Reconstruction," *Dissent* 38 (Spring 1991), 193-304.

74. Vaclav Havel, *Disturbing the Peace* (New York: Knopf, 1990), p. 115.

75. See Alena Hromadkova, "Whatever Happened to Charter 77?" *East European Reporter* 5 (January/February 1992), 69. See also Ladislav Hejdanek, "Democracy without Opposition Is Nonsense," and Jacub Trojan, "Democracy and Its Spiritual Foundations," *East European Reporter* 4 (Autumn/Winter 1990), 96-98, 100-102.

76. George Konrad, "What Is the Charter?" *East European Reporter* 5 (January/February 1992), 36-37. The charter itself is reproduced on pp. 35-37. See also George Konrad, "A Colorful Scene Ahead," *East European Reporter* 4 (Spring/Summer 1991), 27-28.

77. Andras Bozoki, "The Democratic Charter One Year On," *East European Reporter* 5, (November/December 1992), pp. 13-17.

78. Mary Kaldor, Introduction to *The New Détente*, ed. Mary Kaldor, Gerard Holden, and Richard Falk (London: Verso, 1989), p. 15.

79. "Helsinki Citizens' Assembly," *East European Reporter* 4 (Spring/Summer 1991), 72.

80. Mary Kaldor, "Speech to the Closing Session of the Helsinki Citizens' Assembly," in Mary Kaldor, ed., *Europe from Below: An East-West Dialogue* (London: Verso, 1991), p. 215.

81. See Jirina Siklová, "Backlash," and Pitr Pithart, "Intellectuals in Politics: Double Dissent in the Past, Double Disappointment Today," both in *Social Research* 60 (Winter 1993).

82. I do not deny that the new conditions have created problems for the former dissidents, who have had great difficulty adjusting to the complexities of the new environment and the noticeable decline in their stature now that communism has been supplanted. See, for example, Zygmunt Bauman, "The Polish Predicament: A Model in Search of Class Interests," *Telos*, 1993, pp. 113-30, and John Michael, "The Intellectual in Uncivil Society: Michnik, Poland, and Community," *Telos*, Summer 1991, pp. 141-54. Michnik

has himself commented on this situation quite frankly: "Yes, today politics is becoming normal, and for those who did not treat politics as a game but as a way to defend basic values it is becoming difficult to find a space. It will become even harder in the future. This could have been anticipated, and there is no need for despair." See Paradowska, "Three Cards Game," p. 96.

83. Vaclav Havel, "Address to the Helsinki Citizens' Assembly Opening Session," *East European Reporter* 4 (Spring/Summer 1991), 74.

84. Vaclav Havel, *Summer Meditations* (New York: Knopf, 1992).

85. Here Havel's views are close to those of many Western liberal democrats, who reject Hayek's dogmatism. See Robert Dahl, "Social Reality and 'Free Markets,'" *Dissent* 36 (Spring 1990), 224–28; and Dahrendorf, *Reflections on the Revolution in Europe*, pp. 90–108.

86. See Jiri Pehe, "Civil Society at Issue in the Czech Republic," *Radio Free Europe/Radio Liberty Research Report*, 3 (August 19, 1994), 12–18. This exchange recently has been published as Vaclav Havel and Vaclav Klaus, "Civil Society after Communism: Rival Visions," *Journal of Democracy* 7 (January 1996), 12–23.

87. See Jacek Kuron, "Manifesto: Phase Two of a Program for Poland," *Common Knowledge* 4 (Spring 1995), especially pp. 34–35.

88. For some interesting reflections on this theme, see Joshua Cohen and Joel Rogers, "Secondary Associations and Democratic Governance," and the responses by Paul Hirst, Jane Mansbridge, Philippe Schmitter, Andrew Szasz, and Iris Marion Young, in *Politics and Society* 20 (December 1992). See also Hilary Wainwright, "The State and Society: Reflections from a Western Experience," in Kaldor et al., *New Détente*, and her *Arguments for a New Left: Answering the Free Market Right* (Oxford: Blackwell, 1994).

89. Milan Kundera, *The Book of Laughter and Forgetting* (New York: Penguin, 1981), p. 3.

90. Ibid., p. 3. Jeffrey Goldfarb presents a penetrating discussion of these texts in *Beyond Glasnost*, pp. 109–18.

91. Hannah Arendt, *On Revolution* (New York: Penguin, 1977), p. 220.

92. The view of these efforts as fleeting is most often associated with the writings of Arendt, especially *On Revolution*. For the most insightful discussion of this theme in her work, see James Miller, "The Pathos of Novelty: Hannah Arendt's Image of Freedom in the Modern World," in Melvyn A. Hill, ed., *Hannah Arendt: The Recovery of the Public World* (New York: St. Martin's Press, 1979). For the view of them as part of a process of "dualistic politics," whereby the normal routines of liberal democracy are periodically reconfigured by radical movements, see Bruce Ackerman, *We the People* (Cambridge: Harvard University Press, 1991), and Cohen and Arato, *Civil Society and Political Theory*, especially pp. 492–563.

93. Garton Ash, *Magic Lantern*, p. 156.

94. Frederick Douglass, "Fourth of July Oration," in *The Life and Writings of Frederick Douglass*, ed. Philip S. Foner (New York: International Publishers, 1950).

95. For a similar argument regarding the U.S. civil rights movement, see Richard King, *Civil Rights and the Idea of Freedom* (New York: Oxford University Press, 1992).

96. This point is also made in different ways in Claude Lefort, "Renaissance of Democracy?" *Praxis International* 10 (April and July 1990), 1–13; David A. Reidy Jr., "Eastern Europe, Civil Society and the Real Revolution," *Praxis International 12* (July 1992); and Jean Elshtain, "Politics without Cliché," *Social Research* 60 (Fall 1993).

97. See Andrew Arato, "Interpreting 1989," *Social Research* 60 (Fall 1993), esp. 631–46.

98. See Charles S. Maier, "The Moral Crisis of Democracy," *Foreign Affairs* 73 (July/August 1994), 48–64; Herbert Kitschelt, "Social Movements, Political Parties, and Democratic Theory," *Annals of the American Academy of Political and Social Science*, no. 528 (July 1993). With specific regard to the American case, see William Greider, *Who Will Tell the People: The Betrayal of American Democracy* (New York: Simon & Schuster, 1992); E. J. Dionne Jr., *Why Americans Hate Politics* (New York: 1992); and Kevin Phillips, *Arrogant Capital* (New York: Simon & Schuster, 1994).

99. For an interesting discussion, see Wendy Brown, "Wounded Attachments," *Political Theory* 21 (August 1993), 390–410.

100. Harry Boyte, for example, writes about grass-roots community organizing in a Chartist vein in *Commonwealth: A Return to Citizen Politics* (New York: Free Press, 1989). See also Richard Flacks, "The Party's Over," *Social Research* 60 (Fall 1993), pp. 445–70.

101. Albert Camus, "Return to Tipasa," in *Lyrical and Critical Essays*, trans. Ellen Conroy Kennedy (New York: Knopf, 1968), p. 169.

Chapter 8. The Pathos of Modern Freedom

1. See Abraham Brumberg, "At the Russian Newsstand: Suits, Sunglasses and Sex," *New York Times Book Review*, October 15, 1994, p. 39; and David Remnick, "Letter from Russia: Gorbachev's Last Hurrah," *New Yorker*, March 11, 1996, pp. 68–83.

2. Jane Perlez, "Walesa's Nemesis: Aleksander Kwasniewski," *New York Times*, November 21, 1995, p. A1.

3. See Janina Paradowska, "The Three Cards Game: An Interview with Adam Michnik," *Telos*, Summer 1991, pp. 95–96; see also Vaclav Havel, "Paradise Lost," *New York Review of Books*, April 9, 1992; Vladimir Tismaneanu, "NYR, TLS and the Velvet Counterrevolution," *Common Knowledge* 3 (Spring 1994), 130–42; Timothy Garton Ash, "Prague: Intellectuals and Politicians," *New York Review of Books*, January 12, 1995; and George Konrad, *The Melancholy of Rebirth: Essays From Post-Communist Central Europe, 1989–1994* (New York: Harcourt Brace Jovanovich, 1995).

4. David Rieff, *Slaughterhouse: Bosnia and the Failure of the West* (New York: Simon & Schuster, 1995), p. 22.

5. It is difficult to avoid using these ethnic labels, but it is important to emphasize how porous and problematic they are. What I mean to say in this paragraph is that political elites who claimed Serbian and Croation ethnicity deployed that ethnicity against the Muslims (and each other), and that these elites, and those who identified with them and followed their orders, perpetrated great crimes. In no way does this judgment entail the ascription of collective responsibility to all individuals who happen to identify themselves

as Serb or Croat, just as it in no way absolves of responsibility those criminals, of whom there were many, who identify themselves as Muslims. But this does not mean that all sides were somehow equally responsible in either a causal or a moral sense.

6. Much of this story was first brought to light by the Pulitzer Prize–winning journalist Roy Gutman, whose *Newsday* dispatches have been collected into a powerful volume, *Witness to Genocide* (New York: Macmillan, 1993). Among the journalistic accounts, two others that stand out are Rieff, *Slaughterhouse*, and Peter Maas, *Love Thy Neighbor: A Story of War* (New York: Knopf, 1996). Among the firsthand testimonies, Slavenka Drakulić, *The Balkan Express: Fragments from the Other Side of War* (New York: Norton, 1993), offers a liberal Croatian's penetrating account of the descent into civil war. On the policy of systematically raping Muslim women, see Alexandra Stiglmayer, ed., *Mass Rape: The War against Women in Bosnia-Herzegovina*(Lincoln: University of Nebraska Press, 1994); on the extent of Serbian complicity in ethnic cleansing, see Warren Zimmerman, "The Last Ambassador: A Memoir of the Collapse of Yugoslavia," *Foreign Affairs* 74 (March/April 1995), 2–20; and on the mobilization of racism, see Michael A. Sells, *The Bridge Betrayed: Religion and Genocide in Bosnia* (Berkeley: University of California Press, 1996), and Istvan Deak, "With God on Their Sides," *New Republic*, November 25, 1996, pp. 31–35.

7. Francis Fukuyama, "The Primacy of Culture," *Journal of Democracy* 6 (January 1995), 10.

8. See Susan Woodward, *Balkan Tragedy: Chaos and Dissolution after the Cold War* (Washington, D.C.: Brookings, 1996); Kenneth Jowitt, *New World Disorder: The Leninist Extinction* (Berkeley: University of California Press, 1992); and Bogdan Denitch, *After the Flood: World Politics and Democracy in the Wake of Communism* (Hanover, N.H.: Wesleyan University Press, 1992). On the foreign policy dimensions, see Paula R. Newberg and Thomas Carothers, "Aiding—and Defining—Democracy," *World Policy Journal* 13 (Spring 1996), 97–108.

9. Daniel Patrick Moynihan, *Pandaemonium: Ethnicity in International Politics* (New York: Oxford University Press, 1993).

10. Russia's devastation of Chechnya is particularly notable, both because of its geopolitical significance and because of the relative silence and indifference to it on the part of the world community, such as it is. There is extensive documentation of Russian destruction and human rights abuse. For a powerful account, see Frederick C. Cuny, "Killing Chechnya," *New York Review of Books*, April 6, 1995, pp. 15–17.

11. On the Rwandan genocide, see Robert Block, "The Tragedy of Rwanda," *New York Review of Books*, October 20, 1994, pp. 3–8; Gérard Prunier, *The Rwanda Crisis: History of a Genocide* (New York: Columbia University Press, 1995); and David Rieff, "An Age of Genocide: The Far-Reaching Lessons of Rwanda," *New Republic*, January 29, 1996, pp. 27–36. On the wave of refugees, see James C. McKinley Jr., "Hundreds of Thousands of Exiles Pour Back Toward Rwanda," *New York Times*, November 16, 1996, p. A1.

12. Jean-Paul Sartre, Preface to Frantz Fanon, *The Wretched of the Earth* (New York: Grove Press, 1968), p. 26.

13. See Robert D. Kaplan, *The Ends of the Earth: A Journey at the Dawn of the 21st Century*

(New York: Random House, 1996), and Tina Rosenberg's review, "Anarchy Unbound," *World Policy Journal* 13 (Spring 1996), 83–87. On the problems of postcolonialism in Africa, see Basil Davidson, *The Black Man's Burden: Africa and the Curse of the Nation-State* (New York: Random House, 1992); Wole Soyinka, *The Open Sore of a Continent: A Personal Narrative of the Nigerian Crisis* (New York: Oxford University Press, 1996), and Crawford Young's review, "The Impossible Necessity of Nigeria: A Struggle for Nationhood," *Foreign Affairs* 75 (November/December 1996), 139–43.

14. United Nations High Commissioner for Refugees, *The State of the World's Refugees: The Challenge of Protection* (New York: Penguin, 1993), p. 1.

15. The literature on these issues is of course enormous. Many of these issues are usefully broached in Amy Guttman, ed., *Multiculturalism: Examining the Politics of Recognition* (Princeton: Princeton University Press, 1994), especially in Jürgen Habermas's contribution, "Struggles for Recognition in the Democratic Constitutional State."

16. See Hans Magnus Enzensberger, *Civil Wars: From L.A. to Bosnia* (New York: New Press, 1994).

17. See Hans-Georg Betz, "The New Politics of Resentment: Radical Right-Wing Populist Parties in Western Europe," *Comparative Politics* 25 (July 1993), 413–27, and *Radical Right-Wing Populism in Western Europe* (New York: St. Martin's Press, 1994); Peter H. Merkl and Leonard Weinberg, eds., *Encounters with the Contemporary Radical Right* (Boulder, Colo.: Westview Press, 1993); and Paul Taggart, "New Populist Parties in Western Europe," *West European Politics* 18 (January 1995), 34–51.

18. This point has been made, in different ways, by Michael Walzer in "Multiculturalism and Individualism," *Dissent* 41 (Spring 1994), 185–91, and William E. Connolly in *Identity\Difference: Democratic Negotiations of Political Paradox* (Ithaca: Cornell University Press, 1991).

19. See Rob Nixon, "Of Balkans and Bantustans: 'Ethnic Cleansing' and the Crisis in National Legitimation," *Transition*, no. 60 (1993), 4–26.

20. For an interesting critique of such a fundamentalism, see Kwame Anthony Appiah, *In My Father's House: Africa in the Philosophy of Culture* (New York: Oxford University Press, 1992).

21. See Bonnie Honig, "The Politics of Home," *Social Research* 61 (Fall 1994), 563–98.

22. Julia Kristeva, *Strangers to Ourselves* (New York: Columbia University Press, 1991), p. 1.

23. Peter Maas reports a striking conversation with a traumatized, highly educated, and urbane Bosnian Muslim, who declares in desperation: "We are in the center of mass crimes, pogroms and genocide. We didn't believe that this would happen. This is the twentieth century. We are in Europe. We have satellite television here. Even today, when there is electricity, we can watch CNN. We can watch reports about our own genocide!": *Love Thy Neighbor*, pp. 75–76.

24. My thinking on these issues has unsurprisingly been influenced by the writings of Hannah Arendt, especially *Lectures on Kant's Political Philosophy*, ed. Ronald Beiner (Chi-

cago: University of Chicago Press, 1982), and *The Life of the Mind* (New York: Harcourt Brace Jovanovich, 1978), especially pp. 3–16. But her most relevant reflections on this theme are to be found in *Eichmann in Jerusalem: A Report on the Banality of Evil* (New York: Viking, 1963), especially pp. 280–98.

25. See Arendt, *Eichmann in Jerusalem*.

26. See Stjepan G. Meštrović, *The Balkanization of the West: The Confluence of Postmodernism and Postcommunism* (New York: Routledge, 1994), and the superb essays collected in Thomas Cushman and Stjepan G. Meštrović, eds., *This Time We Knew: Western Responses to Genocide in Bosnia* (New York: New York University Press, 1996). The egregious failure of memory involved here is anticipated in Alain Finkielkraut, *Remembering in Vain: The Klaus Barbie Trial and Crimes against Humanity* (New York: Columbia University Press, 1992).

27. See Jean Baudrillard's essays "No Pity for Sarajevo," "The West's Serbianization," and "When the West Stands In for the Dead," in Cushman and Meštrović, *This Time We Knew*, pp. 79–89, though Baudrillard himself falls prey to the same cynicism he depicts. See also Zygmunt Bauman, "The Moth Seeks Out the Lamp," *New Statesman*, November 1, 1996, pp. 21–23.

28. Joseph Brodsky, "The Berlin Wall Tune," in Carolyn Forché, ed., *Against Forgetting: Twentieth-Century Poetry of Witness* (New York: Norton, 1993), pp. 142–43.

29. Reprinted by permission of Farrar, Straus & Giroux, Inc., on behalf of the Estate of Joseph Brodsky: "Bosnia Tune" by Joseph Brodsky. Copyright © 1992 by Joseph Brodsky.

30. In *Balkanization of the West* Meštrović reproduces a 1994 letter from the president-elect of the American Sociological Association rejecting his proposal for a panel on the Balkan tragedy on the grounds that "several thematic sessions . . . while they do not focus exclusively on the Balkan War, take up issues" implicated by it (pp. xiii–xiv). This shocking indifference to what is going on in the service of normal routine, in this case normal academic routine, is exactly what Brodsky is getting at. As anyone who has ever attended a major academic conference is aware, scores and sometimes hundreds of panels are offered. The idea that a single panel addressing sociological responses to Bosnia is superfluous is, to put it mildly, absurd.

31. See Judith N. Shklar, *The Faces of Injustice* (New Haven: Yale University Press, 1990).

32. See Lawrence Weschler, "Enabling Washington: The Coming Crunch in The Hague," *New Yorker*, December 6, 1996, pp. 9–10.

33. On this problem see Tina Rosenberg, "Tipping the Scales of Justice," *World Policy Journal* 12 (Fall 1995), 55–64. For more caustic accounts, see Finkielkraut, *Remembering in Vain*, and Rieff, "Age of Genocide." These issues have been taken up in Tina Rosenberg, *The Haunted Land: Facing Europe's Ghosts after Communism* (New York: Random House, 1995), and Lawrence Weschler, *A Miracle, a Universe: Settling Accounts with Torturers* (New York: Pantheon, 1990).

34. Walter Benjamin, "Theses on the Philosophy of History," in *Illuminations*, ed.

Hannah Arendt (New York: Schocken, 1969), p. 257. This passage is the opening epigraph of Kaplan, *Ends of the Earth*.

35. Hannah Arendt, *The Human Condition* (Chicago: University of Chicago Press, 1958), p. 157.

36. See Lester Thurow, *The Future of Capitalism* (New York: Morrow, 1996), and Jeremy Brecher and Tim Costello, *Global Village or Global Pillage: Economic Reconstruction from the Bottom Up* (Boston: South End Press, 1994).

37. See Jean Baudrillard, *Selected Writings*, ed. Mark Poster (Stanford: Stanford University Press, 1988) and *The Transparency of Evil: Essays on Extreme Phenomena* (London: Verso, 1993); Sherry Turkle, *Life on the Screen: Identity in the Age of Internet* (New York: Simon & Schuster, 1995); Mark Slouka, *War of the Worlds: Cyberspace and the High-Tech Assault on Reality* (New York: Basic Books, 1995); Zygmunt Bauman, *Intimations of Postmodernity* (London: Routledge, 1992); and Benjamin Barber, *Jihad vs. McWorld* (New York: Times Books, 1995).

38. See Ulrich Beck, *Risk Society: Towards a New Modernity* (London: Sage, 1992) and *Ecological Politics in the Age of Risk* (Cambridge: Polity, 1994); and Ulrich Beck, Anthony Giddens, and Scott Lash, *Reflexive Modernization: Politics, Tradition, and Aesthetics in the Modern Social Order* (Stanford: Stanford University Press, 1994).

39. See Aristide R. Zolberg, Astri Suhrke, and Sergio Aguayo, *Escape from Violence: Conflict and the Refugee Crisis in the Developing World* (New York: Oxford University Press, 1989).

40. See David Held, "Democracy: From City-States to a Cosmopolitan Order?" in David Held, ed., *Prospects for Democracy* (Stanford: Stanford University Press, 1993).

41. See Jürgen Habermas, *Between Facts and Norms: Contributions to a Discourse Theory of Law and Democracy* (Cambridge: MIT Press, 1996); and Jean Cohen and Andrew Arato, *Civil Society and Political Theory* (Cambridge: MIT Press, 1992).

42. A voluminous literature on civil society and "social capital" has been spawned by Robert Putnam, *Making Democracy Work* (Princeton: Princeton University Press, 1993) and "Bowling Alone: America's Declining Social Capital," *Journal of Democracy* 6 (January 1995), 65–78.

43. See Sheldon Wolin, "Fugitive Democracy," *Constellations* 1 (April 1994), 11–25.

44. Karl Marx and Friedrich Engels, "The Manifesto of the Communist Party," in Robert C. Tucker, ed., *The Marx-Engels Reader* (New York: Norton, 1978), p. 478.

45. George Konrad, "What Is the Charter?" *East European Reporter* 5 (January/February 1992), 36–37.

46. See Michael Walzer, "The Politics of Rescue," *Dissent* 42 (Winter 1995), 35–41.

47. Weschler, *A Miracle, a Universe*, p. 79.

48. This accusation was leveled by Jean-Paul Sartre and his associates against Albert Camus when he supported a very similar conception of politics in the late 1940s and early 1950s. See Francis Jeanson, "Albert Camus, or L'Ame Revoltée," *Les Temps Modernes*, no. 80 (August 1952), 2076–77.

49. This last criticism was leveled at an earlier version of Chapter 7 by Joel Rogers in his "Response" to my "Poverty of Progressivism," *Dissent* 43 (Fall 1996), p. 56.

50. Albert Camus, "Neither Victims nor Executioners," in *Between Hell and Reason: Essays from the Resistance Newspaper "Combat," 1944–1947*, ed. Alexandre de Gramont (Hanover, N.H.: Wesleyan University Press, 1991), pp. 121, 139.

51. Hannah Arendt, *Men in Dark Times* (New York: Harcourt Brace & World, 1968), pp. ix–x.